What to Do in the Meantime
(and why it doesn't matter)

DR. MICHAEL RICHARD LUCAS

ISBN: 979888336298

DEDICATION

To Anonymous

PUBLISHER'S DISCLAIMER

For legal (and practical) reasons, please DO NOT DO ANYTHING this book recommends.

This book cover was printed for another book by Dr. Michael Richard Lucas. One he never wrote. We've selected this manuscript (at least a couple hundred pages) recovered from his computer and correspondence. That's what you'll find here. We don't believe this material is as coherent (helpful, readable, etc.) as the proposed book [actually, between us, these are random pages with no connection. But we already released the promo material #yolo]. The book has been edited. Somewhat. As you will see (in the manner it was written). It hardly matters.

This book should not be read if you are easily "offended" (in the boomer/evangelical sense). If you don't experiment with dark humor, philosophical thought, and societal critiques (at least on the weekends), you will not like this book. This book is not for everyone. Anyone? Our author didn't want us to publish this book: "Nobody who would *actually* like it, would read it." While difficult to argue, it's not as if anything better was going to be made during this time.

This book was supposed to be a humorous *"What if?"* reflection on the dumbass mistakes our world had been making. But then our world decided to keep making them. Turning this book into a bland historical account. Leave your comments below. [Don't]. Of course, I would have rather written something YOU enjoy. But I don't know what that is. Do you? Please visit us Online for further details. Fax us your Tweets. Teleport your Kurger Bing. To Grand Central Station. By next Thursday. No later. Amen. We have no money. You can't sue us.

Fiddly Doop,

Publishing Board at Michael Arts Good

CONTENTS

1 FORMS YOU'LL NEED TO SIGN
BEFORE READING

Oh good. Another day. If living in absurd times. Ask an absurdist how to live. Out of options? Create your own. If nothing is possible. Everything is. The difference between warm bread with butter. And toast. Is a toaster. The thing about life. You're still living it. I can't believe that was the past. That that is the past now. Language. A peering out(in)side of space/time. Whilmst containing you. Forever? I've got a conflict of disinterest here. It's going to get a whole lot worse. Before it gets any worser. Whatever I should have been. I am not that. Oh good. I'm writing again. There are plenty of thoughts out there. You don't have to think any of them. Set myself up for disaster. Again. If you ever see me in my fancy pants. I need to do my laundry. I said typing into my computer (our character was shifting all over the place). Never plan anything. Ever. Once again. Citing lack of consensus. Nobody chosen for the Annual Philosophy Award. Whatever you are looking for. You will not find it here. Nation would survive plague. But not self-righteous mediocrity. Always take the easy win. You never know when. The next win. Will be. Always down. Never out.

If you find yourself apologizing for being smart. You might need to find new people. Essentially. We have the story of a person. Perchance. Every person who has ever been in a story. So no one. It could have been as much as it was. As it wasn't. And it would have taken place during a specific space/time. In some part of the *world*. All these details would turn out to be important. In some clever way. Our character. Where are they? When were they? And how are they now? Yesterday? Why should we tell their story? Maybe we will discover the answer. If we keep going. [They didn't]. Our author was trying to entertain us the most. In the least amount of space/time possible. A rhizomatic structure. Non-structure structure. At the moment. Our character. Somewhere in space/time. Doing something persons of this space/time did (as far as we know). With the space/time available to them. In short, attempting the *moreness*. Via a paradoxical *lessening*. Our character was contemplating a scenario. In what they considered to be the past. But they are re-experiencing it. At the time we are talking about now. It is both their present. As much as it is ours. And therefore. Our past as well. Maybe they are with us now? It is also their future. Now it is ours. Now it was ours. The blinding. Binding *now*. Opposed to the Depths. The eons. It will take. Growing up. Our character was trained to make right decisions. Not wrong ones. But most of life (as far as our author could tell) our character was choosing between equally undesirable options. Our character was tired of seeking approval. From a world. They did not approve of. No amount of success. Could offset this struggle. Oxygen now subscription based. 24/7 world expects 9-5 lifestyle. But without the pay. And the lifestyle. So just 24/7 anxiety. The worst of all worlds. A visionless vision. A haystack. In a needle.

Our character was watching the TV. It was becoming obvious. An ad positive about anything. Was attempting to get out in front of a PR nightmare: "CVS is pro positive mental health." What did CVS do? The most concerning ads: ". . . and that's what BP is doing to keep you and your loved one's safe." BP, what did YOU DO? "Hello this is AT&T/Buffalo Wild Wings of Sacramento State University… and we just want to say, we have nothing against people of different races… we have always promoted an inclusive environment… we do not believe in dumping batteries in the ocean… we take a strong stance against pet snake abuse… we do not condone punching old ladies in the face. . . we do not do anything. . . we do not say anything. . ." (eyes side to side emoji). Only ditch the crutches. When you're ready to walk. During our character's space/time. Life not conducive to living. This peanut butter is on the right side of history. Deodorant for special cause. These air filters support our troops. "When you bank with us. . . something about multiculturalism." Not exactly sure. Nobody was.

More Greek ruins. As great as Greece was. . . No more new people. Our character didn't trust the associations they already had. Why more? Our character needed to limit. Their number of story lines. Too many situations. Too many characters. Too many motives. "A delightful romp into a world as unintelligible as our own." – The Author. 75% of footage for new Truck Ad provided by terrorist organization. Our character was busy trying to keep the garbage thoughts at bay. They wake up. Oh good. I'm up. Must/most find distractions. Top 1,000 Questions to Ask at the End of an Interview: "Have you already hired a relative for this position?" Our character thought they had nothing to lose. Then they lost more. Etc. Republican Art Gallery. Never built. Republican History Museum. Very confusing. With no safe exits.

It doesn't have to be fun. To be fun. Work smarter. And harder. During our character's space/time. The force. Forcing us forward. Forwarding us forceward. Lurching out of our selves. Nostalgically moving back through our selves. Our character's expectations. Were narrative based. Mainly. Mustard-based. To distract them (pass space/time). But to see space/time? Perhaps in another space/timeline. Little lime. Rhyme lime timeline. Based on nothing. Our spacing/timing? Living? Etc. Maybe we should? Finally! Solid ground! But we can't dig. We have no tools. Our character felt the need to align. With a through-line. Of space/time. Without feedback from the force? Ask the algorithm. What's the question? All this space/time. And no question. Nobody as smart. Was ever as stupid.

As our character. Nobody as far ahead. Was so far behind. Etc. Without a discipline. A craft. Etc. It turns out. Our character. Would have experienced. The exact same emotions. Irregardlessness. Is it better? They never knew. I won't tell them. Will you? [They did]. So who's right about the Middle East? Comment below.

"Popstar takes bold stance against genocide. Once it becomes profitable. Tough crowd. Perfect. Ignorant. And condescending? Perfect. These pickles are iconic. These bombs aren't going to drop themselves." During our character's space/time. Our character. Wasn't able to do much. About anything. Let's not tell them directly. We'll put hints in their dreams. Or something. Circle back on this. Put a pin in it. Maximize average gains. With limited investment portfolios. If there were a second version. Of this story. We could let our character know. But in another book. Let's keep circling. Bone marrow. Our character. Black sparrow. One of the only people. Of this space/time. Who moved forward. With plans? In truth. We don't know. We haven't been following other characters. Things are difficult enough out there. In here. Etc. Our character's space/time. Could we define thusly? Existence is real. If re-enforced. By a progression of events. A narrative. That holds up. Confirmed. Again. And. Against all odds. It keeps holding up. And so on. More than not. Etc. Maybe this traps our character? Inside narrative expectations. Of what? Why did what happened. Next. Have to happen. At all? The way it did? And no other way? You could be a squid. And 10 could be 0.

How long had our character not been our character? How long had they been our character? At some point in space/time. Our character had agreed. And disagreed. With everyone. And everything. They ever knew. Everyone had. Everyone who could be considered an everyone. To exist. It must have an opposite. Fictional or non-fictional characters included. Fictional fictional characters. And fictional non-fictional characters. And functional fictional characters. Pruning. Our history. Our space/time. Throughout the day. Our character was constantly surprised. To keep living. New things can happen. Hasn't enough happened? They thought aloud to them selves. I'm probably the strangest I've ever been. And that's saying something. Sorry. This is my first time on earth. I haven't been on other planets. But this is still my first time. On this one. No matter how much they think about it. Their job. They still wake up. And go there. Again. Today. And therefore. Forever. Etc. It's the same thing. If your future is murky at best. If your muture is furky at rest. At least. To see the next step. How long until everyone realizes. The wrong people. Have always been in charge. Our character realized. Wining a competition. Doesn't mean better. If evil ever won. How would you know? Super specificality. With no payoff in sight. Nothing annoyed our character more. Are they *trying* to make shows bad? AI fires CEO.

Behind every great plan. A great T-shirt. If you don't have an end point. Synthesize a starting point. That will eventually be an end point. Our character needed something different. Not more. Of the same. The sameness. No. They wanted the moreness. A creative bottleneck. Or a point of departure. For more creativity. The direction of difference. This time. Not of more. This time. After the Philosophy of Synthesis. We'll (I'm saying this within the voice of our character) be within the Philosophy of Difference (difference that creates identities not merely identities that create difference). Closer to extinction. Or birth? Why not both?! Combination of two things. Excites character. In advertisement. Our character. Had thought them selves. Out of the day entirely. Our character wasn't sure. What to make of the moreness. An unusually sharp observation. Soon forgotten. Our character noticed. Society was expanding holidays. More people. Realizing. How shitty life was.

During our character's space/time. Half of Freest Nation. Could not comprehend. Multiple things being true. At once. Multiple things being false. At once. Our character's neighbor was crazy. The landlord did not like our character's neighbor. But the landlord was also crazy. It was possible. Both were crazy. Our character didn't have to believe either of them. [They didn't]. Times could be tough. It didn't mean President of Freest Nation was doing a bad job. Times could be great. It didn't mean President of Freest Nation was doing a good job. Not everything that happened. Had happened that day. If anything could be anything why choose worst? Patient still conscious. Enough. To subtract a few beers. When reporting weekly alcohol consumption. To ER nurse. Our character never wanted to be the voice of their generation. But they were annoyed. Nobody had asked. Announcer. Definitely made-up last fact about player. Back-up. Not as good at celebrating. Nance feeling exotic. After ordering bleu cheese. Wearing sports apparel. Lets you get away with a lot more. At this bar. The only problem with baseball is there isn't more baseball. Cocktails. Made with more care. Than public policy. Fact checkers searching for accurate statements by Orange Man. Racist. Doesn't think they are. Want to start a band? Our character was overly friendly. At the party. Again. *Logos* provides us with a now. But at the expense of not being in the future. We have to eventually not be. To be.

Orange Man was the perfect candidate. For people who couldn't tell. When a TV show ended. And an infomercial began. Popular narratives. Propel the assumption. Employment will end via mechanized automation. Or money being divided. Evenly/value-lessly. In a utopian society. Or with alien-overlords. Parasitically living off us. In a comatose state. Only working. Within a false game-like world. Etc. Regardless of this Irregardlessness. Perchance. Let's consider. Working sdrawkcab. Through the problem. Perhaps if we discover. How to live without jobs. We will discover. Why we are addicted to work. The human psyche. Not ready for change. What would our character do? No revered positions? How would we/our character pass the space/time? Our character. Could pursue *work-like activities*. Turns out. People want to do stuff. But without. Crushing anxiety. And depression. Etc.

To be one. With skill. Pure skill. Our character was dreaming. When they had the following thoughts. Although they couldn't remember. When they woke up the next morning. What if it's the opposite. Of what we think? The odds are good. This happened. Before. For instance. Another planet. Like this one. Probably intelligent life. In our oceans. Etc. "What the dolphins are trying to tell us. Tonight at 8!" Entire Beings. In the abyss. Choosing. To be undetected. A higher level. Biological or technological development. Let me talk to these dolphins. Sort it out in a day. Ethical problems derailing us. Our character would rather join the aliens of the oceans. Atlantis. Etc. Bypass. Humans. No longer smartest form of human intelligence. It's happened before. Something prevents it. Every step of the way. But this space/time. It hasn't. Perhaps we haven't gotten this far. I've only just now realized. If I'm the first person to realize. It is too late. Entirely. Right now. Our character. In another incubation period. The self of society breaks. In a cave. To be birthed. At some point. Our character will have more energy. They will have more wisdom. But not now. Now. They are waiting for space/time. A new calendar. Clock. Narrative. Find a game. Everyone is playing. But nobody is winning.

A comedian on TV. Not great. "I hate speaking in front of large crowds. [*Heavy breathing*]. I thought more people would leave. Before I got on stage. You can stay. But half should close your eyes. And plug your ears? Yes. That's better. I didn't come here to do comedy. I'm a classically trained opera singer. My whole life. My opera coach told me. If I want to make it big. Take every opportunity to sing. [*Sings*]. Fettucine Alfredo! Pasta Rigatoni! Jeep Grand Cherokee Laredo! Ciao Bella! Bruschetta! Steve Buscemi! Isabella Rossellini! [*Satisfied with phenomenal performance*]. Do you guys have microphones too? (No, okay). When it comes to singing. You just gotta say *carpet denim*. Seize life. By the seat of your pants. [*Nervous laughter*]. Live life. By the seat of your pants. [*Audible: "Whut?"*]. Putting two years of high school Spanish to work. [*Chortle*]. Okay. A warmup. I've prepared a song for you. Many long hours. All of today. I hope. I do everything. Perfectly. For you." Comedian turns on radio. Starts singing loudly to whatever song is playing. Without knowing words. Major problems anticipating the lyrics. Attempts to change radio station. As if audience won't notice. Comedian admits. Wrong song. Changes to other station. On off chance. Specific song is playing. "Thank me. Thank me so much. I've been such a lovely performer. Follow me. Locations!"

Our character's space/time. Wouldn't allow people to be great. Or people no longer were. For many. The answer was simple. Blur the line between career and self. This scenario. Was already upon our character. *Homo Economicus* supplies the narrative. The goal. Not to eradicate work. But make work time. *Free time.* Leisure. Etc. Collapsing work into play. Eliminating jobs? Jobs would be everything. And nothing. People in our character's space/time. Wouldn't have jobs. Lives were jobs. Our character was on the verge of asking them selves. [In their inner-monologue (our inner-inner-inner-monologue)]: "If the result is the same. Does it matter?" But our character was distracted. Let's continue. Our character could have asked: "Is one way imprisoning them? Within the opposite result?" Working. To not have to work. Anymore. An endless loop of distraction. Or will another path achieve the result? What is the result? We have to figure that out. I mean, we don't. The people of our character's space/time did. You just have to keep reading. I just have to keep writing. Etc.

In our character's space/time. The rich appeared unmotivated. The people should incentivize them. Growing up they taught our character. People could be *good* with money. And people could be *bad* with money. I don't think they thought that anymore. Our character's space/time has a present parallel to ours. Always. In some way. I suppose. You can never truly know. When or how. You have learned. What you have learned. If you have fully learned. You don't know. You are doing it. If you are questioning it. It is neither being done. Nor permanent. In *time* terms. We would call this the *present.* The future is never now. We can only work backward. From what we have already done. Important to unlearn. You are afforded a non-common view of the self. I meant our character. It becomes apparent. But only because. We are no longer *IT.* Orange Man doesn't like brown people. Average citizen. Responsible for nothing. Held to higher standards. Orange Man threatens tariffs. On immigrants seeking asylum.

Fanatic untethered nationalism and anti-immigration policies. Still best way to create generation of revenge. Which then justifies their genocide. Etc. If we continue to build economies on our basic needs, we will never surpass them. There will only always be a lack or a surplus. Good for motivation. Not for change. And not for health. Art critic: "It has too much not-ness to it." Crucial to somebody changing. You letting them. Our character should have been less worried about robots becoming humans. And more worried about humans not being able to become robots. I'm undecided. Living my best. Barely socially. Acceptable life. Few knew our character's beliefs. It never stopped them before. I have no friends. I have no enemies. The mental rigidity. To withstand insanity. And return. "Oh come off it, Gladys. Nobody gives a fuck about your goddamn hamster." Our character had never heard their elderly neighbor talk like that before. Had they always been this unhinged?

This takes a character. Well versed in ambiguity. Otherwise. They would have perished. A long time ago. Our character felt comprised. Of everyone's opinions. Rays of light. We needed to make them feel this way. Even though. Everyone was comprised of our character's opinions. Etc. Our character persisted through moving this light ray body. But the feeling started to fade. Our character never realized their previous thought. Was heavily influenced. By the show they were watching. Our character reflected once more. Turns out. People *good with money*. Have money. The worst is yet to come. Everything that happens. Happens to me. Incorrectly thought our character. Necessarily. But understandably so. Everything that has ever happened. Is somewhere in my brain. Everyone you have ever met is there. Everyone you know. With only one thing in common. They are filtered through you. Our character. As far as you can tell. But also. They aren't. Are they? Sky Wizard wants fewer followers. On TV. A newfound superpower is blessing. And curse. Tension resolved. By cataclysmic event. A new appreciation for humanity. Discovered.

Our character was resolute. To be more involved. With their illusions. Life forces decisions. Decisions force life. Spouse now subscription based. Subscription now prescription based. People are peopling hard today. Our character was relieved. To be upset about something. To get over. Being upset about something. Else. Etc. Repetition. The only structure. Our character wasn't worried about overstating their point. Throwing all caution into the wind. If only. Someone else. Was there for them to tell. I'm starting to think. Things aren't as normal as they seem. Undiscovered. Mountains of shame. Paralyzed. By knowledge. Our character thought coffee would help. [It didn't?]. Banks needed thorough security procedures. To convince our character. Our character's neighbors. Were more likely to steal. Our character's money. Than the banks. Everyone a musical genius. These days. Our character was back to pacing aimlessly. This would not be the last time! Older generation mentality. Everything sucks. It should suck for you.

Person brags about waking up. At 5am. Every morning. Falls asleep. On couch. Twice a day. Don't panic. Orange Man in charge. Values voter. Sacrifices all values. With vote. Our character. Carried their not-ness. Around with them. Their potentiality to be. Or not. A main characteristic of our character. They carried their birthday. And deathday. With them. If you know a little. About a lot of things. You'll be able to piss everyone off. Our character's retirement plan. Finding out they are secretly famous. "We like to think of ourselves as family." Says institution that is nothing like family. Or exactly like family. Depending on your family. Having a mission is fun. Being young was fun. Missions all day long. If you wanted. Now our character couldn't decide. Between a shitty job. Or a shittier job. There is no mission. If you have a mission as an adult. It is probably a bad mission.

And you are probably a bad person. When a person's motivation. No matter what it is. Becomes apparent. We find it unattractive. You're supposed to be motivated. But NEVER show it.

Regional pride is useless. You never see rich people. At the laundromat. And other clever phrases. Another phrase of turn. When we need to break. A cycle. Change roles. *Dissoi logoi*. Vacation. Etc. If this was a serious story. We could dramatize our character's creative (created) pleasures. A pedagogy for laughing at one's selves. So we can hear others. Suppressed in the serious. Creamer: for those who love coffee but hate the taste. Had their grandmother always been this confrontational? Thing dropped no longer exists in this dimension. Was this dementia? Could our character sense their relationship to us? Their relation through creation. Does our character know more about me? Than I know about them? Etc. A Rhetorics of Listening. Who is listening when something is said? Book wins prize for making better listeners. Thing wasn't behind couch. It wasn't anywhere. Anymore. Our character gave up. Don't we all. Smell. A little like weed? I'm just high. I'm not. Like. Stoned. What is the sound of one cheek clapping?

Can't win them all? No, can't win any of them. Our character would have been religious. If only they believed in religion. Our character pushed back. The boundaries of their agency. Took shape once more. It would behoove us. To place our character in a narrative. That allows the reader, and our character, and our writer, a more elastic mind. After reading. Dealing with vast ambiguities. Our character should take on more inconsistencies. More paradoxes. Hold onto more multiplicities. And not crumble. Our character woke up early in the morning one morning. Several years ago. Our character had this overwhelming feeling. Someone. Or something. Put our character to work. While they were sleeping. Was it us? Did we have our character work on some alien spaceship while they were sleeping? I hope not. Let's not make things any more difficult. Than they have to be. And they have to be. Our character. Picked a shit day. To wake up sober. When we speak. An audience in mind. Rehearsed. Do robots have a potential audience? P.A. for A.I? IPA. AI played for PA. Our audience guides these decisions. Our character apologized yet again. For their house being such a mess. Our character started too many sentences. With "Sorry." Progressive linear decisions. Like the bots. But also great leaps. Forwards and backwards. In our character's story. Or our writer's *logos*? Etc. How could we differentiate. Very abstract concepts. And communications. Occurring simultaneously. In this instance. Our character's audience. Was the many selves. We are. We were. We were going to be. Etc.

Fashion out of fashion. Apparently. Bend your knees. Square your shoulders. Necessary for anything physical. But right now. Our character was looking at pictures. That showed a thing happened. Somewhere. A happy couple. Meticulously tracks the other's sleep. For future arguments. Someday, when our character grew up. They wanted to be a regular at a bar somewhere. "I'll start calling everything sauce." They thought one day. Back to the TV. Thing being sold. Was *more than just* the thing. Our viewer might. Have thought. Thing was. Drunk person can make as many bad decisions sober. Our character and their friend laughed. Future will probably look like future. Are there going to be snacks? I never heard back. Militant optimism vs. the infantilization of entire generation. Find out who wins. Tonight at 8! Anticipating people's motives. On a daily basis. Difficult enough. Guessing the possible moods. Of omniscient Sky Wizard? No thanks. Apparently. Alcohol was the only thing. Fueling our character's socializations. Otherwise, they'd rather sleep.

The beginning. Of a strong inner-dialogue. Creating special skills. And problems. Our character could not tell the difference. Could we? They were the strangest person they knew. And that was saying something. Their talent. Being able to get carried away. And their weakness. During our character's space/time. Paradigmatic shifts in healthcare. Never increased the value of life for people. Instead. It allowed old politicians to live longer. So they could prevent healthcare from helping others. While more talented individuals circulated a PTSD infested job market cesspool. Our character couldn't be too disappointed. They would fail to escape it again tomorrow. Nothing but space/time. Our character assumed. As did our selves. If we look out. Into the universe. We see our past. What direction do we look for our future? Space/time spent alone. Motivated by tasks. That interested our character. Training montage. Wherein. Our character learns important lessons. Don't count your chickens. Before you hatch them. In a basket. While running with scissors. To the market. On a full belly. After Thursdays.

Being without work. Questions and Possible Answers. A brief detour. Could be illuminating. Was our character at an academic conference? Envisioning immortality. Through mortality. But why wouldn't there be change? Does difference only exist in narratives? In identities? In a vacuum? A spaceship powered by difference. Given enough space/time. Everything. Ends the same. Should we tell our character? Stock market goes up. Because stock market. Thought stock market. Would go up. Turns out. Stock market was right. Bull market falls to trade and barter economy. Our character grew tired of music. No more musicians. The person-turned-immortal. Now outside of space/time. Or deeply embedded. Everything there is to do. Our character worked. Relentlessly. To avoid. An insane boredom. Let's have them avoid it? The blinding binding now. Bound to conceptualization. Of space/time. And the problems it poses. How to be Beings in space/time. Appreciation. Defying the space/time categories of the consumer and the producer. Nobody has ever won everything. "Say what you want about this book, nobody has ever written it before." – The Author.

Person dies of no insurance. Our character was watching a bank entice new customers. With novel strategies. Like not killing them. Potential employer. Stalks potential employee. On social media. To see if they are professional. [Hot]. Our character ran out of thoughts. Or walked. They went to sleep later that night. During our character's space/time. The ancients. Had a multitude of voices. Or none. Versions of them selves in different space/times. Did a part of this still exist? Within an unconscious self. Constantly amazed. A perpetual forgetting. Maximum happiness. Embrace a total forgetting. Where they originally projected them selves to be. You can only be sorry. If your intent was malicious. Institutions prevent change. By definition. Our character had been trying to get a doctor's appointment for months. They became the wrong kind of doctor. The ruins of modernity. What it couldn't deliver on. A post-post-enlightenment world. The failure of Wine Maker. And Sky Wizard. Etc. No modernism. No postmodernism. *Re-mix Philosophy*. Our character followed this train of thought. A little further. I forget what they said. Or I couldn't hear it. I can't remember. Neither can you. It was clever. In a stupid way. Made with care.

Soap for Feminists! T-shirt for a cause. Civilized debate for losers. Our character's friend. Wonders if they like college football. Or if they just like drinking. In the morning. Irregardlessness. They managed to have fun weekend. Girl leaves group to pet dog. Dark matter. A field of difference. Quantum space/time fabric softener. Producing identities. Destroying them. The abyss. A rising tide. Floats all ships. But not if the ships. Sink each other. Our character didn't want to have opinions. Anymore. But they still must do life. Thought our character. Somewhat absent-mindedly. Completely. And here. Our character let them selves go. From the project. Imagine if everything was free. An economy. Without money. Everyone was emotionally evolved. Being rich. Creates poverty. By definition. And in reality. It was a metaphor. But it wasn't *merely* a metaphor.

If poor people had money. They wouldn't have to steal. A symptom. Not a cause. *Cum hoc. Ergo. Propter hoc. Post hoc. Ergo. Propter Hoc.* Proper hawk. Post marked. Ergonomics. Our character didn't want to have opinions. Anymore. Again. But they still must do life. Again. Thought our character. Somewhat absent-mindedly. Again. And here. Our character let them selves go. From the project. Again. Taxation without compensation. Their taxes paid for roads. The roads were crumbling. Their taxes paid for protection. They were assaulted. Toilet paper requires password. Have you already created an account? Password too similar to previous passwords. Feeding dog requires two-factor authentication. Our character's one redeeming quality. Their moral through-line. Support the oppressed. The patron saint of lost causes. News reporters must be hot. A romantic dream. Behind everything. That needs to be accomplished. Sports training montage. Our superhero. Surviving. Big highs. Big lows. This space/time is compacted. And extreme. Also repetitious. And often uninteresting. The relentless repetition IS the challenge. The price the superhero must pay. An offering/sacrifice to the Sky Wizard. Devil at the crossroads. Push through the purgatorial. They keep fighting. For no reason. Eventually. They will break through. Or sink further into madness. "If I can't piss on my own front lawn in peace, what the fuck did all our soldiers die for?" Our character's neighbor. Probably wasn't too far. From a retirement home. In our character's space/time. If your happiness depended on the decisions of others. You would be perpetually disappointed. Penalty Nation. Freest Country. The early bird gets the worm. Our character was neither bird. Nor worm.

Our character was having a conversation with them selves. "In real life, I'm going to start calling myself *my character*. For example. WTF did *my character* do this time? And. I didn't tell my character to do that! I want to reach a level of pathetic where everyone HAS to root for me. All this. Merely because I could not accept my life. But not really. But maybe. Etc. Still not famous enough to cancel. No! Sisyphus, you're not supposed to enjoy this!" Our character would flirt with their pharmacist. But the pharmacist knew all their medications. Healthcare. Prohibitive to health. And care. In any space/time. Citizens of Freest Nation. Celebrated the downfall of the rich. But didn't want to tax them. To make *everyone's* lives better. Submit. To the cold quiet comfort. Of mediocrity. It's all chickens. Always has been.

Falling. Into a state of total appreciation. No longer. Subjected to binary definitions. Either/Or. Winner/Loser. Etc. A sighting of the selves. Should we provide more opportunities for our character? Or fewer? No matter how unflattering. Idiotic. Uninformed. Ethically under-developed. Pointlessly angry. Etc. On the flipside. A flattering view. Proof they are happy. Meaningful living. Accepting trajectories. Radically beyond. Led by them selves. Led by our selves. To reside. Somehow in space/time. *Proletariat.* Witty millennial team name. Trivia night. Industrial Looking Drinking Place. Our character hopes their credit card isn't declined. Influencer under the influence. The view. A truth. That might as well be true. Cannot hurt. Cannot harm. Cannot be false. It might as well be. Because it is. Not a gain. Not a loss. Artful movement. Helpful in its own way. No judgment. Emotional space/time. Campaign spending. Enough to solve all problems. The candidates debated. Our character could also spend millions. Not getting elected. Anyone qualified for that job.

Viewing the self. As a strange film. Sequences arrive in achronological order. Or a chronological order? Simultaneously. Perchance.

And one at a time. The same space/time. And a different space/time. One of their selves. Looking through the past. With a lens to the future. Stretching in all directions. Your original body. Left to reflexes. The remaining self. Able to peer out. While our character was focused elsewhere. The draft age should be 50-80. They've lived long enough. But we'd lose motivation. No longer seeking revenge for our young men. Old men. Not as compelling. Not tragic enough. Tragedy is motivation. We'd stop fighting. And, along the way, get rid of some of the old men who want the young men to die. Anyone who lives long enough. Has done enough wrong. At this point. Another path. Provides a glimpse. For the unconscious to develop. A space/time. Disconnecting in creative appreciation. Our character as their original person. A stronger connection to self. Viewing our simple. Stupid. Non-thinking self. Without guilt or shame. Without having to take action to remedy. Without having to take action to make things worse. We become everything. That is us. And not us? Where did our character start? And stop? What do we *not* have the language for? Why is everything hiding its sameness? Math will become language. Language will become math. Etc. TV ad supposed to make our character feel better. Sets them back. A few million years.

Our character's children's children wouldn't die of old age. The Immortal Greeks. In their own way. Creators living beyond. No longer useful. But to confirm our thoughts. To save space/time. Emotionally infinite. Everything will be ourselves. Retrieving endless possibilities. When the day played. During our character's space/time. Drugs had to be illegal. The potential for violence. Must surround the drugs. To weed out. Anyone progressing. Up the ranks. The drugs didn't cause paranoia. Our character's space/time did. We've all been wrong. About the majority of the things. In our lives. We've all been right. About the majority of things. In our lives. Sometimes. It's good we are powerless. With agency. We could steer the ship. In the wrong direction. Maybe our impulsive. More wreck-less selves. Are looking out for our best interests. Our character was at a point in their life. When they were overly polite. Apologize. Rather than confront. Our character said they understood. They didn't. They wanted to move on. But it never made sense to begin with. And it hardly mattered. Or maybe it did. This was our character's fatal flaw. Or it meant nothing. Difficult to tell.

Our character needed more confidence. We gave them more self-doubt. We weren't a great Sky Wizard. Neither were they. Sky Wizard created heaven. Wanted a mulligan. Maybe we need to lower our standards. When defining the human spirit. And in general. Our misplaced will to succeed. An annoyance. Or working best. Right now. We deserve exactly what we should get. Is this an illusion we want to live with? A chemical state. Outside the daily grind. Our character needed that moreness. The only thing our character remembered. Shouting. At the end of an argument:

"People still starve to death!" They had no idea why. Who they said it to. If you think. You do not have a choice. You don't. Irregardlessness. Project the assumption you have a choice. Forget you don't. And now. You've made a choice. Back to bed. Create the possibility. Of fruition. Something resembles footholds. From above. The original intention. Is not nothing. But might not be something. Explaining a joke. That doesn't make sense. Rhetorical and pedagogical challenge. *Par excellence.*

Imagine a society so bad at communicating. They need to teach sex. In school. The legal drugs were the ones that made the most money. To out freeloaders. Prisons now required an application. Filled out by hand. And a CV. And a cover letter. And five *current* letters of recommendation. Antagonizing hours. Formatting perfect documents. Yet implementation must remain in a state of pure chaos. "Why is this prison a good fit for you?" "If accepted by this prison, how would you utilize our facilities in a creative way, different from some of our local competing prisons?" "What are you bringing to the table?" "No, seriously, empty your pockets." But to reflect on our character's all-too serious self. The type of person. We usually are. In life. The business voice. A narrow focus. Unable to see individuals. As individuals. Around them. Through them selves. They find more insights. No longer truth-seeking. Winning or losing. Loved or unloved. Etc. Our character thought they were helping prevent. The end of days. However. They were speeding it up. And they were the main cause. Let's not tell them this. Yet.

When children. We have fewer *selves* to think a thought. Simpler. Chronological. Moving from one. To another. No competing perspectives. To derail you. Everything was beautiful. And terrifying. Back then. Almost a state of appreciation. Things could be settled. Not that they were. But the possibility existed. Perhaps with dementia. The past and future aren't as heavy. We carry less. Nomads once more. The extreme order of our days. Keeps us distracted. Adding up to ourselves and others. Logical through lines. Through logical lines. To improve the economy of self. Our character could be right that the world was going to shit. But wrong about why. They could know the *what.* But also not know the *when, where,* and *how.* It was possible to be right for the wrong reasons. And wrong for the right reasons. It was also possible. These are only distinctions. We are projecting on our character. The only thing wrong with drugs. They wear off. If you don't do drugs. You'll still feel like shit in the morning. Our character was learning this lesson. As we speak. Please text this number to your state officials fax number to receive the code to unlock the next chapter. Service fees may apply. Sign up for a new account! Today!

Classic our character. Such an *our character* move. Totally something our character would do. Discarded first pages. If ever they wrote. Our character. Always writing the first page. Everything was somewhere else at one point. Everything was sometime else at one point. The change you thought would happen. In your lifetime. Will not. News reports. Didn't say explicitly. But we can assume as much. This type of thing happened often. Our character. Now in the backseat of history. Influencing. Again. No perfect ending. I will end. It will end. Nothing will change. So far as I'll be able to see. For others it will change. That can be motivation. Kicking the can. Further down the road. Kingdoms built on character flaws. Our quantitative processes. Leaving the task of description. To metaphor. Ascribing character types to parts of the cell. Maybe the stones fall. Because they want to. I want to work backwards. Reverse engineer. A theory from a metaphor. Live in a manner. That creates a past. Helpful to your future. A categorical semi-imperative. Our character would remember this. And then forget it. And then remember it. Again. Etc.

Our character remembered a space/time. They had to keep a checkbook. Cursive was mandatory. There wasn't a college football playoff. People complained about wearing seat belts. And then. This space/time. Never existed. Will AI be like this? The challenge remains. Survive. Procreate. Etc. But it has always favored a certain type of person. *Homo economicus* is created. And recreated. *Ad absurdum*. Undoubtedly. Our character was one of these types. At least. Outside the safety of their domicile. One of the books our character was reading (coincidentally?) was saying something similar. Although not unheard of. Resistance was futile: "What we see as *successful* is merely that which is doing a good job of meeting the *challenge*. But what if the *challenge* was different? What kind of people could we re-create ourselves to be?" If you can learn it. You can learn it. Time. A measure of mental digestion. Our character was full. And couldn't move. The horizon. You can go no further. Thinking yourself into non-understandings. Thinking the essential nothingness of existence. Understanding without understanding. The brain can do no more. Our character thanked their evil ways. For protecting them. From their more evil ways. That causes this but what causes that? Etc. Please fill out this survey to let us know how we did!

I got myself into this mess. I'm going to be the one. To get myself further into this mess. The "I" that wanted identity. Our character wanted their story to be remembered. But why? Why this? This Being I body? All day. Everyday. Everything and everyone. Emphasizing the This-ness of this body. The space/time. Why not be a squid? And so. Our character went on caring. Or not caring. In relation to what they can only assume. Is a world external enough to differentiate it from them selves. Our character thought. Shit. I do all the bullshit. I hate others. For doing. "You're the most motivated nihilist. I've ever met." Nihilist Party. Yet to put forth a candidate. Absurdist not sure they are absurd enough. Everyone says something. You must become fully stuck. To become unstuck. Our character realizes the importance of *Dad Naps* during holiday celebrations. Our character is less psyched. Each birthday. *Going senile* retirement plan. That feeling you get. You pack something ahead of time. Forget you packed it. And then later. It shows up. Exactly where you put it. You were wrong! You can defy your own mental capacities! If life appears to be a game. It is! Games are life. Was this a fact about the planets? Or about me. "What? No! We don't have time to buy presents! We have a parade to catch!" Something from our character's past. "Long winded. But ultimately. Somewhat rewarding." – The Author.

Our character's life. Was in boxes. Once more. Moving. Was killing them. Turns out. Sharks could survive stillness. Our character didn't have a job. During this space/time. Not having a job also meant not having healthcare. This is when they needed healthcare. The most. A lot of things were very stupid about our character's space/time. Pharmacies were closed on Sunday. Why? Nobody needs medication on Sunday. The spray-paint was behind lock-and-key. So were the condoms. To be successful in this space/time. In any way. Our character knew. They needed to draw their audience's attention. Away from the fundamentally mistaken nature of *logos*. Our character would appeal (like many others) to consistency. Consistency is evidence. Of the fixity of truth. *Logocentrism*. Limits the audience's ability. To understand the rhetorical maneuvers. Of the logocentric dialectician. This is how profit/tragedy was created/generated. With a universal truth. We can appear to agree with our selves. No room for our audience. To agree or disagree. Erasing the conflict itself. If our character appealed to a consistency within their own process. They can appear to appeal to a consistency within the reader. And the space/time outside the reader. But no invention facilitated. Within the reader. Only a reaffirmation. Of the consistency. The reader is already looking for. This is what our character needed to do. To have a job. To have healthcare. Etc.

Our character would have to take advantage. Of their audience's need. To construct and confirm. Their own self-consistency. Shouldn't be too hard? [It was]. The desire for consistency, necessarily, permeated their *logos*. This didn't lead to self-awareness (nor appreciation). Method appears to offer us the ability to act with consistency towards Truth. Maybe it does? Our character didn't know. But then again, our character wasn't thinking any of this. On a conscious level. They may have stumbled upon it. It was statistically possible. Probably. But not probable. Possibly. If Orange Man was wrong about the plague. What else could he have been wrong about? Only those with no allegiance. Could tell the truth. Our character. Had no allegiances. But they also had. No motivation. Our character thought to them selves. If you're going to date me. You've got to be cool. About a lot of shit. And fast.

Just because someone had a stupid idea. Once. Doesn't mean we have to keep doing it. Our character knew without knowing. This desire to act in the world. The ultimate rhetorical position. Consistency demanded from the inner world they created. Consistency demanded from the outer world they created. We forget which side it originated. Our character did too. And therefore. We demand the consistency. We have assumed. Is demanded from us. From others. Perpetuating the cycle. Motives must be silenced. To learn a dialectic. And gain self-consistency. Within us. That will respond to a self-consistency. In others. Motive balancing. Recycling the obsession. Getting rid of mistakes. Instead of listening to them. Apparently. Sky Wizard just letting tragedy happen. At some point, there will be a good reason. [There never was]. Our character wanted to write a book that was universally unappealing. [Mission accomplished!]. The ultimate aesthetic challenge. Conquering chaos. Monumental monuments. Appreciation. A valueless value. In neoliberalism. But. "Don't shirk off the responsibility of your art."

Texas catching up with Florida. Our character asked: "Is it good?" "No. But it's better than country music right now." Our character bought two. Nation's flag permanently set to half-mast. Again. Extremely Normal Political Party bases public policy on bad interpretations of old book about Sky Wizard. Extremely Normal Political Party doesn't accept bailout money. Except. Everytime. Liberal media doesn't want you to know Orange Man. Won Gold. In the 1993 Alaskan Olympics. Winter Games. Institutions. Claim their path to appreciation is the correct one. But an individual's appreciation is paradoxical. And purposefully pointless. It is a pedagogy. Our character must learn for them selves. Our character knew this. In some vague way. For institutions. *The Method* becomes *The Way*. The rituals and traditions. All through the lens of attraction. Keeping up. With the Joneses. A competition. With no winner. Self-explanations. Provided by the perpetuators. Of the motives. An economy needs. The never-ending pursuit. Of attraction. Our character was arriving at a similar conclusion (edited here). If we appreciate everything. We won't be motivated. To compete. Take financial risks. Etc. Even institutions that appear to be in conflict. Find common ground. In resisting. Appreciation.

The only time. Our character gets a security warning. Is when THEY. Try to sign into THEIR ACCOUNT. Everyone had to be a politician. In our character's space/time. Limit the periphery. "All there is.

Is all there is." Our character's success was directly proportional. To their belief in the illusion. How else could others agree? However. This wouldn't help others. Become better listeners. Our character's illusion of the real. Didn't depend on the others. Inability to hear. The rhetorical nature. Of their grand narratives. Whether knowingly or not. Our clarity. Marched towards seriousness. Silencing the dissonance. That could help us hear. Our own thinking. Our character's thinking. Etc. The rhetorical stylist (absurdist) imitates the serious by appealing to the clarity. We desire. Demonstrating the absurdity. Within clarity. If nothing else. They've more than likely. Banished their nomads. To clear a path. For grand narratives. A favorite of dictators and tyrants. A long-standing tradition amongst the elite. Rhetoric causes impotence. Politicians put blinders. On the people. They rode. Some people. Just have good hair. Get over it, Debby.

Popstar is pissed at Popstar. For talking shit. About Popstar. After Popstar. Broke up with Popstar. In order to date Popstar. And is making new music inspired by their love for Popstar. In the Popstar galaxy. In the dimension of Popstar. You don't have to be. A marginalized community. To be fucked over. By Freest Nation. But. That's an easy place. For most politicians to start. The moreness our character sought. They never found. We might always fail. To get past this point. Past the past. As *humans*. Although we could get past this past. As Beings? During our character's space/time. The most brilliant trick the rich have pulled: making us vet ourselves. To death. Our own characters. Our own people. While they remain unqualified. But alone. At the top. Nietzsche tragically and unwittingly. Misinterpreted in commercial. For home and auto insurance. Our character's favorite Nietzsche quote: "Fuck John Wayne." Second favorite: "Think outside the bun." The television had an important announcement. WWIII Sponsored by Butter.

Our character simply didn't relate. To the person you think they are. How do they know who you think they are? I told them. Yesterday. The T-Mobile/Mountain Dew Concert Series is coming to NBC/Netflix next Wednesday! Comment below. Band "has a good sound." According to guy. Standing next to me. At the concert. Hibernation sounds great. This time of year. Homework is bullshit. People dancing in commercial. Look like total. Fucking. Idiots. Real people. Not actors. Are really actors. Because people are people too! Freest market. Can't fire Nance. She's been here for so "goddamn" long. Hot girl not impressed. People. Being really productive. In commercial. Guest room smells a little pukey. Great movie ruined by human emotions. Nothing matters. Want to buy stuff though? Perchance? Our character was fading in and out of a documentary. History makes a lot more sense. When you realize. Everyone was on just as many drugs. As we are now.

Popular person. Still too cool. For our character. Person trying to be popular. By pointing out. How other person is trying to be popular. Only ten people dying tragically in easily preventable catastrophe seems hardly newsworthy at this point. Nothing ever happens at 4pm. "Am I that much of a dick?" Wonders guy who is. New style of cultural group dancing. Where apparently anything goes. The only thing we agree on. Is that we have to compromise. Our character thought. They were. Really turning the corner here. In fact. They were rapidly spiraling. Downward. To their eternal demise. Our character. Was still waiting. To be *discovered*. What if. They were quietly becoming. Nation's Next Top Model? The Millers are milling. About their mill. While milling. If I were reincarnated. I'd probably. Come back as myself. "No. You're the asshole!" Candy is good. For you to eat. Movie. Really long trailer. For sequel. But this might have been. When our character was dreaming. ["What might have been when? What? Huh?"].

But that's not as interesting. As how Popstar. Saw Popstar. At Popstar. And they all Popstarted. All over again. Our character disrupted. Our dependence. On the fixity of language (if this was a good story). Revealing. That which is not easily communicated. That which is closest to us. Our relationship to *logos*. Concealed by familiarity. By habit. By method. By repetition. By Sky Wizard. Therefore. Our language (our character's language) should paradoxically turn on itself. To highlight. Limitations and possibilities. We don't. Communicate the things. Out there. To our neighbors. However. Saying what cannot be said. We can hear. What cannot be heard. The concealedness. Of the unconcealed. And the unconcealedness. Of the concealed. Attempting to keep our character's inability. To control *logos*. Concealed. In order to conceal. Our own ultimate inability. To do so. In our character's space/time. That spring. The NCAA Ivybridge/Doritos FedEx Conference will play for their sixth consecutive national championship. Recent Survey of Most Effective Interview Negotiation Questions Compiled by Pew Research Center and Citizens United: "How much do I have to pretend my research is directly related to 'important' causes without having to address any of those 'important' causes in my research?"

If you knew everything. You'd be rich. If you knew everything. You'd know. It wasn't worth. Diddly poo. This is why. Best to be rich. And know nothing. Our character. Realized. They haven't heard anyone. Use the word *hyper*. In a long time. "I'm announced to be thrilled. By our updates. The latest of which. These are. Versions. Sorry. Let me start over. It's the versions. That have been updated. Not the. The. Hold on. Okay. Let me. Let me. Show you some numbers. Here. On this diagram. Did we bring it?" Our character. Hated public speaking. Popstar. Has new clothing line. New study. Finds. Perfectly normal. To feel like total dogshit. 100%. Of the time. Young dad. Jogs less. Watches WWII documentaries more. Our character overheard this somewhere. But they couldn't place it. We need. Our illusions to align. Regret is growth. Growth is pain. The only motivation is public humiliation. Our character hated public humiliation. Above all. Not for the act. Itself. But for all the times. Their mind. Would play it. Back for them. In the future.

To the Capitalists' credit. They founded. Something. Semi-constant. To get any consistency within the universe. Difficult and rare. Markets provided a scheduled consistency. Patterns in crop growth. You can now make *plans*. In the *future*. Now. You can now. Bet on them! Create ceremony. Monumental monuments of monumental meaning. For everyone! Do you realize how difficult that is to do? Thus far. Only nations and religions have accomplished this. And probably some books. United by stuff! Our character felt satisfied. For the first time. In a long time. Cautimistic. Science Fiction. A public pedagogy. For theoretical experimentation. Helping to normalize. If possible. Our character's future. At least. Collectively preparing. But the task. Overwhelming. An infinite number? Of possible futures. But worth it? Any narrative is a prediction. Disguised by. And originating from. The past and present. The present. Moving away. From the past. Walmart! Prodigal Son. Returns. Just in case it wasn't clear. Absurdist also thinks. Being absurdist. Is absurd. Let him cook! If all that exists. Is eternal chaos and pain. What difference does it make. If our character is distracted from these truths? How can you translate this meaningless-meaning? Into a view of space/time?

It's fish-sticks for breakfast if you haven't eaten your corn mash hash yet (TV audience groans). Potatoes the new carrot. Orange you glad to see me? Pastel bathrooms. With toilet warmers. To space/time travel. Our character branched off into different selves. As when daydreaming. Our character. Didn't know. They didn't know. Nor did anyone else. That we know of. In our character's space/time. The only authentic gesture is a mistake. Molded by mistakes. Not our hero narratives. Are we the subconscious? To our world. Of mistakes? A parasite living off our mistake-self-host. It is the *real self*. We haul around. All day. Our conscious self thinks we are *their* subconscious. Are we even asking an interesting question? We don't. Yet know. Who we are. Does our character? The baseline. We are not all the things. We think we are. Necessarily. We are. Some of the things. We don't think we are too. Pushing through. Being released from. The binary. Bouncing between the extremes.

During our character's space/time. Taxes shouldn't have been sexy. But they were. They shouldn't have been gamified. But they were. They should have been boring. And simple. The IRS and CPA's should be one entity. They calculate how much they owe you. You owe them. It's math. No paperwork. Your employer, bank, and this new *tax institution* should report to each other. It should be federally regulated. It should be one thing. State governments don't need to be involved. No arcane infinity. Of particularly regional tax rules. This new *tax institution* will create jobs. To streamline the process further. And aid in implementation (software innovation, help desks, Etc.). Like the post office. When the post office is properly funded. The same thing should be true about voting. Picking candidates. Should be boring. Make America Boring Again. I've got good news. I've got bad news. You are not as bad as you think you are. You are not as good as you think you are. I assume. Our character would be the same? Sky Wizard. Assumes we are the same. Etc. Philosophy is ambiguity training. Our character almost thought this once. However, their friend was closer to understanding it.

Buzzfeed's Top 10 Questions to Ask Your Future Employer (sponsored by the Tobacco Farmers of America): "Do you pay employees in legal US tender or spirit points?" But where/when was our character, without singular judgements: information, taxonomies, details, charts and graphs, data points, Etc. All adding up. Knowing their ability to improve. Our character's social capital. Viewing the others. Their multiplicity. Not claiming to *know*. But knowing more. Than knowledge. Even anti-establishment antidisestablishmentarianism. Was part of the establishment. Normalized. In neoliberal competition. Stay away from Iceland! You don't want to catch pneumonoultramicroscopicsilicovolcanoconiosis. Words like supercalifragilisticexpialidocious were examples of floccinaucinihilipilification. A hierarchy of not having to listen. Socioeconomic groups. The highest not having to listen at all. The lowest having to listen all the time. They must hear everything. They are often. The least capable of doing so. Yet. They faithfully report back to the highest ranked. Our character. Did this impulsively. Without knowing. Although others. During this time. Were smart enough. Not to betray their own people.

Our character wasn't a bad person. But they were stupid. But so was everyone. Our character wanted to write a book. That made (most) other books. Unnecessary to read. This was actually one of their better ideas. Currently they were too busy fighting battles to sleep. Oh well. The next life would be better. "Name one person who doesn't like donuts. Name me one person! You can't! Can you?" The inefficiency of our character's space/time baffled future generations. And past generations. Abolish. All the red tape. Laws historically established to disenfranchise. Skimming off the top. Cowboys vs. Farmers. The nomads. Are we winning yet, son? Tune in. Tonight at 8! Too many characters. For our character. To keep track of. Ryan 3. Kelly Blonde. Kyle Bar. Guy Might Have Job Opening. Don't Call!1(1). Steph Craigslist. Bree Camera Return. Jason From? Denmark Hank. We can imagine these people. But we won't.

Our character knew how to be disinterested. To interest people. Crucial to their livelihood. Often mistaken for confidence. Or competence.

What does this person choose not to know? That I don't? A gap in knowledge. A power dynamic. Repulsion. Necessary for attraction. Only the potentially uninteresting person will act. The disinterested person doesn't act. Therefore. Two mutually attracted people. Are less likely to end up together. People of this space/time were more interested in confirming logocentric hierarchies. Than they were. Being happy. Or doing anything potentially interesting. How well are they competing? Playing catch-up. Rationalizing after the fact. And now. Viewing the future through the past. Take the averages. Our character was hoping. Their self-image was stable enough. [It wasn't]. Our author failed. DM for creative brand solution management. We can start calling it the 20's. At this point. Historians won't differentiate. Our character tried. To follow every religion. And every form of scholarship. We made them fail. For some reason. Maybe. It was to teach *us* a lesson? Them a lesson? The one way. Was always one of many. Insanity Tour. Popstar's new summer concert series!

Our character's paranoia and psychoses were not wrong. Just wildly inaccurate. Making assumptions about the consciousnesses "above" them: our reader, writer, Etc. But they couldn't let it go. As long as it almost kept adding up. A mission! Some big mystery. Maybe. Their mind was bored. The consciousnesses "below" them (them and us), was now awake. They were thinking. So we were reading. I'd like to use a metaphor here. But I don't know all the metaphors you know. Our character didn't either. Neither do you. "Oh you know English? Name every word." Each day. Morning. And Mourning. Not necessarily the fall of Rome. As much as the burning of the Library of Alexandria. And the death of Harambe. Etc.

Oh good. Another day. Fighting back. The eons of stupidity. Single-handedly. And no thanks. Breaking news. HR department. Not for Humans. And not Resourceful. But demanding the singular self. Our character was split into several selves. But usually. They only listened to the main ones. To save space/time. To save space/time we won't either. Or. We couldn't. What if our character. Could hear peoples' motives? Faster than speech. Speech dethroned. Listening. Lessening. Lessthething. Conquered in the sun. Epicurious in the shade. Notwithstanding wind resistance: S(peed) x D(istance) x T(ime) / M(otive) = RP (rhetorical position). Irregardlessness. Better understandings. Of everyone else's selves. Must exist? You can know when. But not where. Etc. Must our character take the most paranoid position? We'll try to sprinkle it in. Here and there. These else selves. Elves on shelves. Viewing all voices. Even the worst. Speaking to a person at their best. The listening speaker. As their best listener. Talks to the other's best listener. Of them selves. A speaking of listening. Speaking of listening. . . Etc. The New York Time's Top Questions to Ask During an Interview: "Which Very Normal Older Generation employee is going to complain about me not getting to the office at 4am every morning? How much time do I have before they try to convince everyone I'm lazy (all young people are these days)? One week? One hour?"

So there were aliens during our character's space/time. Apparently. It wasn't very big news. For some reason. ~~There were enough genocides ("not") happening around the world. For it to hit the news cycle. Soft enough to not terrify the American consumer. Too much. "Did I say that last part. Out loud? That's the part you don't say. Strike that from the record, Your Honor.~~" Elongated Musk. Ox. Axe. Lingers in the air. Popstar starting to "really sound like" Popstar. Postmodern Basketball Guru. Instead of trying to pass the ball to the other four players, these four players should provide a man-made rotating shield around the point guard in the middle. We will have to practice it. Every day. The unit will have to move both forward and side-to-side. As the unit moved. The four players will be sprinting in a circle. A zone of complete indiscriminance. For the body of the other. More Electrons. Than players. At this point. A proactive protective shield of human flesh. A circular human chainsaw. The point guard. Could probably shoot it. From anywhere. They wanted. At this point. "There. The perfect joke. That's it for me. Until Next time. See you at 8!" Other things characters from this space/time said!

"Today, Orange Man really became president!" Again. After accomplishing. Easiest achievement possible. Generation's Trophy Wives, unite! Our character. Had this uncanny ability. To attract potential mates. But only. When the end of the world was nye. Some impulsive. Genetic disposition. To make offsprings. Offerings of spring. Ever tried Onsprings? Might work this time. "This impulse had a kick!" And wouldn't butt out. Ass up. Etc. Obvi. No Boomer. No Scrubs. To the left. Etc. News makes it seem. As if people really care. About Popstar. To get people mad. About people caring. About Popstar. Then [yes, there's more] the news. Could report on whether people were supporting or not supporting. Popstar. Our character. Was a Hot. Mess. And also. Obsessed! You must see people at their worst. To allow them. To bring out their best. Amongst. Your selves. Our character's seemingly *random* actions. Motivations. From another person they are. You don't have access. Maybe they don't either. Access denied. By the singular. Meaning. Only one interpretation. And it's wrong. But at least it's something. Limited to communicate on one level. However, reaching the higher levels of communication, our character could evolve. Through them selves. They will move light years. Their skill to listen to all the voices. To come to terms with our destructive persons. Those that work against us. Without our knowing. Knowing without knowing.

Make it the slogan. Not the saga. Profoundly stuck in the moment. You have to be a prisoner. To be free. To understand. What you're a prisoner of. The glorious incoherence of youth. Somewhere there is an understanding of everything. Hallmark movie. Really hamming it up. All ham. At this point. During our character's space/time. There were only three movies: nostalgic superhero, nostalgic remake, nostalgic bio pic. Is purple 3? So many new ways. Unlimited number of platforms. To search for a movie. You can't watch. Person from Very Normal Older Generation. Mad. At apparently. Fucking. Everything. At this point. Yet. Nothing. Important. Yet. Our character was now well-rested. And ready to be fully depressed. Dog disappointed. Our character couldn't smell thing. Dog generally disappointed in our character's sensory abilities. LGBTQ+ Confederate flag. HGTV Divorce Court. Internet Televangelist. Doesn't understand. Their own double-entendres: "Always let Sky Wizard come inside you." The winning agenda. Our character knew their opinions were controversial. But they were brave enough. To hide them. From everyone. Including them selves. Our character believed we should limit the number of deaths caused by viruses. And we should help the poor. And not be fascists? So brave. This!

A systemic failure. Our character was reading another article. Top 200 Questions to Ask at the End of a Job Interview (sponsored by the Ham Council): "Given what you know about me so far, should I continue to waste my time with this lengthy, traumatic process?" "Oh no, I'm just regular normal. Thanks!" Who are the people. Telling women. To go hiking? Popstar goes to war! Is there anything she can't do? Popstar heard. Of boyfriends. In the middle east. Locked and Loaded. "War Times." Probably. Not great name. For video game. Right now. In War Times. Hard to market. One would think. But Christmas is coming up. War can wait. It'll be there. After Christmas. Our character could get better. At communicating with their denied selves. Learn to compromise. With them. Their *gut* feeling. Another them. Trapped inside them. In their stomach. Of all places. See through that merging of consciousness. What we will want. In the future. Assumptions of our future. Narrative expectations. Or subconscious (unconscious?). Mainly focused on food. If our character. Could communicate. To their stomach-self. Eliminating the dissonance. Your otherness. Your own other otherness. The otherness within you. It makes you whole. To generate the push and pull. Carrying us to another realm of consciousness. And after that? And after that? Etc. Can we arrive. While alive? In opposition. To the neoliberal pursuits of representation. In religion, law, politics, Etc. Empty traditions. Empty methods. Territorial disputes. Conquering and converting natives.

[*Heavy breathing*]. Student majoring in English Literature. Writing paper on identity politics. And social justice. North Pole. Ain't nothin but ice. And broken dreams. Great Wall of China never failed. Perfect immigration policy. For our character's space/time. Christmas. Another great time to be rich. Existential crisis. Underwhelming. Our character was reading another article. The Top 69 (nice) Questions to Ask at the End of a Job Interview Volume II ["Volume 2 11" – Spinal Tap]: "Who in upper management looks like an atheist. Talks like an atheist. But is really. An evangelical follower of Wine Maker. And going to judge me. Like Old Testament Sky Wizard?" "Who in upper management is going to walk into my office. Unannounced. And start insulting the books. On my bookshelf. The art on my walls?" "What changes would your department need to make. For it to be. A fully functioning group of adults?" "Who could you fire today. To make this department semi-functional?" "If a client shows up at my office. Unannounced. Without setting up a meeting. And I'm not there. Are you going to call me in the middle of a sale. To tell me. About how I should be in my office? When I shouldn't be. Are you going to tell my client how bad I am?" The Sublime. Future orientation. Darkness. Its own certainty. "The beautiful soul. Affirms everything." *Amor fati*. In love with your life. Art critic swallowed by thesaurus. Bad Doctor of Medicine. Has saved fewer lives. Than decent Doctor of History. Person solving international mystery. Must not need day job.

Data can only generate the past. But hey. It's something? Fireworks. Adult. XXX. Videos. Fruit stand. God Saves! From the other things? Must be in Florida. Next Exit. Tonight at 8. In our character's space/time. The scientists. Attempted to measure how people act. However. Based that prediction. On what somebody else said. About that prediction. Our character recognized a pattern. Barely. Or it was their paranoia. Others during our character's space/time. Were better able to articulate this. Not that they did. It's good at what it does. But it doesn't do much. Simply. More problems. Not the moreness. Our character was looking for. [*Classical music starts playing*]. Making the problem universal. And semi-predictable. Was not the same as solving it. Our character got distracted here. If only. They could have stayed on the rails. With this train of thought. To break free. From our addiction. To language. Our character. Was trying to get away. From this panic attack. By them selves. It was a road. Impossible to go down. Only someone. On the very edge. Remembers memories. They never had. To understand perfectly. You don't understand. When the binary mind. In our minds. Fails. Allows us to think. One step ahead? Or one step behind? Which is more important? Fuzzy connections. The five-paragraph essay. Takes the shape of a synapse firing in your brain. The visualization of all thought and structure. The warm glow of light. Off the dark wood. Both sides. Do not. Have good ideas. One side has decent ideas and poor execution. The other side. Is in the Middle Ages. During our character's space/time. Parents had to pay children. Not to swallow their teeth.

We will not tolerate obscurity! Except. Everywhere. At all times. Apparently. A world currency. How to capitalize on obscurity. A history of history. Through the tolerance of another's *logos*. One might understand them selves and others. If our character didn't have any problems. They would create them. Luckily. Our character didn't have to create many problems. During this space/time period. The problems were bountiful. And perpetually unsolvable. Just the way we like it. However. Other characters (as far as we know). During this space/time. Were better at generating problems. That need not be problems. Everyone has to be good at something. While problems were plentiful. Few were very interesting. If any. A sudden commotion. Attention back to the text. Our character had tried to read this book. Several times now. But couldn't get past the first chapter. [Understand the feeling]. It was prestigious. So they continued. Who is the master of one's words/worlds? [Was our character?]. Who is speaking. When something is spoken. Who is writing. When something is written. Etc. Write that down. In a way. This is obvious. We do not create the language we use. The *logos* has developed over space/time. Through others. And other others. And others of our others. Etc. [Several pages later].

Most Effective Questions to Ask at Your Amazon-Huawei Interview Interrogation: "How long do I have to pretend your company is prestigious to avoid offending the out-of-touch Very Normal Older Generation who haven't experienced the outside world since the Reagan administration?" Listening. Essential to speaking. A lack of tolerance for obscurity. Leads people (like our character) to exclude the *other* in their work. And therefore. The listener. And the listener's happiness. Hopefully. Our character. Would not exclude us in their reading. For some. Our love language is venting. Best come to terms with this. By all means. Still love (vent, complain, critique, Etc.). Just make sure your audience knows. The who. You are being. And they are comfortable. Make sure. You've introduced this character. Beforehand. Though. Again. This is why you should never meet new people. But all people. Are always new people. Every space/time. Our character was always close to this realization. They would probably be able to think this thought again. In about five years. If the settings were similar. Enough. Or perfect? Or the opposite?

Nation bases economy. On promise. Anyone can get rich. Fitting as it is. Fitting in is all there is. Everything is good. Everything is settled. There is music playing somewhere. No matter what. Someone will disagree with you. Our character. Found that oddly comforting. Instead of demanding. Their logocentric listener. Follow one true narrative. You can also wake up too early. To contact your doctor. Again. It wasn't unprofessionalism. It was Fascism. That destroyed our character's space/time. Cops are people. People who are able to get so mad at somebody stealing (something that isn't theirs) that they go through day(s) of "training" so they can stop everyone from stealing. Ever again. They need no context. To make bad guys. Bad guys. Everyone who is stealing. Is stealing from them. Personally. Except rich people. Can you imagine the kind of person it would take. To make this logical leap. Everyday they wake up. Is it any wonder they are wrong? More than not. Cops are people. People who are able to get so mad. At someone driving fast. . . Etc. Cops are people. Who want to get other people in trouble. Can you imagine the kind of person it would take. Is it any wonder. They are wrong. More than not? If they put on a uniform. The government (that you hate) says cops have power. To be Sky Wizard. All day. The same people who can't fix your bridges and roads. The same people who can't provide you healthcare (in some cities clean drinking water). Again. It's a wonder. Anything. Was accomplished. During our character's space/time.

If our character could articulate this. They'd probably be able to write a fairly interesting book. If our character could ask their audience. To consider more than one reality. But not an infinity of them. Invite the listener to look at words. Not just through them. But also. Not just at them. Etc. Calling attention to their tricks. The order our character's audience will see. Is the one they impose on them selves. As much as the book itself. In a way. I guess. I did keep myself alive. In one narrative form. Or another. Our character. Visited their friend. If my dogs had to name me, they'd call me *Dog Who Can't Bark*. [*Subtle laughter*]. If my dogs had to name me, they'd call me *Animal Who Poops in One Place*. [*Laughter builds*]. If my dogs had to name me, they'd call me *One Who Walks Around the House Erratically*. Top Questions. EVERY. Successful Professional. Should Ask. Spring Edition: "Is most of the workload 'office politics' and/or 'unforeseen vision quests to other galaxies'?"

Our character's current retirement plan: waiting for the FBI to tell them they were the only one qualified to save the world. Turns out, they've had superpowers this whole time. Electoral College still exists. Back in my day we didn't even have days and we ate dirt. Will my performance reviews be based on my performance or on my astrological sign? What obfuscating and antiquated software system will I get minimal training on that this entire operation will be run through every day? What form of medieval torture would you compare your work environment to? What random, pointless method will be used to "measure my performance" and how has everyone else already found their way around it? Who has slept with who in this department? How many marriages has this department ruined? What percent of marriages are sham marriages within this department so they could get hired *as a couple*? How much do I need to pretend. I'm married. To get this job?

This call may be monitored or recorded to ensure quality service is not provided. A story of maxims. But aren't they all? Built to pass. No lessons. Just learning. You like challenges right? No. I do not. You'll see it as an opportunity. To apply all those clever psychology terms. You learned in college. Our character was currently a living psychiatric experiment. Please send an email! ASAP! Think about the fun! Prosperity. Always a day away. Various institutions supposedly allowed our character economic ascent. But. Forever. Prevented them from (literal) prosperity. That would affect change. That would be helpful. Etc. What administrator/colleague pretends to be the nicest but is really the meanest? And what administrator/colleague pretends to be the meanest but is really the nicest? Don't let your job. Get in the way. Of you. Making money. Every day. Now memorial day. Tragedy encouraged. Tragedy enforced. Mandatory tragedy.

3 IRREGARDLESSNESS. PERCHANCE.

Everything designed around something. And other topic sentences. Tonight at 8. Traveling through "space" is designed. Around the limitations of holding your breath. What other examples? Everything is designed around us not dying. That's not true. Our character thought. What else could we design around? Is necessity learned? Can it be unlearned? Our character was looking for another goal-oriented individual. Who enjoys accomplishing things. A little competitive spirit never hurts. [It always did]. And don't worry. I'm going to be a very important person. Very soon. Debt was supposed to pay off. For them to be able to pay it off. Etc. Again. Great for keeping things going. But where will it end. . . A strong emphasis on charity for everyday people. To give money. To everyday people. The small print in bank transactions. Financial rewards for "settling down." According to country song. Happiness. Right in front of you. Etc. A strong emphasis on marriage. The individual. In the family. Remains. In their tax bracket. Predictability. For the housing market.

The chaotic nature of life. Makes it difficult to focus. Make mistake. Mad they made mistake. Mad they are mad they made mistake. Etc. Limited technological advancements for the lower class. In ways that genuinely matter. In our character's space/time. You needed to spend money. To make money. Leading to debt. And now we've come full circle. Again. It keeps rolling. Down the hill. Gathering steam. And mass. The *prosperity ascent narrative*. A steaming pile of shit. Rolling down a mountain. Followed closely. By Reagan's trickle down Pissanomics. What you know is all you know. You can't know what you don't know. And you can only "gain" knowledge. Of what you don't know. You are. What you don't know. But at least that's something. A collection of not knowing. A collection of moments. Unknown. Of moments unkept. Within these biological forms. An interface-less. Interface. Merely another level. Of abstraction. For distraction. I'm not sure. If it's even possible. To manage THIS interface. Let alone. A completely new. And even more pointless one. Bound to necessarily and perpetually. Confuse cause and effect. Something our character will understand. In the eventual? Perchance? If they reach the moreness? Irregardlessness. Our character wouldn't sleep that night. Orange Man's recession. Going to be biggest. And greatest. Recession. Ever. Just wait and see. Our character was applying for a job. Again. This happened often in this space/time. Although we haven't been able to figure out why. Which culture wars are raging throughout the department? Follow up. Which side should I take? "Could the principle of my actions be turned into a universal law?" "How does one manage not to know. What everyone else knows?"

By denying their reader the obscurity necessary to recognize their relationship to *logos*. Our character fails to take advantage. Of the therapeutic qualities of rhetoric/narration; i.e., providing their listeners with the possibility of moreness. Potential being. Our character must create new ways to perceive them selves in the world. We remain blind to this. When we consider our narrative. Only heading in one direction. If you can't veer off course. If there is no course. *Dissoi. Logoi.* The trip. The festival. The event. Etc. "Can I get three letters of recommendation from junior faculty assessing your department's workplace environment?" For the composition of a religion/moral *ethos*. A moral home. Another must be conquered. Our Sky Wizard is bigger than your Sky Wizard. Religion now football team. Another way to block us from our unheard self. It's been more than five minutes. You've been logged out.

Your life is circular. You need to figure out how. And why? Etc. Or don't. Our character couldn't. Neither could we. If it's cycles you must break. There's a bicycle right here. How many times. Can we dissolve our world. Completely. A death. In life. A narrowing of the space/time. The event. Possibilities closed off. Forever (at least the unforeseeable). Might as well. Be the same. Start again? Become a new person. How can our character provide a practical way for their reader (remember they were trying to write a book) to break free from the familiar? To find new ways to perceive them selves and their world? Should our character be a social chameleon? Becoming the people around them. *Homo rhetoricus par excellence.* A harmonious understanding of a text. Accepts the obscure. As always possible. A yet unheard language. The inaudible. The inaudible in what is said. The intent. The intentions. A language of intentions and motives. Hear the unheard. A rhetorics of listening. Our character. Started reading Bible. Ironically. Have I not hit rock bottom yet? Asks our character [They hadn't].

Perhaps our character couldn't comprehend the nuances of another person's personality. After a certain point. Within a certain timeframe. Our character based many of their interactions with people. On similar people. They knew before. Expectations applied accordingly. The past will conform to the future. The mistaken *logos*. That allows everything to keep "moving forward." Our character's expectations will necessarily be shattered. THAT they will be shattered is given. Finding yourself where you are. Remembering that you are present and will be future. And so what? And so what? And so what? Etc. Needing proof and not needing proof. They find common ground. Neither are the bigger sense. Of being that could exist. Our character was reminded of the *moreness*. But it didn't last. To be the main character of our story. Not to be too much of someone else's main story. Isn't it your fault for not bringing reading material to the barbershop? Reversing the problem. The pedagogy of *dissoi logoi*. Reverse Engineering.

Simultaneous. Quantum ones. And zeros. Zero-sum. Some zeros. The further out I go. The more I can bring back.

First they say. Have you eaten all your mashed potatoes? Now they say. You have eaten too many mashed potatoes. Our character was fed up. With mash potatoes. War on Christmas. Funded by terrorists. Prescriptions. Greatly overestimating. Our character's need to operate heavy machinery. The main thing wrong with our character's generation: the previous generations. You know what's better than a viral video of a soldier surprising their family by coming home? No war. Full potential. Fully wasted. Americanized-biopower. Now. At your local gas station. Narrative expectations. Compatible to the individual's best interests. In a system systematically preventing their best interests from being achieved. Stories about overcoming poverty. More common. Than people overcoming poverty.

Freest Nation's origin story. People during our character's space/time. Hadn't turned it into a cliché yet. It wasn't for lack of trying. It appealed to a very primal need. To survive/thrive. And that is the essence of biopower. A bill approved by congress and the senate. Full of highly motivated secondary causes (the parasite). Not at all related to the bill (the host). The narratives and the motivations. Combined together. Almost seamlessly. The individual cannot separate out. What is good. And what is bad. Radicalism. Becomes a currency. When everything becomes a currency. The prosperity narrative. Focused on progress. While it moved. In the opposite direction. Is it a cliché yet? Possible epitaph for our character: "Considering the odds against them. They did an okay job. It was fine." Only by accident. Do we impress the future. Go to conflict. It is easier to conquer a house divided. Trouble is never hard to find. And other pointless aphorisms. Allow yourself to profit. Off other people's trouble. This is merely the definition of profit. Profit from profit. For prophets. So now you see. Everyone is guilty. And we spend all our energy distancing ourselves from this guilt.

We sacrifice the *other* on a daily basis. Limited mobility. And the constant threat of dissention. Late payments. Unplanned pregnancies. Hospital bills. Losing the undesirable job. You already have. All possible. Through practices of over-self-policing. The burden lies on the individual. The burden is the individual. They start to believe this narrative as well. To become masters of their own destinies. Temporarily embarrassed trillionaires. People voting against their best interests. Charging phone. Our character was feeling productive. If you're enjoying your day off. Congrats. You're a socialist. Our character was looking forward to repopulating the planet. In all their communications. Our character was trying to cryptically reassure their FBI agent. They were too dangerous/important an asset. To eliminate: "Damn it Johnson! They are more valuable to us alive than dead!" When some unsuspecting muggers threaten our character's life in a back alley. FBI agents will take out the muggers. Smash/cut/next scene. Something bizarre is about to happen. Our character's FBI agents: "No, hold on a sec. . . Let's see where this goes. . ."

Would our character choose (without choosing) to find interesting questions? Or defend uninteresting conclusions? Ponder in ponds. Falling in love. Makes a lot more sense. If we think of it. As accepting the particular-kind-of-terrible. A person is. How do you come to experience your primordial-self? That ancient brain-matter we can't access. Our character sleeps to join this pre-human-self. A jobless-self. A nation-less-self. For some reason it works. Will the primordial-self be left behind. When we are uploaded to computers? Is this good or bad? We don't know. What we don't know about ourselves. Work to allow your primordial-self to be appreciative. Give it enough time to BE. The primordial-self will do whatever it can to make you stop. This is enough. You can go no further. "Who's with me! I'm with me!" If you can think of it. It can happen. Everyone Says Something. And other repetitive aphorisms. If this doesn't work. Something else might. Keep moving forward. If this doesn't work. Something else might. Keep moving forward. If this doesn't work. Something else might. Keep moving forward. If this doesn't work. Something else might. Keep moving forward. If this doesn't work. Something else might. Keep moving forward. If this doesn't work. Something else might. Keep moving forward. If you want to dazzle. You're going to have to put up with some razzle. Extremely Normal Older Generation do not understand. And cannot participate in. The world they have created. They created a global economy. And chastise culture. The greatest generation. Cannot be great. If they created. The worst generation.

Our character discovered a way to draw. Every chess game. They'd never lose. But they'd never win. But they'd never lose. Etc. Radicalization must be channeled. And practiced. And then sold for a profit. Narratives co-opted. Through the dichotomous structure of Nation's morality. The emphasis placed within the narrow confines of sexual promiscuity. Or hair color. The baseline morality is set at a fixed position. To transgress it. Not an accident or mistake. But the way people during our character's space/time regularly operated. Proof that the system was "working." Who was it working for? Cars? People? People never knew. People were overdosing on drugs. It was working. People were being arrested. It was working. Suicide and genocide? Check. All working as planned. But nobody was planning it. Oh well. Film ratings. Life ratings. Differentiating how we act. Contrasted with revered ceremonies. At work. At play. The dichotomies that limit our response. Necessarily. Aristotle's wet dream.

Movie will inoculate our character for the inevitabilities of life. Sci-Fi helping normalize the future. Allowing our character to comprehend it.

Aliens (is that us right now?). Etc. Just don't tell the conspiracy theorists. Freest Nation doesn't need conspiracy to disadvantage the disadvantaged. Sci-Fi government fables. Our character loved it. All the combat training. When Freest Nation's population goes to war. They'll be ready. Not that deriving pleasure from anything. Is bad. Any pleasure. You can get these days. Go for it. Furthermore. It is highly questionable. Whether our character could make them selves aware of the power dynamics at work in everything they do. Nor necessarily desirable. The power of illusion. The illusion of power. Need not be demonized. The goal then becomes. Separating and dissolving the dichotomies. Pursuing a project of regenerative enlightenment/curiosity. Finding joy in the journey and not the destination. And other clichés. Making these empty clichés into something they are not. Eternal return of difference. "Which acts would I repeat an infinite number of times?"

If people have told you you've gone insane. You haven't. Yet. It's when they stop telling you. Your insane. That you have to start worrying. That's good news for all of us. If you "went" insane. It implies that at one point. You were sane. Who else would be better at pretending they are a sane person? An insane person! Ergo. . . ["My car go. . ."] It's fine to be insane! If you pretend long enough. You'll forget you were pretending. As we all forget everything. Most of the space/time. And then you will actually just become sane. Even your cells will have all been replaced by new cells. The Ship of Theseus. If you can decide to be insane. Then you can decide to be sane. Just act like you acted when people liked you? At what point did they stop liking our character? Had they ever liked our character? Spiral. Not insane. But unsane. Our sane. Who's sane for ice cream! Hussein for I scream! Etc.

Pain and suffering. The baseline existence. The Universal hint. We are not welcome. We are intruders. Within this context. Freest Nation's institutions look impotent. Amateurs. They often unknowingly eradicate us. By accident. They are good at it. Because they are bad. At everything. But the universe *wants* to eradicate us. On purpose. Nation's institutions should take notes. [Please, don't]. Humans trying to survive. Hanging on to whatever they can. Once this is your understanding. Everything makes more sense. Rather than less sense. It allows us to make sense of other things. Does it? If all has not been that which we are sometimes to command the friends of friends to react in such a manner. But it was not our character's fault. They put the liquor in the oven. Get traditional with your cooking! Go ahead! As I have never understood it to be anything other than the worst of the best favorite time in the summer when you can cruse with your friends and everyone is having as much soda products to keep you well and stimulated with the best vibrating chairs for sale and are half off until labor day and night night and day and night night and day and night time is the right time if you feel this then please let me know it's real darling you are just too good to be true cannot take my eyes out without walking down the goddamn street and seeing these fucking hippies did you even read the bag of fresh potatoes you get at the store around the corner and turn around every now and then I get a little bit lonely and I got to just break down and cry. Cry baby cry.

Popstar wins feminism. Military appreciation month. Month appreciation month. Civilian appreciation month. "We're giving you guys a pizza party!" Heaven is just a pizza party. "Thanks, God Boss!" For whom does our character exist? Them selves? The reader? Our character could be explained. By describing the objects around them. This became. This has become. Even more difficult. Than figuring out when. Where. How. And who. This person was. Is. Could be. Did the objects have agency too? Can we avoid the fate. We've chosen for them? After a while. Everyone got fed up. With not knowing anything. "Exhausting and ultimately unsustainable." –The Author. Standardized testing. Let's get back to motives. Maybe. Our character had many similar motives. To those around them. But they also had more particular ones. All of these things combined. Made our character a person we could think. Once this was established. It followed. This is This. This is That. This is Not That. This is Like That. This is this. This is That. This is Not That. This is Like That. This is this. At the end of the day. Our character hardly knew who they were. Did we? Our character grows another layer. Of emotional skin.

During our character's space/time. They'd able to answer a lot of ethical questions. If they could define consciousness. Stock market. Looking at ourselves in the mirror. But not well. Purposeful obfuscation. So there can be a market. An extra something. A not knowing. The not knowing that everything revolves around. That makes money doing nothing. The Gig Economy. Property value. The zero. The nothing. Everything revolves around. The placeholder. The McGuffin. "But is it interesting, remarkable, or important?" Breaking news. Character building experience #1 cause of death for poor people. Free T-shirt totally worth it. Our character. And I'm sure their friends and family. Would like to skip to the point where they could reminisce. About those good old days. Poverty days. Money buys happiness. Cover band sucks. Local smart person organizes talking points before meeting with friends. Bartender not getting off anytime soon. Settle for less.

It doesn't have to be as emotional. Does it? At all space/times? Everyone has to find what works for them. And other obvious aphorisms. Buy local. Our character was practicing their plots. Long before they happened (except for the ones we haven't told them about). Repeating plots. That already happened. Practicing them differently. What's it all for? So much effort and focus. Mere distraction? Our economy of self? Our new attempt at immortality? Glass Door's Top 11 Questions to Ask Your Boss on the First Day: "This job sucks pretty bad, right? Answer honestly." Let me start awkwardly. In an unusual spot. [Too late]. What is our story now? Can we give up yet? We could. But our reader. Is reading about our character. Who were these people? Identify yourself! Could they be our character? Might get old. And they would know everything about their story if that was the case. Would they? Almost impossible for them to experience their life. If they are reading it. Popstar takes strong stance on violence (against it). "What everyone already knows: the dogmatic image of thought."

Fosbury flop. Works every time. Our character's neighbor was at it again. "I didn't come back from fighting in the Korean War for you to tell me I can't run over innocent civilians in my car!" There's always money in the Banana Stand. [There wasn't]. Being able to do things skillfully. A decent way to pass the time. The pure meaninglessness of meaning. Philosophy was supposed to be performed. And appreciated by an audience. The state of awe was the only purpose. There was no solution. Purposeful nonsolutions. A solution undermines the practice. Appreciation requires forgetting. As much as remembering. Instead we took the end result. As the end result. But there was no there. There. People in movie trying to save the world. Our character was just trying to sleep. "The smell means it's working." Don't rub it! Religion causes two-state problem. With no solution.

If our character could envision them selves standing still. They could move anywhere they wanted. So, as with everything. Something led to something else. Made possible by distinctions. Between things. And other things. We could go on making these distinctions. For an entire book. [They did]. As is common practice. One of the main difficulties facing our character. Being able to tell the difference. Between merely adding one thing to another. And building toward something else (not the thing it was originally). Often our character thought these things were big things. That led to small things. Or just as likely. Small things that led to big things. But there were only a certain number of combinations we could include before this appeared repetitive. And led nowhere. And again our character turned into everyone. And no one. But our character. If they were real. Wouldn't be able to think about any of the things in the way we are thinking about them now. Otherwise, they might lose interest in their own story. Who else would care. If they didn't? If we didn't?

Being surprised by the answer was the experience itself. In stand-up comedy. And sit-down philosophy. Answers of the unknown (of the previously forgotten). The buried punchline. The other foot. Etc. Breaking news. Big truck. Also loud. And driving fast. During our character's space/time. They simply weren't THAT kind of society. "Aunt Teffa done it!" Our character was starting not to trust the process. "New" "Year" great marketing scheme. Extremely Normal Political Party the most obsessed with other people having sex. Unfortunately. They couldn't provide sufficient criticism of science's military industrial complex and big pharma. Progressively Regressive. New piece of shit computer thing. Supposed to make you more creative. Or something. Freest Market approves opioid epidemic. Dow Jones wishes he had different name. Man being kept alive at most advanced hospital in Nation. Believes in literal interpretation of Bible. Members of The Extremally Normal Political Party aboard Titanic aren't convinced it's sinking. "Living best life" no longer viable excuse. Our character started a pointless conversation. With a pointless question.

First day of preschool. Impetus for parent to practice caring about child cursing. Our character couldn't remember the last time. Someone told them. They could be whatever they wanted to be. When they grew up. Our character's life will be defined (in part) by overcoming roadblocks to creativity while simultaneously highlighting particular aspects of the creative process that will hopefully allow our reader to resist problematic rhetorical stances influenced by a highly competitive capitalistic society. In Inverness. Unorganized crime. Bag Dad. Slipper family. Only reaching the masses. Pays the bills. If you don't care about expertise. You don't care about expertise. Can't save the unsavable. The truth. That is true. In the simulation as well. A shared truth. A social contract. Agreeing to be agreeable. Agreeing to be a part. Apart. Ape art. The stimulation simulation. What could our character do in the simulation to make their life easier? What could we do? For our character? Could we do anything? Nation mourns as it kills heroes. Popstar and Athlete give birth to new brand experience. See how far you can go in all pursuits. The drive to repeat what you did. And the inability to do so. We are the thing. Crashing through our plans. The audacity to think you know the future well enough to be disappointed by it. Everything was someone's grand idea. Every story is the same. How they are the same. Will tell you something. About yourself.

Our character's Professor suddenly stopped talking in class. They sat in silence. Everyday. The entire semester. Students adored this professor. They were soon fired. Remembering a future memory. Forgetting a present memory. That world outside your Being in space/time. A you outside yourself. Iconoclast controversy says images fine. Dalmatian spotted. Difficult to tell if Professor has lost their mind. Or merely misplaced it. Again. Oh good. Another day. Again. Beating the cosmic odds. It's a fine line. Our character did not walk it well. Book too aware. For its own good. Book too aware. It's trying to be too aware. Hamming it up. Pig fat on your face. Everything our character had ever seen. They'd seen in a movie. Freest Nation unsure if they can trust experts who work with precision in highly specialized peer-reviewed fields requiring decades of education and training. So they believe random Internet opinion. US News & World Report/Fed Ex Top Questions for an Academic Job Interview: "Which co-workers have Daddy Issues?" World no longer worth saving. Invest now!

Future's past is today. Our character's surprise. They can still do something. The moreness? The joy of remembering. Space/time forgotten. Remembered. Revealed to our relief. Everything will be done for the first time. The realization. There is more space/time. A beautiful forgetting. A never-ending party. A perpetual remembering. Everything will be new. Everything can be appreciated. Full of wonder. In this remembrance of forgetting. We stop projecting our-selves. Onto the world. And the world onto our selves. We are able to listen. To the lack of everything around us. The great silence. The silence of infinite appreciation. Our character wasn't trying to think of clever things to say anymore. They just put random words. Next to each other. It worked. More than not. You're seeing those words next to each other. More than not. Confirming our shared reality. Everything is a reference to a movie. We forget we've seen. Language. A lost reference. Simulacra. We forget what we are referencing. Lost Fragments. All we ever do. Process references that have always been.

The thing about this book. Is your still reading it. Appreciate worth for its worthlessness. Understanding our nothingness. The state of appreciation. And appreciating. The understanding. Of our nothingness. You can't plan on being within this space/time. Finding of a self. And hearing the nothingness of everything. Confront the idea you accomplish nothing. You are doing everything you have ever done. Appreciate your lack of consciousness. You are the subconscious to a greater consciousness. Our character was our subconscious. The subconsciousness under the illusion they are the conscious one. There is more consciousness to you than you can be aware of. Perchance. But it is blocked by our sense of superiority. This prevents us from the other selves.

Study finds people who hate others for their race are more likely to be racist. Extremely Normal Political Party thinks slavery no reason for slaves to not have had decent, respectable jobs. Most of the time. People just say stuff. Encouraging and beautifully crafted message of hope. Does nothing. To stop the inevitably horrific end of humanity. But it does sell cars. Wine Maker returning wheneves. English Department vows social justice. Still nothing conservative about Conservatism. Nothing natural about Nature. Nothing free about Freest Market. Etc. The mantra. The centripetal force. Generational wealth competition. Generational Wealth Complex. I didn't have it easy. Neither should they. Neither should our character. Nation barely avoiding existential crisis. All teenagers go through it. Extremely Normal Political Party. Held together. By the belief. All who follow Wine Maker. Are in this together. [They weren't]. Statistics proving statistics wrong. Our character couldn't believe the news.

Handle your business. Or someone will handle it for you. Incorrectly. Style is accidental. English Department devolves into super bitchy book club. Autocorrect takes hardline stance against cursing. For religious reasons. Have you tried unplugging Nation? And plugging it back in? Conquered people excited for change. Health Insurance on trial for crimes against humanity. During our character's space/time the concept of creativity (like everything else) was leveraged as an identifying feature to market the self. Or market a thing. [It was the same thing]. *Sua sponte.* Were we trying to make our character mad? During our character's space/time, medicines were marketed with the same care as cola and shoes. Consumer technology commercials were selling the product's ability to transform the individual into a productive consumer and entrepreneur. Reducing creativity to an empty marketing catchphrase. Making creativity synonymous with productivity. Cutting-edge technology severs artery. Revolutionary! Game-changing results!

Progress. Not progressing. During our character's space/time there was a strong demand for results. They didn't know what the results should look like. They didn't know how to get results. They just knew they wanted them. And now. Results for the sake of results. Freest Nation busy being busy. But not reimagining and implementing new ways to produce a vastly more healthy, helpful, and meaningful society. In a space/time when creative ideas were desperately needed. Creativity was relegated to an empty catchall term. At best. And at worst to the realm of productive technology. Not to improve the lives of each global citizen. To make us better consumers and entrepreneurs. To better compete with China. No acceptable plan of action possible. The private and social aspects of our character's life must reinforce the image of them selves as an entrepreneur. Of them selves. And of human capital. Don't we want our character to do well? Are overly-limiting rhetorical stances inevitable? "Who was the shithead that opened the cereal like this?" There is the way the box was meant to be opened. And there is the way our character opened it. The two seem to be at odds most of the time.

Our character wanted to be a Trillionaire. But the news said Trillionaires might be taxed more. So our character was totally disincentivized. And they became lazy. And THIS is what was wrong with Freest Nation. Need to abolish Trust Funds. They disincentivize people from entering the workforce. Forcework. Extremely Normal Politician has problem with "procedure" to remain racist. And keep foot on throat of poor. New study. Shows Every study. Wrong. Studies show. That studies show. That studies show. That studies show. That everything. Is probably good. And bad for you. I dunno. Dark chocolate. And wine. Or something. If you feel like you've read this before, you probably have. Give your secrets to the person who will always remember. But forget to tell others. Our character forgot everything. Our character remembered everything. It only existed through them. So whether it was or it wasn't. It was through them. Whether or not anything was possible. They had no control over it. That's what this whole game is for! In appreciation we see the extremes converge into their common nothingness.

The truth that might as well be true. Could our character go back. To seeing their native language. As they saw it for the first time. As a mess of indistinguishable lines. What prevents our character. From reverting back. To meaninglessness. Irregardlessness. Afraid to move outside of *logos*. Forever? Fornever? Fore ever. Before ever. In space/time. Everything will be seen as necessary. Maybe our character's dimension was space/time and language/math. Other dimensions could be different. Everything that is. IS space/time/language/math. And the unknown. Everything that is. IS unknown. The only way to win. Is to believe the game isn't over. For a while. Our character's President. Who was not our character's President. Was President. But he was wildly unqualified. He ended up making a terrible President. [Etc]. I think this explains a lot about the space/time our character lived in. You can never leave the cult of self-improvement. I have come to terms. With the chaotic collection of tasks and trips in and out of collective consciousness. That ask me only. To learn how to drown with dignity. Please die quieter. You're going to wake the children. Easier to say our character did something wrong. Than admit we made it up.

Another day. Spent treating the symptoms. Not the problem. At/during our character's space/time. Everyone knew what was wrong with our character. Nobody offered viable solutions. It surprised our character. How much everyone. Thought they knew them. Perpetually projected onto. But necessarily. Otherwise. They wouldn't be our character. Both wave and particle? How. But not why. All bachelors are unmarried. But the sun will rise tomorrow. Self-explanatory or experienced. Analytic or synthetic. Gasoline. Fill it up? Probability. Probably. Young men no longer willing to fight wars of old men. Will the future conform to the past? Faithful to no assumptions. No stage. For our character. No *stasis*. How will our character exist without you? General generally a generalist. A nomadic journey becomes necessary. Dynamic motive. A reexamination that sets our character adrift. Solutions elsewhere. A caricature of *logos*. Who would attack next? And why? "A meditation on the limits of *logos*." – The Author. The boundaries of Truth. Was our character merely an imitation of dynamic motive? Are we? Leave the form open waiting to be realized. But close the door. You're letting all the warm air out. Illuminate the reader's own contributions to the text. Our character vowed to be better prepared when asked/required to put forth their own thoughts. Freest Nation diagnoses mental health crisis as laziness. Oh good. The book is writing itself! The news should be boring. The information is disturbing enough.

Our character was trying to remember. To not say. The first thing that came into their head. Or the second thing. Or the third thing. In fact, just wait until the conversation moves on without you. Maybe write it down later. Physically fiscal. Fizzically fit. Missing teeth. Charts and graphs in congress. Debt, the price of liberty. Older generation apologizes for nothing. Only ten people can afford to live in Freest Nation's big city. But millions work there. You're an economist? Name every dollar. Influencer not influential. Monk but not religious. Exile on lame street. Work costs money. Fire and mice. Of ice and men. Forced baptism. What good is seeing the future if you can't do anything about it? Flying too close to the sun while crawling on the ground. Always erring on the side of the oppressed. Erroring. With dignity. Viewer discretion is advised. Spoilers!?! That's not the definition of retaliation. Dictator not bold. Just very stupid. Trauma. Only thing Older Generation passes down. What proof is there. That fish don't think like us? The good news. If oppressors haven't changed their tactics. Neither do we. Our character was feeling down. But then they watched clips of Orange Man. And felt better. At least they weren't them. Tune in at 8! For cool marriage trick. Tough love. Hints of insincerity. Our character wanted to be defined by their hate for person. Some day. They'll all see! [They didn't].

Much was concealed from our character. Did we know what they didn't? There was much they concealed from them selves. Did we not know that neither? [They didn't]. Everyone has disadvantages. Everyone has advantages. Does our character need more motivation? Should we provide them with a few tragedies? Maybe that will help them. [It didn't]. Dictators not even trying to hide it anymore. Creativity. A step forward. Backward. Into our selves. Our character's self. An overarching/demanding narrative expectation lifted. Allowing us to see. Alternative perspectives. To creatively respond. To highly motivated and invested communication. Allowing us to create/critique in ways that account for our dynamic and multifaceted selves. Our character's many selves. Lost count at this point. Never attempt to make others believe your interpretation. Start them on a path. Toward *thinking* about their relationship to *logos*. Embrace your muse. Create a beginning. An impetus. Narrative of possibility. For others. Instead of thinking towards closure. Facilitate an opening. In this way the writer goes beyond what they *know*. Showing how the *logos* conceals and unconceals itself. The individual can deal with *logos* outside the confines of the writer's own creation. Should we tell our character? Perchance.

"Gun owners celebrate victory." This only made sense during our character's space/time. It would take too long to explain. Made in Vietnam. Should we have our character narrowly identify with one of their selves? To market this self. For an overly specialized career? Career is being generous.

In our character's space/time. Indentured internship. False choices bountiful. Over-identifying our selves. Our character's selves. The narratives we champion. The heroic stories of inventors. I'm hooked. Were there inventors anymore? In our character's space/time. They seem to have gone missing. Overly romantic notions. Saccharine. A receptive audience. Are you? Able to carefully listen to a multitude of voices that offer opinions on the project at hand? Re-envisioning the rhetorical stances. We take. Our character takes. Forming opinions. Directing our actions. Acting our directions. Our character's actions. Etc.

Wine Maker's Top Ten Questions to Ask Anyone. At Any time. "Which person in the department is the fully-functioning, emotionally-developed human, and what steps have you taken to ruin them?" "Do you reward people for doing a good job? Or do people only deserve insults?" Our character wanted to be remembered fondly. As that one person. Who listened to jazz. And spoke real quiet. Our character thought of this. After watching a movie. Cheese wine. For women. Meat wine. For men. The devil is in the details. But also never sleeps. There's more than one way to skin a cat. But they have nine lives. It takes money to make money. But a penny saved is a penny earned. Two in the penny is one in the hedge. I don't know what you can do with this information. Historians: "Today's lecture is on 2010's – 2030's. A continuation of our lecture series on The Dark Ages that lasted from the 5ᵗʰ Century to the 22ⁿᵈ Century. A period of intellectual and spiritual depravity." Our character's professor continued: "However, the years 2019-2024 all technically count as a full century each. Although no progress was made. As far as we can tell. They attempted to eradicate the virus with. . . murder hornets. Divorce? And a female dance-ritual (wearing tight pants) on a Vine knock-off."

Unsubscribe from all. Our character's younger self. Thought they'd be taking off and landing on more aircraft carriers by now. And much more involved with pyramid adventures. Now it was pyramid schemes. Which turned out to be everything. Childhood fear of quicksand. Disproportionately irrational. Any more or less than our character's current fear of nuclear war? Difficult to say. Childhood fear of people. Spot on. There's a lot less James Bond stuff that happens in real life. Our character had never even been in a street race. Meaningful monologues during straight-razor shaves. Also never seemed to happen. Person driving fast. Also playing loud music. Amateur human. Extreme Amateur adulting. Gold, but for birds. Challenge yourday everyself.

Our character often forgot. They had to keep living. That there was still an outside of them. Skeptic not genuinely skeptical. Enough. Septic skeptic. Suspect. Slosh fest. Our character wasn't very famous. Were they? Maybe they were. And we didn't know. They didn't know. Is that more delusional? Or to be a famous person. And not know it? Our character didn't have money though. So they couldn't be famous. Our character was now trying to be sold on multiplatform exposurement in a point development context. They will guarantee return investment on structural policies. Channel your challenges to develop optimum D.R.E.A.M. capacity among team leaders. Find qualified candidates. Responsive investing communities provide growth opportunities for conglomerate collaborations with footholds in dynamic expenditure dividends. Principled growth needs daily attention. Principled growth standards need maximum attention benefits for qualitative results. Invest hard. Micro. Soft. Macro. Hard. Discover. Inspire. Enjoy! How well do you know your butter? Tonight at 8! The creative strategies we wanted to develop for our character would enable agency in an individual's everyday relations with dominating power dynamics and improve their ability to both articulate and think about their world more creatively. Should we do it?

4 WHAT THE STOCK MARKET IS SAYING BEHIND YOUR BACK AND WHY YOU SHOULD BE EMBARRASSED

The purposeful (therefore practiced and habitual) undoing of purposeful procedures. Aleatory moments. Beyond analysis. An invitation to create. "Thinking as discovery. Rather than interpretation." Should we make our character be the person other people wanted them to be? So they can get what they want? What do they want? How could we ask them. Sky Wizard must make a lot of unfounded assumptions. Marriage final scene of movie. Freest Nation failing civic duties. Infrastructure becoming unfrastructure. Not every thought our character thought. Was worth thinking. Or *interesting*, *remarkable*, and *important*. Not every conversation our character had was worth analyzing and re-playing millions of times in their mind. Our character had been accused of worse. Our character needed enough drugs, merit badges, and visual stimulation to make them think everything was either "fine' or fundamentally unchangeable. They had always admired the pacification of organized religion. Our character was racing along the fault lines of false dichotomies. To allow them selves the ability to look back on a space/time. When they weren't an unapologetic opportunist. Our character was typically never this lucid. Or well spoken. Are we surprised? They continued darkly. We are merely attempting to apologize for the apocalypse we weren't able to avoid. French pop music playing faintly. In the background. Over opening credits. A late-night scene. People talking. Overheard in conversation. Our character was having with them selves. "Huh… Five-year warranty? Pretty good."

You can never see where you are. Everything remade. Writer's room sacks plot where amoral, lawsuit riddled, failed real-estate/casino tycoon from the big city is out of touch with farmers in heartland. It was too predictable. Hallmark movie indistinguishable. "No! You do NOT have time to clip your toenails!" Weird domestic arrangement. Domestic arrangement getting weird. Apparently normal. We made our character search for what was real via evidence. But just as important. Our character recognized their thought process in another's thoughts. Were they our thoughts? Should we make everything productive for our character? Creating *logos*. Allows us. Not necessarily certainty. But the reproduction of thoughts. Freest Nation runs on gossip. Gossip Nation. Embarrassment. And shame. If we called him Donald. Nobody would take him seriously. Nation unhelpful. In every way. A lot happens once we realize how un-dramatic our lives are (whether they are or not). This is being rhetorically un-positioned. Our character was only able to accomplish this occasionally.

NRA suggests outlawing schools. Rainbow in sky is surprisingly homophobic. Couple looking for mid-century modern house. Open concept. Kitchen with space to entertain. And a clawfoot bathtub. Reality TV competition is why humans never deserved consciousness.

Which household electrical appliances are trying to murder you? Tonight at 8! New candle scent: laser tag room. Drones are just remote-controlled airplanes. Big deal, our character thought. We move through stories. The narratives we generate for our selves. For others. For our character. Keep going after we are dead. But how would we know? Living through dead stories. Is this the only place we live? Our data will live on. Perchance. If we can make stories out of it. Could they re-compile us from our collective data? Through our character's Google searches? Are we/our character better able to move through our stories/data without a fixed reference point? A fixed reference point that we have come to learn is our individual self? There are people you know. That you will never see again. After today. This is not forever. Great art is reality. Nothing worth knowing. Could be worth knowing. Our character got close to making this connection but couldn't quite. For the religious person. Everything is evidence we need more religion. For the atheist. Everything is evidence we don't. Our biggest fear is having nothing to push against. In the future. We won't say "They died. Now they are with Sky Wizard." We will say. "Now they are with Google."

Our character was doing a lot of talking. For how horny they were. If only our character was this witty sober. I'm like a fine wine. I'll get you drunk. Let's get high and go to the grocery store. You can really do a lot with eggs. Freest Nation rationing. Rationality. The ability to abandon one's faith. In their own presuppositions. When signs of failure appear. Our character read this somewhere. If you live long enough. Time will kill you. Our character had to be the favorite person of someone. And therefore. The least favorite of someone else. But this was in constant flux. When they became older. They were surprised so much could change. How much more would have to change? Hadn't enough changed? We had no answers for them. Our character was thought of. As much as anyone else. And with similar sentiments. Our character bounced around in the heads of others (especially ours). And in their own head. A layer. A stage. A *stasis* of reality. One that made sense of their senses. It appeared to have always been like this. As far as they knew. As far as we knew. We/our character knew there were colors. We couldn't see. Sounds we couldn't hear. And years we'd never live. Still. Everything somehow still made sense to us. Odd. Life apparently not that important. According to Freest Nation. Freest Nation vows to explode world peace "all over your asses."

If we have no problems to deal with. We will make up our own. Out character too? Makes our job easier. Are you better able to tell your 3

Or are others? Are we better able to tell our character's story? Or are they? Person wasn't told they died. An administrative error on heaven's part. Bored Sky Wizard creates purgatory. Terrible parenting. Leads to raising a psychopath. Really great parenting. Leads to raising a psychopath. High fashion. Taking something poor people do. Out of necessity. And turning it into something optionally-mandatory for upper class. Without poor people there would be no culture. Addicted to poverty. Parenting automatically qualifies you for a career in hostage negotiations. Cat man don't. Our character unnecessarily worried their confidence was holding them back. [It wasn't]. Our character's memory was always supplying a now. You can't know the last step. Otherwise you would be an infinity. I don't know what this means. Logic isn't circular. It's spherical. Everything is working to become spherical. You are the in-between extremes.

People who drink wine. Are 100% guaranteed to drink wine. People who drink more wine. Tend to drink more wine. Our character wasn't drinking tonight. They were just going to have a couple glasses of wine. Somedays. Parents agree. They weren't ready to have children. Other days. They were drunk. Our character had grown tired of their married friends. Our character would probably attend the next holiday gathering. But none thereafter. It's very difficult to convince someone you're not an alcoholic. It's very difficult to convince someone you're not a serial killer. It's very difficult to convince someone you're not a total psychopath. It's very difficult to convince someone you're not a habitual liar. But it's also very difficult to convince someone you're an artist. Our character had tried for several years. But to no avail. They would give up. And start again. Innumerable times.

Sky Wizard blames devil for banishing devil. Sky Wizard creates devil. To make Sky Wizard. A failure to pinpoint the problem. Its causes. And the solution. Company blames employee. A way to form a conclusion. Without having to address anything fundamental. That could cause a total reworking of the system. That would make everything better for everyone. Idiots still in charge. An unhelpful conclusion. Many minds. Or mini minds. Freest Nation vows to never learn from experience. Our character did not have the luxury of staying mad at others. World's average quality of life is abject poverty. What's the matter with people? Represent the unrepresented. Resent the unrepresented. Represent the resented. Compounded problem. Older Generation offended. Not as entertaining as professional actors. Should our character perpetuate these misunderstandings? A generalization of another generalization. Very Normal Older Generation asleep on couch. Blames younger generation for taking naps. Heidegger unnecessarily confusing. No summarization. Just transference. An attempt at reproducing the same.

[Captions Auto-Generated]. Our character was undefeated. At

being alive. Parent starts pointless conversation with pointless question. Unqualified person comments in the comments section. Unqualified person does not know they are unqualified. Self-advertising and advertising. A *logos* of event. Of accomplishment. The "tonight" of tonight. So much self-interest. Interest charged on self. The assumption we can progress. Or gain. You can multitask. Question the thing that brings someone the most success. Question your ability to question. You have to be something. To grow out of it. Regret is growth. We are a new person. We would have done it differently. Appreciation transcends regret. Regret is tied to Tick-Tock time. Appreciation is *kairotic* time. Cathartic time. Assigning significance to what our perception makes significant. Everything that is. Is necessary. Our character didn't connect with seasons anymore. Don't spend yourself in the first. The awareness of creating memories. Dreaming is knowing. We will not be able to connect these thoughts. Later. Why should we let something like reality get in the way of a good thing? Our character laughed out loud in their apartment. Eventually, we came to accept this version of events. If at first you don't succeed. Try again. And then stop. She's never coming back to you.

Our character feared death would be boring. Self-punishment is reflection without appreciation. You are the boundaries you set. To maintain what you think you are. Your economy of person. The moment. Our character saw their perspective tilted. In a way. They did not consider. Always another game to play. All *logos* works to explain itself. It flows out. It comes back to itself. We stay still. We are the thing in circles. In cycles. You travel alone. Our character could only change something. If they could change something. Everything is water. It isn't. But imagine if it was. It is. [It wasn't]. Etc. If you suspect someone is a con artist. They aren't. Our character needed to see the effects of their private idiosyncrasies on others. Helping or harming? Listening to the *logos* of motives. The motives hidden in familiarity. Rewarded. In other instances. Riveting departure monologue. Through the background music. The viewer understands the setting. Modern Nation. Still no health. Or care. White people. Am I right?

Music getting too mainstream. Our character started listening to recordings of plates being scratched by forks. Our character was asked if they believed in Sky Wizard. They didn't even know if careers existed. Music getting too mainstream. Our character listened to animals. Because they have a lot to say. We have much to learn from them. Not really. I dunno. Brave men and women have died for Freest Nation. To protect your right to get shot. Minding your own business. Show some fucking respect. You worthless shit. Our character should work to complicate their *logos* of motivation. The best equipped to understand this relationship. Have the most difficulty. In dealing with it. We don't want our character to be blind to what is right in front of them. The suffering of others. Our character's perceptiveness. Prevents them from understanding. Their inability to perceive suffering. It is their confidence in *logos* that conceals their relationship with *logos*. The notion that somewhere. Someone is recording all of this. Some Sky Wizard will remember. Some Being. Some View. Some Perspective. It understands. Watching us watch ourselves. Watching Sky Wizard. What we cannot overcome. Also defines us. This is where we are. Subjected to subjecting. The next evolution. Will be beyond this.

Nothing will change my mind. My mind is my heart. And my heart has been taken. By you. My arms are my upper legs. My hands are arm feet. Etc. Trash Nation. How cute. Stitches get snitches. "My mosquito! Fall into my soup of the day. Drown in lovers' broth. Is it no wonder? I am your love prisoner?" To be completely insane. But never believe you are. To believe that the best part of life is death. To be totally dependent of nothing. Except your dependence on nothing. To be sad about nothing and happy with everything. Therefore neither. Our character could maximize their time. By not believing in time. Thereby minimizing it. There is nothing to understand. Except what you understand to be nothing. When you are alive. To believe you are dead. And when you are dead. To believe you are alive. Death lasts longer? A judgment that rests solely. On the confirmation of an external reality. Based on a clearly recognizable visual representation. A judgment complicating judgment. Judging our character's ability to listen. No easily determinable criteria. No easily accessible evidence. That can reaffirm our confidence in understanding *logos* and ourselves. To hear the unheard. Listeners of *logos*. An impetus for listening. Concealed from us.

"Even a broken clock is right twice a day." Our character didn't understand. When they were younger. "If the clock is off, it will never be right." But they meant the clock had stopped moving. Our character was the most generous. When nothing was at stake. Women are women too! It seems as if. From a very early age. Our character learned. Being good. Would never be good enough. Joining our dream state. Our character was no longer a step behind space/time. We are space/time. We run with space/time. With everything through us. Fragments of thoughts and memories. No longer fragmented. We are them. Our character. They are everything. Etc. No more questions asked. For the sake of your dreams. Follow your fancies. Only follow what's magical. Irresponsibility is derived from holding on to fancies not pursued. We should make our character smart enough. To realize they are an idiot. You are an idiot? We are an idiot. When everyone becomes their own Sky Wizard. Developing a complete moral rationale. Atheism should be believed. To eliminate theism. Believe in anarchy. To eliminate hierarchy. Based on poverty. Starbucks store opens university. Princeton Chevy Truck Corporation. Stanford Doritos Airforce University. University of Wisconsin—Bud Light Lime.

University of Amazon Ohio wins another championship. "Shut up Joseph. You're not my real dad!"

If ever reproached. For not raising your child to be follower of Wine Maker. Respond: "Wine Maker wasn't raised under teachings of Wine Maker. And look how Wine Maker turned out." Classic White. Greek Architecture. Not white. Asking someone on date. Still most likely way to ensure rejection. In the end everything was built for nothing. Will the process remain essential? To mentally retrace the path. In prison. Would our character have enough thoughts to think about? To have enough lives to re-live. Prison is the only place where they give you time. But they take your space. Living in nation takes your time. But gives you space. Barely. It's not theirs to give. Nor to take. But they do. Can't just have random people living a good life. The only goal. To perpetually generate inspiration for yourself (and others?). Consciousness fundamentally flawed. Sleep a necessary detox. Life the poison. Periodically silence the inside voice. Of our character. Also ours. And yours. Etc. One cannot separate them selves to view them selves. Dreams allow this view. Our experience of ourselves. Mediated through others. And mirrors. Our unconscious dream state. Another self?

Our character invested millions. In waffle themed office supplies. It's called Office Waffle. We will sell: waffle staplers, waffle office chairs, waffle paper, waffle printers, lamps… made of waffles. You can die. But you have to do a lot of pointless shit before that. Our character liked this show. But sometimes found the jokes confusing. And weird. Always only do. What people will think you'll do. The least. View of our selves. Denied in consciousness. Evidence of existence. Incomplete and paradoxical. Space/time. Fundamentally flawed. Correct understanding. Of what we consider to be space/time. Present only in dreams. In consciousness. Everything based. On something else. When something fails. It sets downward. All holding on. To *logos*. Only copied. And slightly modified. To fit the individual's needs. Only borrowed. Borrowed space/time. Modification is illusion. By covering all possible possibilities. This view might be flawed. But it is present. For our character? For our selves? Our character ran their fingers over their lips. To check if they were saying these things out loud

Our character wondered. Could there be any newly discovered continents? Fans love new Popstar. Spelling a hoax. Created to embarrass people. Independently poor. Starting new religion. If these hot people don't screw. I'm not watching another episode. Second season of show. Scraps creative concepts. To focus on lame character development. Kid can tell when parent skips pages now. Wasn't coffee supposed to be bad for us? Pouring thing into different container. A fucking disaster. Beethoven brought to you by Honda Stage and T-Mobile Concert Series at Bank of

America Stadium Auditorium. Parents still waiting. To see if their child turns out to be total psychopath. Before publishing self-help book. Our character still not sure why all their friends had kids. It was a race. Our character was watching the news. Lucky despot gets retaliatory violence they need to justify genocide. Of powerless socioeconomic class. Taxation without representation doesn't make list of Top 100 Human Atrocities. Not even close to the Library of Alexandria. Staunch political party loses interest. During sports season.

A major driving force in the creative process. And self-inquiry. The suspicion. Everything you are doing is terrible. While not pleasant. Doesn't it help me the most? And what I promote the least? The most self-blinding rhetorical stance. Thinking everyone else. Thinking our character (as you are now). Is missing something. Only you can see. Essential to creativity. Truly brilliant people. Never create anything. *Logos* is mimetic. They know. They aren't the only ones. Who have thought the thing. We are thinking now. What did this say about our writer? Our inability to hear many things. At once. *Logos* with its own translation/instructions. What would that look like? How could you make *logos* the simplest. But still fantastic enough. To provide illusions. So others (maybe even our character?) are able to build worlds. Finding the universe in anything and everything. Obfuscation or expertise? Being able to understand the difference. And how it acts as a steering strategy. Away. A way of protecting intellectual property. From outsiders. Our character got the absolute shit kicked out of them. Wasn't the first. Or last time. Wasn't going to make the healing happen any faster. Down but never out. But definitely down. Our character hadn't heard much about the Bermuda Triangle recently.

The story of a murderous filmmaker. Only they don't know. They are. They murder in their sleep. Or while suffering a psychotic episode. Etc. Their unconscious. Has launched a heroic revenge narrative. On unsuspecting people. They had never met before. Everyone is innocent enough. Maybe not. Sky Wizard says sin original. But this character is on a mission. Of internalized is self-preservation. They are the victim. And they might be? Their unconscious disguises their actions. Even from them selves. But not from us? The filmmaker makes a film based on the murders. They cast themself in the lead role. By accident. Until opening night of the film. They realize. They are the murderer. They try to stop the film from being played. But others assume the filmmaker is merely nervous. The film is a huge success. Everyone raves about how real the acting was. It becomes famous. Maybe they all eventually realize it was real. But we could just leave it at that. Hotcakes are selling like hotcakes. This crack is like crack. The Taj Mahal of itself. Sliced bread is the best thing since itself. Have you seen that one car commercial for butter? Remember that one dream I had?

Perchance. Our character felt. Actions helped erase the wrong. By holding up mistakes for inspection. Some people wished they could see more. Our character wished they could see less. Turning mistakes into advice for others. Either way. We finished the novel. And there I was. At the place when consequences become reality. No more speculation. Fear only works. As a temporary power. Inquisitions making a comeback. Make Inquisitions Great Again. Inquisition Nation. We aren't supposed to be this old. And have this good of eyesight. We can see too far. Able to hold onto the anxiety of youthful competition. Unable to let it go. As we let our vision go. We can still see a potential mate in the distance. We can still see a potential competitor in the distance. The heightened awareness remains. We remain anxious. When you get older you are supposed to only see what's in front of you. Only concentrating on not tripping. The competitions are blurry. In the distance. Technology. Always doing something our minds cannot account for.

Oh good another day. Our character had to out crazy. The crazies. Our character's password situation is seriously fucked. Passwords are useless. If you can't remember them. Turns out fascism. Not unprofessionalism. Caused latest genocide. Our character was constantly running scenarios in their head. A computer. Accidentally left computing. Probability scenarios. The average. Would be the through line they could walk. Armchair quarterback. Backseat driver. Fortunately. Everyone was too caught up in their own story. To remember ALL the stupid our character had stupided. Or all the stupid. Our character suspected. Everyone thought they did. Engineer who "lacks people skills." Also a shitty engineer. Our character felt fortunate. To have been part of the child's development into adulthood. During that commercial. This would all sound better. If you read it in a British Accent. Nation's Christianity. Mainly judgment. We thought we survived the horror. We were wrong. Again. Popstar sounds like department store looks.

The music had been building to this point. Somewhat too obviously. Am I going to have to do everything for myself? Yes. You are yourself. Oh right. PhD in Fast Food Services now required for entry level positions at McDonald's Haliburton University. Assistant Director of Economically Expedient Nourishment. Audience intelligence insulted by pandering. Did they know? Is this commercial selling phones? The concept of transcendence? Nationalism? Or Popstar's next movie? Thing said to prove a point. Doesn't address point. Playing hard to get. Hard to get. Big ending. Our character has big band playing behind them. Then maybe some desert setting with more traveling. If the answer to everything came to our character. They would not have to speak it. But they would. They'd write it down. At least. That's all there is. Coming up with stuff. And writing it down. But that's why the answer won't come to our character. As opposed to the lie of Truth. When the Truth is a secret. It becomes untrue. Becomes guarded. Becomes ritualized. It does the most harm. And least good. Only fools believe answers exist. Narrowing to one. Rather than many. Deduction. Rather than induction. Crossing out. Rather than brainstorming. Mind hail. Hail brain! Broken car windows. The posthumans might be disinterested in running ancestor-simulations.

Nation decides cars talking in children's movies is normal. College freshman writes essay that settles abortion debate. Our character was over group dancing. We get it. You're all doing the same thing. Our character only wanted to be good at everything. And didn't think this was too much to ask. Turns out. It hardly ever matters if you are right. Our character hadn't learned this lesson yet. Would they ever? Find out. [They didn't]. There is always truth to a conspiracy. But again. Conspiracy theorists should never be told this. I haven't been outside long. My coffee is still hot. Our character's new measure of space/time. Our character was starting to listen to only half the thoughts they thought. Not sure if it's working. Or it's just working half the time. Therapy works great. If you can get an appointment. And you can afford it. Therefore. The people who need therapy the most. Almost never get it. Mission accomplished. "He really lost the thread with this one." – The Author. Entertainment is shit. But the comments section has never been better.

News segment pandering too obviously to women. Cringe. I'm going to murder the next person who eats celery around me. Our character wanted to think they knew just enough. To be really dangerous. Did our character even really communicate with anyone? Or are they in a hamster bubble of spherical self? Greenhouse effect. But for emotions. And thoughts. Perpetually adding our interactions together to construct the wall of the bubble. Allowing us to differentiate our selves from others. To get outside our selves. You and everyone builds the bubble. The ever-present surrounding perspective looking in at you. The eye of the panopticon. The eye is you. The you of everyone's perceived perspective. Your eye is the bubble. You plaster these perceptions onto the wall of the bubble. Achievements. You surround yourself in this sphere. Everyone helps build the wall of the bubble. Success is your ability to construct a bubble. Preventing others from seeing. Everything inside. Not knowing. They already can (at least. We can). In regards to our character. Nobody can see the gaps in who you are. So you can't see the gaps in who you are. Our character's bubble was the only measure of how they fit in. Commendable attempt to carry many things. Fails immediately. Person with power abuses it. Our character tried to go to sleep. But couldn't. If only they could remember the thoughts they thought they thought. Etc.

During our character's space/time they had ceremonies. They built monumental monuments. To say. This was the space/time. These are the people. Our character vowed they would never talk to that person again.

They talked to them the next day. To avoid social discomfort. Not *cogito ergo sum*. But 'if interested' *ergo sum*. If interested in something. Then you are. Or you are not. That's you. *Cogito ergo all. Et al. Etc. E.g.* Eggs. Dinosaurs came first. What gets you interested. Will tell you more about yourself. Than what you tell about yourself. To yourself. And others. Our character could not fake appreciation or interest. If it's there. It's there. The most *now* you can be. Rhetoric inseparable from philosophy. From *logos*. Gaining the interest of others. A thread that pulls apart. And brings together. Our space/time. *Logos*: an evolution of dichotomies. "It was more difficult than the first books I wrote. Not sure if that means it's better." – The Author. "Read this one. Not the others. But don't read this one either." – The Author.

What will the posthumans be interested in? The prehumans? Not chasing the past. As if it expires. We want to be narrativized. Addicted. The only solution to self. We know/can perform. Relieving our anxiety. About death. Emptiness. Being non-narrativized. Our unconscious (our character) is simply the narrative perspective we deliberately choose not to see. Must be ignored/forgotten to move. "Forward." The narrative we are attempting to tell about our lives. Narrative expectations. Always. Almost out of reach. Although with practice. You might avoid chit chat. A circular understanding to widen our vision. The expansion of the self. Into everything. The dramatic turn. The world as it isn't. Our character makes the mistake. They're never going to do it again. They might do it. Sometime in the future. They might do it a few days a week. They make the mistake again. They're never going to do it again. Etc. Somehow. It just keeps going. Eventually. Our character hoped to be in the right mind. To let it take them. But this is difficult. Giving up one's selves. To something else. Should we make our character do what everyone told them to do? The self without self. With thought. Might as well. What our character needed to get. To be the person. Other people want. So they could get. What they want. People didn't want honesty. They wanted to not be anxious. About everything. All the time.

During our character's space/time. Other's wanted proof. Our character would be subordinate. To something. We wanted proof of this too. Otherwise. We'd stop reading/writing. At least. The most terrifying thing. Was someone who had no Sky Wizard. They wanted proof. You were serving someone. A cause. B cause. Because. Be a cause. Because. Etc. An "ethics." A "morality." B (plus). Believing. Be leaving. Bee living in Sky Wizard was the easiest way to assimilate into normalcy. A list of requirements. The people would continue to be "shocked." When others transgressed. This normalcy. That wasn't a good indication. Of anything. Normal. Normalcy was necessarily transgressed. For them to feel. They weren't transgressing. [They were]. Cause and effect. Simple. Brutal. Our character had crossed the actual line. Legitimately acting against the pact.

Against the past? Between them selves and society. That which ensures harmony. In a non-harmonious Nation. Nation of discontent. Agitation. Rumor and Justice. Sudden death. Overtime. Underspace. A pact they never signed. The landslide of reasons. Justifying. Didn't matter. And there they were. Again. In what can be considered their present. At the place where consequences and actions become reality. Not merely constant speculation. "If you don't usually read books like this, you're probably not going to like this book." – The Author.

We had our character considered optometry school. At some point in this book. There are only two things in the universe. What is currently shit. What will become shit. A species of feces. People aren't getting faster. More people are joining the competition. Eventually we will plateau. Or else. We will have people running 1 second miles. Then nobody will beat the fastest time. They will only be able to tie it. Insane people. Have too many souls. Two mini-soles. When there is a fine line between enough and insanity. No matter what you do in this period. It will be great. [Not necessarily]. So at least there is that. Space/time is emotion. Etc. Our character should order space/time. Not as rungs on a ladder. But by emotion. Stress of tasks. And calculating their worth. Their length and their mass. By how much feeling-gravity it displaced. We allowed. Our character to hear. The conversation in Beethoven. All emotion. No language. Our character told them selves. Don't throw away that box! We might need it for something! Once again. Our character entered the room asking a pointless question. To nobody in particular. They realized. They did all the things. Other people do. That they hate. Our character was growing tired of this lesson. It stretched them too thin person-wise.

Our character did everything. Everyone asked them to do. But very reluctantly. Perhaps over hundreds of years. They made sure its completion was undetectable. They didn't want to raise expectations. Tardigrade elected President. Lack of sleep and indigestion. Caused by everything. How do you connect with this conscious unconsciousness? We grow out of ourselves. Stretching elastic. Recoiling like a spring. When completely focused on the task/thought at hand. Our character will be leaning out of them selves. Completely silent. Thinking no thoughts. Nearly being in the same space/time. As your self. Perfect alignment is death. Our character was comprised of this progression. Moving forward and backward into them selves. The middle. A medium amount of awareness. In the medium. Thing isn't just thing. It's a culture. Etc. We have ways of sneaking below. We can't sink all the way down. Staying above creates consciousness. The ability to sink down far enough. To propel us up the other side. Teeter-totter. We stay in the middle. If our character arrived at the extremes. They would find. They are traveling in a circle. The two ends meet up. Being the same thing. And other. Not opposite. Can you go back to a different state of the self? Multi-spaced/timed. Going back and reading this. I am in the future. And looking back at this space/time in the past. That is happening now. We just don't have a strong enough connection to it. Anymore. Small towns cannibalizing. Via the "event." Perhaps a metaphor can provide a visualization.

Your life becomes habited. You forget people will know you forever by this. Scientists discover yet another way to destroy humanity. Person overcomes tragedy to win TV contest to win TV. There is nothing before birth. There is nothing before waking. There is nothing more terrifying than animatronic Disney characters. New artist is different. The longer a power structure is established. The less space/time it has. Historical trends. History of trends. History tends to trend. The rise and fall of empires. Inevitable. The inability to gain self-certainty in a role that is other-than-self. In the dramatically "serious" moments it is unconcealed. They lack a sense of belonging. Eventually the constant swapping out of identities catches up with our character. But not yet. God watching Christian masturbate. Wait. Why are they watching? Who's the pervert now, God? Follower of Wine Maker praising Sky Wizard wrong. Chubby. Less charming man. Will probably be more faithful in movie. Speaking of speaking in tongues. Joseph disappointed in Wine Maker's lifestyle choices. I guess every artist gets to this point. Desperate enough. To throw everything against the wall. When they are the most broken. They can come back from the dark. And retrieve it for us. In communist countries you don't get to choose. In the USA. It's AT&T. Our character went to an art show where the artist was attempting to *create a dialogue*. A move toward the obscure. The only way to momentarily allow our character to question the clarity of their motives. An imitation of dynamic motive. Not restricted by the *mise-en-scène*. But instead compliments. Our character. They were going to lose. They had to lose. To be controlled. By torturous hours of routine paperwork. And official documents. Blue collar crime was embarrassing. And all consuming. White collar crime got you a two-hour special produced by Netflix Apple Inc. What color collar did our first caller wear? Be the second caller to find out! At 8!

Nation only keeping score. When they are winning. If our character knew what they didn't know. Maybe they would spontaneously combust. Our character wasn't necessarily an idiot. Rather. It's possible they were merely more aware of how much of an idiot they were. And were better equipped to handle the realization. Than others. Our character suddenly remembered. They forgot about something fun. They were going to do next. The "dead" time. In-between. Moments of socioeconomic importance. The moments that propel the narrative "forward." The only reason you still read. And we still write. And our character still characterizes. It's the words you don't say. Performance artist's performance starts to collapse on itself. Trapped in performance. Maintaining identities. Extremely Normal Political Party rushes to make same horrible mistake twice. Too much content. Imagine the works that move you. And your favorite teachers. Encouragement to create/think differently. *Free Spirit* makes waiter take food back. And doesn't tip. Wears a lot of bracelets. Tries to look homeless. Has trust fund. Zeitgeist. Naps. Truck Month somewhere. Deep State cover blown by retirees Frank and Debbie Smith from Homestead, South Dakota. In five years. Everyone will live in South Dakota. We are all just one bad/day night a way. From leaving civilization. And starting a cult commune in South Dakota. In desperate need of an authenticating myth. Urgency of perfection. The joy of attempting an authentification. That will (thankfully/hopefully) always fall comically short. Truck won truck award. According to truck commercial.

Look to texts that provide not mirror (not mere) images of ourselves. But a view of our exaggerated selves. Caricatures taken to logical absurdities. *Reductio ad absurdum ergo sum*. Not merely a belief in "knowledge." Started to feel like Fall today. Our character thought. I don't want to think. All beauty is born from grief. But it might be. What do you want to know about our character? Furthermore. Perchance. WHAT do you want to know about our character? What DO you want to know? What do YOU want to know? What do you WANT to know about our character? What do you want TO know? What do you want to KNOW about our character? What do you want to know ABOUT our character? What do you want to know about OUR character? What do you want to know about our CHARACTER?

During our character's space/time. It was unnecessary to play a role in their financial transactions. Yet they did. And it took up most of their space/time (hence their stupidity). Our character's work. Should communicate with our character's bank. Who in turn. Should communicate with our character's bills. And to close the loop. The government should be recording everything. And communicate all of this to our character's work. For their taxes. Since they all. Already did this. The missing link. Preventing this from happening? Our character shouldn't be involved. It would be more efficient. But would our character be who they are? Perhaps they never were. Their identity. Their economy. The wasted space/time it takes. For money to move around. The never-ending cycle. Value is our character's inefficiency. Value is wasted space/time. Or poor investments. Carelessness, stupidity, Etc. To create wealth. Create poverty. Create stupidity.

It is easy to calculate. The amount of money our character needs to live. That others need to live. Schedule time for them to work. And leave it at that. They were all already trying to do this. Let them? There was a gap in their knowledge. Flowing underneath. The unconscious. They didn't know.

Creating value. By devaluing. Elsewhere. The problem with *logos*. Is the problem with money. We can't solve one. Without the other. What is preventing us from realizing this? The thing preventing this. Is propping up everything. Hopefully we will know what it is. Before we knock it down. [They didn't know]. Why we didn't know. Why others didn't know. Why our character doesn't know. Etc. It is preventing our selves from understanding the pointlessness. And therefore. The purpose. It IS *logos*. Find the scapegoat. They will tell you who's in charge. The only one. Who can tell the truth. Has nothing left. If AI could replace our character's job. Why couldn't it replace their boss's? Let's ask AI. [They couldn't].

5 WHY TO BE UNSUCCESSFUL
(TIPS FROM AND EXPERT)

Sitting on toilet still favorite place to plot the death of loved ones. Sitting on toilet still best place to generate social media content. Shitting on toilet still best place to generate social media content. Someone who drinks pee: a piss-cetarian. Parent spends 75% of bathroom time to GET A FUCKING SECOND TO BREATHE. Sky Wizard in open relationship. I'll pretty much eat anything at this point. "A poor man's Voltaire." - Author. Love. Smothering our character. To death. Our "choice" in purchasing what we want. The freedom the Freest Nation was founded on. Building/enacting our identities. Prevents us from realizing them. Everything generated by this circular cycle (when we should be spherical). We haven't been able to get out of the circle. For long enough. To realize other ways of Being. The more space/time you spend poking your head out of the circle as you go by. The harder it is to go around the circle. Looking slows you down. You have to be bad at playing the game. To understand it. Only the poor know how to be rich. So they can never be rich. Only insane people understand consciousness. But they can't do anything with it. Everyone has a biopic now. Asking poor people for money was probably one of the stupidest things they did during our character's space/time. Holy shit! Did our character actually know something others didn't? This was odd. It also meant. Nobody was in-charge. [We weren't].

Being right. Had almost never helped our character. Being right had almost never mattered during our character's space/time. It was a decent way of getting people to take their foot off your throat (sometimes). No assurance in insurance. Statistics proved our character wrong. Statistics proved those statistics wrong. As if statistics held a Truth. [They didn't]. Merely a way to show our character something they didn't know. Or couldn't think. A means. Not an end. This would plague our character's space/time for some space/time. Nobody believed our character. Therefore. Our character was the only one who could tell the truth. Capitalism necessarily short-changed deep space/time. The problems of Capitalism. Were not solved via Capitalism. Nation would realize this. Too late. Pennies on the dollar. Committee gets it wrong. Again. Turns out. The one they chose. Was the one. Nobody wanted. Again. Democracy only as good as education. And not the education. The committee members had. Our character finally caught up to three weeks ago. It's not a proper tangent if you remember where you were going. Are there any Hollow Earthers? I could believe it. Full cavity cavity search. I'm done with the grind. When do I get healthcare? For the teeth I've been grinding?

Our character was suffering. They must be making great art.

Otherwise. They assumed they weren't suffering. That much. Our character wasn't even close to waking up. Every living thing: "Let's make more of me." Most lives were spent fulfilling requirements created by idiots. Need more field trips. If you think people are talking about you. They are. You are. We are. Etc. "When our world needed a hero. More than ever. They got this book instead." - The Author. Our character tripped over what must have been a chair (they never saw it). They spilled their glass of red wine. All over what they assumed could have been their soulmate. Then they mistakenly mumble something incoherently romantic. To the person sitting next to what could have been their soulmate. And never saw their soulmate again. Interesting. Our character had grown tired of these stories. They would start reading it again tomorrow. Oh good. Another day. Again. Too pissed to sleep-in.

Sometimes the hardest thing to do. Is the wrong thing to do. Commercial telling our character to be "bold." Doesn't know about restraining order. Fork wrong utensil this time. Did our character fail because they were too honest? Probably not. But regardless. People never want honesty. They want to be right. And to conform the world. To their pre-established suppositions. It was much easier to do this. Requiring no creative thinking. *Homo economicus* had convinced them. Impossible to do otherwise. Space/time simply wouldn't allow it. People don't want you to be humble. They want you to act like the you they think you are. They need evidence you're serving a higher purpose. Other than yourself. If only. Your past self. If not. They fear you. They can't trust. You will follow the rules. This dementia can't early onset fast enough. Older Generation on TV again. In my day. The government didn't bail you out. And I had to cook our dog for dinner. And marry our cat. Freest Market chooses socialism. I've caught the plague. Or it's Tuesday.

Our character could only fall asleep. When they woke up. Person suffering from addiction. To public radio pledge drives. Our character takes leap of faith. Moves digital porn collection to the cloud. Our character was always trying to get into soccer. But they never knew if they should root for T-Mobile? Or Hyundai? Or Fly Emirates? Maybe our character was writing for redemption. Was our character writing this? It couldn't not be. Turning their mistakes into advice. Maybe this helped erase their mistakes. [It didn't]. Either way. It changed nothing. They still wrote/read. And needed to finish. Our character was wondering how to act as a person. In the outside place. They assumed they were doing it wrong in the before times too. Someone much smarter than them has probably already said this. You ever find yourself shitting and eating at the same time? That doesn't even make sense in human.

How can the finished design maintain the status of a sketch? Allowing the user to reperceive their relationship with the design. And the designer. The medium. Intentions. The sketch must retain the elements of a finished product. Instead of trying to make the design *look* like a sketch. Make our finished design *act* like a sketch. Allowing the audience to abandon a sense of finality. Without pandering. Providing ambiguity within the design. Deciding what not to close off. Making connections. Leaving some connections unfinis. . . An invitation to create. A sketch of the proposed "event." Barely finished. Enough. We don't tell our guests. Everything that should happen. A costume party. Where our character was. It was fine. Some people they knew. Others they didn't. Good conversations with some. Offended by others. At least they didn't over-share. For once. They would. Next space/time. Drink every time a commercial refers to "these times" as "difficult" or "uncertain." Carbo loading for the apocalypse. End of world anticlimactic. If the world were a better place. Our character would absolutely be an idealist.

Our character was surprised. They weren't as bad as person. They thought they were as bad as. They also weren't as good as others. But they didn't need to hear that now. We'd tell them later. Our character went to the movie theater. The movie's main character had skills/strengths based off mistaken perceptions. Accidental happenstance. Fodder for comedy. Preventing them from perceiving. A certain way. They weren't. A cascade of perspectives. Keep caving in. All narrators untrustworthy. Untrustworthy readers. Person who claims they are "Independent." Really Republican. "Hustle." "Culture." Really just Older Generation. Regifting trauma. And applying to "new" industries. [It didn't work]. Freest Nation heavily surveilled, censored, policed, and imprisoned. [It didn't work]. Etc. Movie allowed our character to survive the trauma. Live through the tension. Without effecting the story. Others would tell about them.

In the movie. Situations based on flawed perspectives. Relatable. When science fails. It was all too human. And contextual. Science too religious. And too political. An excuse for science not being a science. Only as good. As the humans who use it. Nation too emotionally illiterate to develop alongside technology. Crust is bread peel. The kids are right. No crust! No crust! No crust! Nobody starts reading a book. They open it. They tell them selves. They'll look at the first couple pages. Then they find them selves. Reading the book. A lot was probably like this. In our character's space/time. When space/time is the price. It isn't given freely. Only begrudgingly. And not often. If at all. Author tells them selves they'll sit down and work on a couple pages. Then they find themselves. Writing the book. Our character had to purchase insurance at the restaurant before they got their meal. During our character's space/time. You had to apply for everything. They made industries out of it. They didn't realize. Just because you *could* make an industry out of something. Doesn't mean you *should*. Password prevents healthcare. Again. Child puts down payment on candy. Baby leasing crib before buying. Older generation says. That's the way things work. Around here. After making things work. The way they work. Around here. Parent has to choose between food or vaccine for child.

Background check needed for dating app. Paperwork prevents procreation. Lifestyles of the poor and unknown. Something as arbitrary as money was seemingly significant. During our character's space/time. They praised some people for having "more" of "it." Life was a lot like High School. And a game show. Where nobody won. Most of the contestants didn't want to play. And the same people kept winning. Our character was still trying to figure out how to monetize their problematic ability to disassociate. "I wanna be hard-core. But still super safe." Our character thought. Maybe they'd get a tattoo. We are all on our way to becoming something else. Multiracial skateboarding crew selling cars, cellphone service, and hard seltzer. Billionaires running out of ways to spend money. Our character had to pretend the majority of things happening. Weren't happening.

Looking back. Our character couldn't understand why. Never the problem child. So how? Why all this? Because it could happen to anyone. It didn't matter. Good people did good things. Bad people did bad things. This explanation. Was good enough for Older Generation. It wouldn't be for anyone else. This made even less sense now. Older Generation watching TV couldn't differentiate between infomercials and news. Let alone. News infomercials. Lawyers thriving. Older generation. So resolute in their cause. They didn't care if it made less money or violated democratic principles. They were cracking all the eggs to make their omelet. Then they cracked the pan. Then they cracked the stove. They didn't stop until the house was swallowed by the earth's molten core. Hallow Earther's furious about this assumption. They couldn't understand. What they purposefully prevented them selves from understanding. People banning books in Freest Nation. They didn't get these "new" jokes. This "weird" sense of humor.

Bank: "We need more of your money." Our character: "Why? Are you poor or something?" Did the stars even fight a war? Are pirates Irish? Hold the line to the moon. Wrong answers only. Domino's phone app is "actually pretty neat." Our character's date says. Weekend warriors walking around hardware store like they can actually build shit. Have you even chopped wood, bro? Driver drumming to vocal melody of song. And not the goddamn fucking rhythm. What happened in our character's life. Had happened. And they had to believe that. In order to still be them. To act so drastically against one's own experiences. That could only happen to someone disassociating. Or religious. It never made sense to our character. To go out of one's way. To make life harder for someone. Who does not pose as a threat to you. Extremely Normal Political Party thought everyone posed a threat. Their club became so exclusive. Nobody could join. A very narrow sense of self. Mission Accomplished? You do you. [Please don't].

Our character's first inclination was to like someone. Before they hated them. It was their best feature. And why people liked them. Our character barely knew this during their lifetime. Our character gave everyone a blank slate. This was not common. Our character hoped. Other's could learn this. Or. If our character wasn't actually doing it. They could learn it. They wanted to be unopinionated about all existence. Our character didn't like it. When others were afraid. This made them uncomfortable. Which made the person more uncomfortable. And our character could tell. Which made them more uncomfortable. And the person could tell they could tell. Which made the person more uncomfortable. Etc. To get out of the feedback loop. Someone had to say something else. They both offered up strange nonsensical chit chat. It didn't solve the problem. At all. But it tricked them into thinking. They did. They could leave the feedback loop. It wasn't great. But I guess it worked?

"Wasn't it like U-Haul trucks. That only made U-turns. Every turn. So they'd get there faster?" Our character was too distracted to continue. They had been giving up. Mid-sentence. Mid-conversation. A lot lately. Who cares anymore? The world was probably ending anyway. I feel sorry for the rich children who never had hand-me-downs. Maybe this is what others don't like about our character. Our character's disregard for the other's existence (our character was merely preoccupied with other things at the space/time but couldn't communicate this effectively). Unless the person was in front of them. Or useful to our character. Or posed a threat to our character. But isn't this how we all act? Is this human nature? The economy of space/time? Or maybe our character was the one. Who wants to feel important. By saying that others go out of their way. To make our character's life harder. It could have been. As much as it couldn't. *Reductio ad absurdum ergo sum!!!* New Popstar is different. New Popstar artistically influenced by car and cellphone sponsorship. ABBA aficionado cringes when Nance brings up her love of *Mama Mia* in casual conversation. No starving children in Somalia nominated for Golden Globe Award. Professor trans-splanning astrophysics.

Our character was attending another mandatory training session. At least they weren't the last one to arrive late. Let's network! Stay safe out there, folks. But more importantly, stay professional! People will always forget if you died from the plague. But they will never forget if you did it unprofessionally. Let's network! Don't be afraid of going insane. Be afraid of thinking you're normal. True insanity. Let's network! They were attempting to convert our character. Yet again. But our character failed to see the connection between their current fall from grace. And the historical and theoretical inadequacies of organized religion. Our character's (super) powers of disassociation. Were the only thing keeping their relationships together. It was a competition. Who could be the most stressed about the most things. The person most stressed. Would have that to fall back on in arguments. No matter what happened. The ace up the sleeve. It struck hollow.

Suffering is Being. *Suffering ergo sum.* Thriving (via illegal drugs)! Legal drugs. The main problem. Bar never set so low. Could be a good thing. Surely this cake will make me feel better. Our character was working on working on them selves. Normalize nocturnal. You know why authors drink a lot? Because people drink a lot. Authors are people too! Cheat code: Bumbling Idiot Dad. Quickest way to be left alone. Recovering academic. Oh shit. They're at it again: telling the youths they can be anything they want to be when they grow up. Is potato love? Yes. I'm probably that one guy from that one time. There are hundreds of people alive today that looked exactly like our character. There are hundreds of people that look identical to our character's soulmate. There should be enough people. To like the way another person looks. The problem. They have no way of meeting. There isn't a shortage of people. But a shortage of appropriate times to approach others. No space/time was appropriate for this. Apparently.

Instead of apologizing for mess they made. Older Generation diverts attention onto younger "troubled" generation. Which they were able to get away with. Until that generation was adults. And then it rang hallow. How could Older Generation have seen this coming? What? Space/time passes?! Had they not worked hard enough to infantilize an entire generation of people? Apparently. Nancy Reagan. Throat Goat of Hollywood. The most evil people appeal to Sky Wizard. Works every time. Are serial killers not religious? Are suicide bombers not religious? The atheist does not have to provide evidence they don't believe in Sky Wizard. But that's how religions get away with not having proof. Saying the other side can't provide proof. Even when. The other side can. And doesn't need to. Perfect time to join my cult. Let's network. "I feel like life is probably just a highlight reel to show chicks in heaven." Let's network. If the government/higher being/Etc. has put me under constant surveillance, can it please tell me where I put my keys?

The birdy economy. Our character helped birds who made a nest in their shed. They believed it wasn't detracting from their own wealth. So generous. When we believe it costs us nothing. Most generous. When we have nothing to gain. So either it costs us nothing. Or we have to believe it costs us nothing. In order to be generous. Our character had grown tired of hearing their colleague philosophate (our character should have been listening more closely). Our character hasn't had an "I'M A FUCKING GODDDDDDDD!" moment in a while. Does anyone else have several weird bumps all over their head? To see if they were cancerous. Our character was able to get an appointment. In 6 months. All these years eating a humble pie full of crows. You can make the right decision and still be wrong. Our character set the following automated message: "I can't communicate right now. I'm currently out of brain space for human interaction. I'll get back to you as soon as anything matters again. Please leave a message." Our character was out of excuses. If you never hear from our character again. They ran out of storage space. On their devices. And gave up.

All calls recorded. In Freest Nation. Freest Nation needs healthcare. Instead they got a pre-recorded phone menu. They were on hold. For hours. For ever. Freest Nations receptionists are killing us. If our character has to make one more username. Or one more password. They are moving to the Australian outback. Our character felt no need to convert others to their belief system. They weren't sure their belief system worked. This was one of their best features. But it wasn't promoted during our characters space/time. There was no competition to be the most unattached. There was no way to measure it. Religions and governments cannot exploit you. If you believe in nothing. So instead. Our character was ostracized for not believing. In a religion they did not need. To be a good person. Did you have enough potato today? Our character thought. Nothing matters. The Extremely Normal Money System replied: "Want to buy stuff tho?"

Older Generation blames Younger Generation for allowing Older Generation to destroy everything. Climate change is a conspiracy that benefits. . . wait. What's a conspiracy again? Adventure is #1 cause of death for poor people. There are always synthesized emotions that creep into every dealing. With others. Like the pink apartment building. Next to our hotel. Unnatural. A terrible attempt. To one-up nature. Some falseness lies. At the bottom of everything. It is becoming more apparent. To our character. Everyday. Now a person. With no ambitions. Their dreams. Beaten out of them. They now only existed. In the middle of the night. To write down these words. To bring vengeance upon the minds that tore their soul from them. Ghosts of Founding Fathers: "When did cocaine become illegal? None of this works without cocaine in the morning. And opium at night." Great time to double down on failed casino owner. Culture losing culture wars. No, I'm the President! I assume one of my biggest flaws is being too sexy. Our character thought this was pretty funny. If you see something, smell something.

Extremely Normal Political Party was the party of personal accountability. For people who have the least control over their lives. PERSONAL ACCOUNTABILITY. Except for Presidents. And rich people. Also police. Oh and insurrectionists. And white supremacists. Oh also Nazis. But Hitler had some bad ideas too, right? Slave owners are also fine. Let's not be too quick to judge assault rifles. Rapists are okay as long as they follow Wine Maker. Orange Man announces candidacy for sainthood. Nation botches suicide. Fiscally racist. Also socially racist. Our character felt a true void of light. The only true reality. Others have become numb to. We are all just walking talking contradictions that eventually fade into the vastness of space/time. The happier you are. The better you've been able to lie to yourself. This isn't true all the space/time. And it was difficult to admit. But it might have been like this during our character's space/time. Our character felt it at space/times. But the sharp fading. At 4:10am. Everything is numb. Our character wrote. Because. Our character didn't sleep.

LinkedIn-Planet Fitness Top Questions to Ask During Job Tournament: "Is your workplace millennial hunger games? Is there a prize for winning? Will it be televised? If televised, do I get residuals? Are there opportunities for branding or a series spin-off?" Mango Cocaine Seltzer. I don't want my taxes paying for things my taxes wouldn't be paying for anyway! Our character's neighbor had been growing more and more vocal. But they made less and less sense. Everyone loves a good pull-yourself-up-by-your-bootstraps comeback story. Unless it's someone you know. And then you want them to fail miserably. Because who do THEY think they are? As long as you stay in-between the lines. For the most part. You'll probably be ok? Whenever you can remember to do it. Do it. Always take a step back. Think about who you are trying to please. Sometimes it will be the right people. Sometimes it will be the wrong people. We wish we could tell our character which was which. [We couldn't. And even if we could. We couldn't]. Could we? States and corporations. Have more rights. Than people. Eating solids difficult without dental insurance. Public health experts recommend not eating shit. Extremely Normal Political Party responds with Poop Fest 2024. Virus not adhering to news cycle. Pro Virus and Pro State's Rights!

Bad acting. Inspired by. Bad writing. A hodgepodge of antiquated social theories. Wanted one more golden moment in the sun. Before falling back. Into the fires of hell. From whence they came. Extremely Normal Politician is furious. About hypothetical issue they imagined. Who is our character serving? This would help us understand what direction they are headed. Our character was doing fine. So long as they didn't claim to have any answers. The Right co-opts the Left's rhetoric of victimization. The Left co-opts the Right's rhetoric of absolute Truths. Etc. Our character had a quip about a third party. Libertarian really Republican. With extra steps. But they weren't able to follow through with it. Imagine all the crimes we don't know Orange Man is committing. Our character couldn't tell if naps were making their sleep better or worse. Their sleep appeared to be bad regardless. Nobody likes their cage. But some people work within it. Cave cage. Where we are with consciousness. Only animals are smart enough to remember they are in a cage. The lizard tried to get out again. Despite all my rage. I'm still just a rat in Plato's Cave. The cave is *logos*. We built it for our character. When should we let them out? By staying inside the cave. We get outside the cage. We remain. *Logos* helping and preventing. Our character belonged to the only species (of feces) who could cmprhnd wht Im typin wright knoww.

Truth arrives when we are ready. Advice arrives too late. We prevent ourselves from seeing. Before we are ready. The exact amount. The average. Is reality. What we can handle. If you feel like you've read this before. You have. Our character had. Probably. I am the edge point of reality. We are the edge point of reality. It is the edge point of reality. They are the edge point of reality. I am the edge point of reality. We are the edge point of reality. It is the edge point of reality. They are the edge point of reality. I am the edge point of reality. Our character thought they were joking. Because others thought they were joking. Our character needed a win. So they took it. Always pause. And explain your universe. If others don't understand you. Was all this. Merely some tortuous inside joke with our character? Life. There has to be more ephemeral stuff. Damp grass in the dark. During our character's space/time. Presidential candidate runs on bringing troops home from War on Christmas. With puppies. Etc. Extremely Normal Politicians worship Sky Wizard and Orange Man. Our character thought about writing some of this down. They forgot what they were going to say.

If you write a book about how scholars don't take humor seriously. Scholars might not take it seriously. Does your boyfriend even shop at craft stores? Extremely Normal Money System creates competition. Which breeds innovation. Which is why we haven't been able to move beyond Extremely Normal Money System. Wait. What's innovation again? Extremely Normal Money System is trauma. Trying to have a weekend every night. Does your boyfriend even have a microphone? People aren't machines. They don't operate with exact consistency. Neither do machines. Apparently. Our character had car trouble. Once again. Our character was using facial expressions inconsistently. And unknowingly. How could we tell them without them freaking out? All the throw away lines. Chit chat to fill the air. Barely meaning any of it.

Never not extra. Offer only. Our character wanted to tell people. They met our character at a strange space/time. In our character's life. But honestly. Our character's life has all been very strange. Both sides have good points. Says "Centrist" (Republican). Postmodern auto mechanic. Hear me out. Alaskan NFL team. Investing too much in particular things a person has done. Instead of taking the person as a whole. Instead of consulting the source. The quest for perfection is futile. Also undesirable. And at times. Unattractive. Activities that were only supposed to bring people together. Then people invest too much. Now there is too much at stake. Activity breaks people apart. Science only as good as the people who use it. We all play games. The ones our character played. Showed others. How much space/time they had on their hands. Or so they all thought. Get rid of one-word descriptions for people. People riding in car. In independent film. Really getting away from it all. Getting out through the vent. Saved countless plots. Climate change's extreme weather is a great way for (poor) people to get out into nature. Our character thought they could get away with just doing a really good job. [It never worked].

Who spams regular people? Who would benefit from this? Sure, Older Generation might be taken advantage of. Not because they are technologically illiterate. But because they are not smart. But they are the most persistent, have the most time, and the most money to fight back. So it can't be too lucrative. Making communication unnecessarily difficult is necessary in fascist nation. Sorry, Freest Nation. If people were able to communicate clearly. They'd realize. How badly those in charge were doing. People need to miss appointments. Drop calls. Be late on payments. Unable to schedule doctor's visits. Technology needs to break after a certain amount of years. Misread the fine print. These aren't "accidents." These are the capital generating strategies of a police-state. The secretaries become police. Floor managers become police. Teachers become police. Any and every authority. Must become police. Over policing. The selves. Accept. Nobody: . . . Extremely Normal Political Party: "What if we made everything a gun?" Faith-based small-batch organic free-range green energy. Cyber security. Good at. Locking people out of their accounts. Helping Disney take down copyright violations. Bad at. Apparently everything else. Our character understood. These were first-world problems. But still. Do better. There is no first-world. Only last-world.

Wrong/right now. Our character didn't have interesting things to do or think. So they made an annoying sound instead. Our character plays an unproductive circular game. To pass through the space/time. For example. Dating, Etc. Nothing more. Nothing less. Not a given. One person. Will find one person. To live with. Their entire life. Our character's dissatisfaction in the way things are. And their reflex. To change the world around them. To fit their idea. Of what should lead them. On a never-ending path of dissatisfaction. Scrap it. Or fix it in post? Did our character get smarter or wiser with age? Blaming our character for their shortcomings. Became too convenient. For too many people. Mental laziness. Not included on list of enemies for Older Generation's War On Laziness (disenfranchised peoples). The unemployment department asked our character how much they made this year. They didn't know exactly.

Then the lady told our character how much they made. Our character couldn't figure out. Why did they ask them in the first-place? Or worst loser?

Slippery slope not slippery enough for Older Generation. To curb the mental health crisis during our character's space/time. The news decided to only report when politicians agreed. They didn't report for a couple years. Nation racists. On principle. Devil not advocate. Just devil. Devil offended. Hey! Leave me outta this! Character not necessarily smarter/wiser with age. But they recognized sooner. When and how to get out of bad situations. They'd still make the same mistakes. However. They'd cover them up better. It wasn't a great system. But it worked for most? [It didn't]. Politicians should never be hired to carry out a particular policy. They should be hired to be able to see the way the THINGS ARE. And act accordingly. Some political parties encouraged this. Others did not. Again. They were not very smart during our character's space/time. Politics should have been boring. It was their main source of entertainment. The entertainment must not have been good.

To be creative. Our character had to come up with a lot of ideas. Some good. Some bad. Show people the good. Hide the bad. Etc. They could come up with one good idea. For every 100 bad ideas. So they only had to hide the other 99. You have to fail miserably in order to succeed. And as long as you keep your head above water. More than you fall under. You will do just fine. [They didn't]. In a community. Our character was forced to participate in consciousness. Our character must have started. At some point. As a blank slate. *Tabula rasa*. In which it is possible for a Head Voice or Personality or Identity or Unconscious/consciousness to evolve. Outside of possible future communication, would it be necessary for our character to have a Head Voice? How could we find out? The Head Voice medium. What audience does it address? Communication must be practiced and repeated within the individual. To be used with others.

Anyone talking shit. Is talking in turd person. It's magic and mischief that keep this whole thing going. Our character remembered saying this to someone. Upon repetition. Our character was revolted by the inauthentic whimsy. Smug. Smaug. Smug Smaug in the fog. On a different schedule. Midway through a conversation. Is the worst time. To remember. You are socially awkward. And only pretending to adult. Fraud depends on other frauds. For others. Not to realize. They were a fraud. Impossible to tell who was a fraud. And who was not. During our character's space/time. Someone says "craft beer" at taproom. Everyone realizes. People who drink craft beer. Just call it beer. Many of the people our character met today. They'd never see again. The rest of their lives. No cause worth dying for. At least during our character's space/time.

Oh damn. People in charge. Really are that stupid. Always take the train. Auto Correct biggest setback for human/AI relations. Spike in 76ers jersey sales. Apparently. Mission not all that impossible. 40% of a human's life spent trying to charge phone. I want healthcare to be expensive and insufficient! Our character took a shower with clothes on. It felt like they were breaking every human law ever. People who always follow the rules. Are the most terrifying. It is necessarily impossible to always follow the rules. You can't do anything. Without breaking a rule someone has set. Someone somewhere. Has outlawed what you are doing. Religion is merely convenient. Because people assume they know. What set of rules. Another person is living by. Were they? [They never were]. Pobody's nerfect. Catholic not voting for Catholic President because Catholic is Catholic. If you actually thought about things during our character's space/time. It would hurt your head. So most people were trying not to. [It didn't work].

Our character had to become their own role-model. They didn't realize that was a thing. Everything a thing now. Every word now the name of musical artist. I guess it was our character's time to lead. They had to be the strong one. Odd. They did not want to be in charge. Which made them good at being in-charge. Fig futons. Big Crouton. Lobbies for more salad. Holidays make it acceptable. For adults to eat as much candy as possible. You're not a real parent. Until you've woken up next to your child in the middle of the night. Soaked by their urine. And said "Fuck it." And fell back asleep. When the single head voice has been lost. The original purpose is lost. To a multiplicity. Multiplied personality disordered. Only a tool for communication. The need for a head voice is repeated. When it has already been achieved. The problem remains. Whether 2 or 200,000 different personalities. The original personality was not strongly established. The individual is not being reaffirmed of their reality. Nobody was. During this space/time.

Our character had to beat them. At their own game. No matter much they didn't want to play. You don't have to be offended by everything. You don't have to be offended by anything. This pandemic has given our character a good opportunity to evaluate their post apocalypse team. When quarantine is over. Dogs will be able to talk. We aren't going to like what they have to say. All Memes Go to Heaven II. Lol. Imagine if Orange Man became president. Lol WTF? Failed Casino Owner. Surprisingly makes bad leader. Art must create the want. And deliver on the want. Provide the quiz. And the answers. Each piece needs its own *logos*. A new world. A new form. A new style. Etc. B form. Beforming. In the mind of their audience. Every time the art is displayed/performed/Etc. In every sport there is a counter-intuitive but necessary flick of the wrist. It determines mastery. It is the threshold. It feels almost the same as when you fail. Except for the flick. Find the angle. Repeat. Over and over. A million times. Routine is Sky Wizard. Money can absolutely buy happiness.

All of our character's current problems could be solved with money.

Incuriosity. Running from what you know. Instead of running to it. Perpetual concealment. From your selves. A constant fear of failure. Mental cowardice. Mental laziness. Older generation doesn't understand. What they don't understand. Older Generation doesn't understand. Why younger generation isn't buying houses. Older Generation could add things up. But could not knock them down. When they no longer added up. Confirmation bias. In an echo chamber. Inside an ivory tower. Waking up. A second wind. Another chance. Run Lola! Run! Alarmist nation. Our character was on trial. Everyone was. At all times. It wasn't fun. It was also counterproductive. Our character never decided to get up in the morning. They just couldn't put their mind back to sleep. Symbolism symbolic. Abraham sacrificing son. Never sat right with our character. What else was like this? That our character couldn't agree with. But accepted. What kind of love is that? A love of betrayal. Cruelty of Old Testament Sky Wizard. Only surpassed by cruelty of New Testament Sky Wizard. These examples were given to young people. Only during our character's space/time. Who can have the least amount of fun? Wait. Why is this a competition.

President good for economy. Stock market did *blippity doop da beep*. President bad for economy. Stock market did *filippity dipplty whoop*. Poor people still poor. Orange Man not a good President. Also not a good person. Nation. Failing group assignment. Low power mode. I will respond to your message. After monthly reboot. Time travel with definitive "now" points. Conceals everything as a constant happening. At once. In/at all space/time. Flowing through us. We inhabit all. For however long. People. Realities. A universe. Plants. Animals. Etc. The space/timeless. Formless. Ineffable fabric of soul. Can you be there in 4 hours? No, but does 1mm growth of my carrots work? The transition from polytheism to monotheism. The multi-voiced individual. The singular individual. Placed into a mold. By one all-seeing. Omniscient Sky Wizard. The singularization organizes. Now the individual can be disciplined. By law. Career. Romance. Etc. Otherwise. How could we know if our character was winning or losing?

Sleep is the most important thing. If you want to be a lazy fucking loser. That amounts to nothing. You piece of shit. Capitalism would rather be inefficient than empathetic. Randy takes a shit in the office toilet at 8:45am each day. But Nance was in there. Goddammit Nance. Our character never wanted to see any of their colleagues for the rest of their life. If you're unemployed. Monday is your Monday. And your Friday. Our character didn't ask if things were good or bad anymore. They skipped to bad or worst. Every day is a weekend. If you're high enough. Applewood smoked bacon tastes nothing like apple. Or wood. Pretty much just bacon. In most of their friend groups. Our character figured they'd be the getaway driver in a heist. They could really rock a leather jacket. Top Seventy Questions to Ask the Seventy-Year-Old interviewing you: "Have you hired so many bad/unqualified employees that clients hate us before they meet us?"

6 HOW TO STOP YOUR BOOMER FROM DOING ANOTHER JANUARY 6TH ON FACEBOOK

Our character found it funny. If attacked by a murderer while turning a corner. Their last words would be something like "Oop, sorry about that, my bad. . ." as our character would attempt to awkwardly step back. And do a stupid wave thing. That only white people do. Starting a vlogcast. Everywhere books are sold. Subscribe on Tinder. Or call your local fire department. Our character wanted to be famous. But they didn't want anyone to know anything about them. No longer a young "young professional." No longer professional. Never was. Never wanted to be. Neither was anyone else. "Professional" was one of the terms they kicked around during our character's space/time. *Carte blanche* for getting rid of people they didn't like. Like standardized testing, Etc. An easy way to reject. Without having to think much about it. Popstar wins local Popstar cover band award. Stop dancing. Everyone. Stop dancing. Given the inevitability of pandemics. Throughout human existence. One would have assumed. Extremely Normal Money System would factor this in. Don't you hate it when you see an exclamation point coming up, and you're forced to raise your inner-voice at the end of the sentence!

Luckily our character didn't trust them selves enough. To stay mad at people. It was one of their only redeeming qualities. Or they were too stupid. And forgot. Those were the two options. Either be perfect. And smart all the time. And never get anything wrong. Or find a way to get over your wrongness. When do we tell our character they are being stupid? But not to offend them. And make it worse? Our character decided to make important things. What things would they make important? Things that would provide lasting rewards. As long as they had a purpose. A goal in mind. They would be fine. Our character had gotten better at recognizing the self-construction. They learned how to arrange them selves. Environment was hostile. But it had the blessing of Sky Wizard and Orange Man. So it couldn't have been hostile. If it were hostile that would mean things were going wrong. And needed to be changed. And obviously that wasn't true during our character's space/time. [It was]. So it couldn't have been a hostile environment. #Logic. Ergo. Air go. Escargot. My car go. 150 swiftly.

Just because you can do things with super-human strength. Doesn't mean you should. Our character only used what they used. Personal accountability a pyramid scheme. All the good Wine Maker's principles don't require you to follow Wine Maker. There were no socioeconomic classes in Freest Nation. But our character sent their kids to private school just in case. Our character was going to change the channel. But they kept it on. Our character was creating an invitation. To their costume party. Without a theme their guests would ask: "What's the point?" Conversely, our character shouldn't pick out costumes for each individual. Our character needed to provide direction to create. A sketch. A sketchy sketch. A stretchy sketchy sketch. Incapable Political Party trying to find a candidate that will change nothing. And lose election. Not a great alternative.

Fanatically Conservative. Chaotic Order. Wildly Calm. Inconsistently Consistent. Buttchugginginsane Rules. Impossibly Possible. Existentially Istential. Liberal Conservative. Climate change and evolution do not need you to believe in them. But if you want to be able to do science… Anything can be anything. But that doesn't mean people will read an academic paper written by science deniers. [They didn't]. Person from Extremely Normal Political Party attacks shadow. Extremely Normal Political Party wants to limit access to healthcare and expand access to guns. This made our character pause. And think. But they soon wandered off topic. *Big Bang Theory* has hardest working laugh track since *Friends*. Jokes without punchlines.

Throughout our character's life. They realized. They put as many limitations on things. As other people. Arriving at these realizations. Was one of their best qualities. But it was not rewarded during our character's space/time. So our character didn't fully develop this trait. But when they did realize this. Our character was able to be friends with more people. And more people within those people. Hippy college kid spent hours debating the homeless Sky Wizard prophets on campus. It was inauthentic. Shaking hands and pretending to be friends afterward. Is easy when you never have to see that person again. Our character only had space/time for those who had space/time for them. It wasn't a great system. But it was one. "Save the whales! Sign this petition!" Just don't make eye contact and you'll be fine. Our character went through their life being more judgmental sometimes. And less judgmental other times. It used to be easy to know who the famous people were. Now, our character found them selves constantly asking: "Am I supposed to know who this is?"

Our character vetted projects on their ability to like them. Then dislike them. Then like them again. Etc. If a project didn't go through this process. Our character doubted others would like it. Other people will come to the project with different opinions. So our character should as well. If our character hasn't changed their mind about a project (or a person). It meant they hadn't thought about them very carefully. A "finished" project was never finished. It was merely abandoned due to other demands from space/time. This mindset communicated the openness of a sketch. An impetus for creativity. The finished work can/should still be edited. For the next project. At least. It is still open to permutations. Not a period at the end of a sentence but a. . . Refusing to spoon-feed or patronize the audience. Our character let go of their projects. Always before they were ready. Asking their audience to consider, not a singular message, but a message that opens up possibilities for the individual that lay beyond the singular work. Not merely reinforcing the audience's habitual rhetorical positioning. But reminding them to look around and consider the context. Not merely getting their audience to do something. But to undo something as well.

Our character had to become the strangest they had ever become. Before they could become normal again. Our character realized the importance of what they were doing. And therefore. Had to learn how to stop. If you put your audience at a disadvantage. There better be a payoff. What you need to know about what you don't know. Tonight at 8. "I sure hope there isn't paint in my protein shake" is something our character never would have thought to think before having a child. Crowbar or Bar Crow? Cheerios has a pretty good customer service hotline. You guys should check it out. What's your skin care routine? Difficulty in obtaining prescription for anxiety medication made our character anxious. Defeating its own purpose. If our character was going to be crazy. They might as well be a good writer. Or maybe they weren't? Never certain. Nearer curtains. Work to eliminate possibilities. When there are too many. Prove the null hypotheses. Put forth the thoughts you hide. See what validity springs forth. If not. You will be forced to. Get your house in order. Before the inspectors come.

Life during wartime. Freest Nation pretends nothing is happening. Freest Nation's ability to disassociate. The only thing keeping it going. Defeating its own purpose. If you must beat the refs and the other team. Then you must beat the refs and the other team. There is no such thing as fair. Inequality is nation's foundation. The End. At Least. For now. Only treating the symptoms. Not the causes. Life being the disease. If you're counting on technicalities to get you out of your problems. You'll never see the end of them. You're nothing until you prove yourself. And then you'll never stop having to prove yourself. Nobody ever arrived. They were all always in transit. Our character refuses to fill out customer survey. On principle. There weren't many principles left. They were collecting all the data. But they didn't know why. Nobody knew what to do with all the information. So they used it to sell more stuff. Etc. *Ad Infinitum.* Ads infinitum. Unfortunately. It was as bad as our character thought. During our character's space/time.

Our character needed to work on becoming a better salesperson of the self. Our character needed to create a character out of them selves. Our character's character needed to interact with the characters the other characters created. Everyone could drop the charade. But the rich people wouldn't be able to purchase a fourth house if this happened. The character's salesperson characters needed to be hyper-aware of everything. At all space/times. They needed to place a character of them selves (or two) amongst the audience of salespeople characters they were constantly performing for. To see how they were doing. Every sentence. Every word. Was being read into (this is a book after all). A perpetual state of anxiety, being offended, and being pointlessly mad. What did they think about this? And what did they think about that? Form an opinion. Quickly. Defend it. With the rest of your life. Attacking became a defensive strategy. Everything had to add up at the end of the day. Even if it didn't add up. Cooking the books. Of the self. It didn't help anyone. In fact it hurt most. But they had to win. Everything was a competition. Nobody could ever win. They could only lose. [They all did].

If every space/time period is unique and different. None of them are. Our character's British professor was saying *logician* but it sounded like they were saying *magician*. That lecture was wild. There are no wrong answers. So long as you provide an impetus to create. The idea of a finished project used to identify our selves can be intimidating. Find a way to break it down. Trick yourself into starting. Not having to fully identify with the project and all the baggage that entails. Maybe you'll publish under a pseudonym (but don't)? Maybe you won't publish it at all (but do)? Try not to worry too much about getting all your selves to align. So they agree with each other. Because they won't. Necessarily. Big Mac too small. Everything is a Science now. Biology. A brand of lotion. Philosopher doesn't publish due to religious beliefs. Update. One cannot bore oneself to death. Our character usually tried to avoid talking to others at the gas station. Our character's epitaph: "Surprisingly dedicated to pointless causes." Everything is glitching. One red flag. Should have been. Orange Man's casinos lost money. Freest Nation. The Karen of Nations. Fly wins. Our character defeated. Again.

We don't know what happens after we die. Because we haven't a clue what we are doing. When we are alive. Loosen your grip on end-results. Move outside the narrow expectation of logic and reason. Subjugated to an all-encompassing utilitarian purposefulness. Pointless purposefulness. Mountains of data. Rotting in the sun. Loosen but not abandon. The grip of one's cognitive orientation toward the world in favor of another's. Jettisoning the perpetual calculation of *homo economicus*. Our character was ready to stop being a crazy person. The world didn't agree. The crazy remained. Do less. Big energy energy. Dedicated to my addictions. Eat enough toast tomorrow. How do I people? Why did we ever let humans drive cars? Once again. Our character should have been wayyyyyy less honest. In 99.9% of their interactions with humans.

Nothing appropriate. Remind me later. Self-help workshop at 8pm in the main ballroom. Oh shit! I just have to BELIEVE in myself? Moon fed up. Iowa. We grow corn. We eat fried sticks of butter. And we decide who the leader of the free world is. No. Not just a Boy Scout. An Eagle Scout. Our character was stunned. If it's not rated TV-MA. I've not wasting my time. Symptoms for one thing. Also symptoms for other thing. Studies show. You've been doing it wrong this whole time. You're probably sleeping wrong too. Here for a long time not for a good time. If my socks are inside out, who am I to stop them? Our character would turn them right-side-in. In the middle of the night. Enough experimenting. I need to sleep! Was it Lennon, Lenin, or linen who did the bed thing? Culturally authentic performance boring AF. Bud Light commercials now streaming on Netflix. "Oh, but I like THESE ones!" Our character's friend claimed. They weren't friends for long. We need to fear fear itself. And everything else.

Our character had been so concerned with everything going on. They forgot to be perpetually irrationally afraid of volcanoes killing them. Our character had given the Extremely Normal Money System countless opportunities to exploit them for their over-educated mind and stupidly relentless work ethic. If you need me. I'll be in bed. Election sex. Nation thinks health is cool. But likes rich people more. Nation believes money trickles down. And altruism trickles up. [It didn't]. A beautiful night to start a bender. Creativity requires a deep friendship with one's selves. All the selves. To inspire creativity in others. We need to first be able to be vulnerable with our selves. Critical of our selves without taking offense. With the understanding. We have our own backs. And will see our selves through the process. We gain the confidence. Necessary. To play with the end-result. And therefore. Leave it open for others. Instead of merely responding to our own vulnerabilities. That convince us we need to direct others to one singular answer. To limit our audience's ability to question our authority. If we avoid this. We can allow others to be creative. When they interact with what we have made. A sacrificial lamb.

Raisins inexpensive. According to trail mix. Forgetful people remember they were forgetting. Isn't that more impressive? Our character was today years old today. Drowning in neoliberal inspiration. "Crazy." "Musician." Boring music. Did I just hit on my wife? And yes, I can drink on the job. Are my fingernails growing faster? Lol. Wait. Why is anything the way it is? Masquerades hit all time low. Don't lift a grift horse in the mouse. One in the ham is better than true in the brush. A cloaked clock is wrong for days. Our character. A *tabula rasa*. To have the many value systems played out upon them. Within them. Etc. What they bring. Experiences. Narratives. Into the situation. They don't think of it as "them selves." Because they can change their minds. But for others. Our character's *logos* (or perceived *logos* = *ethos*) is all the others have. To think about our character. All they can use. All they have learned to use. But our character is the thing that can change their minds. The *ethos* cannot. Necessarily. The attempt to create a human through artificial means. Will therefore fail. We would be attempting to create it through an *ethos/logos*. A value system we have discovered. Been taught. Used repeatedly. Normalized. However. This does not allow them to create with the blank nothingness. People who write. Are already dead. Writing is the disease that keeps them going. Creating *logos* for others. After *logos* is finished with us. The world agrees. Too much stuff. I work really soft. I'd rather have a "twice in a lifetime" experience. Do everything as much as possible. So you won't want to do it for a while. What's your favorite car season? Maybe it's not a great idea to have the worst people in charge of everything. Have we tried putting the best people in charge?

Cantaloupe still shit melon. Easter every fucking weekend bro! This had them rolling in the grass. Shit. It was nice to finally get together and do this. Let's get wasted! It's Arbor Day! Great time to invest in Furbies. You don't have to advertise the thing I'm using. I'm already using it. What more do you want from me? Our character forgot everything. So they could change their mind. Lowkey epic bender occurring somewhere. Our character's 1:00 am rationale: "Tomorrow is going to suck regardless. There might as well be a reason." Sharts are not always just farts. To a parent. An electric scooter looks like an ice pack to the face all night. Now, more than ever. In these difficult times. The sheets trap my farts for you. How to create a *tabula rasa*. By definition impossible. On which we operate. Not a *logos*. Merely multiplying the number of responses. A computer can provide. Duplicating what is already known. It can only generate *logos*. Not the *tabula rasa*. Only responding to what we know. Which is all it knows. But our character was never fully their own response. They were not their *logos*. *Logos* was only one of many selves. Circumstantial.

Our character couldn't make out what the delivery driver was saying. Too many fridges. Or two mini fridges? CEO fails drug test. Again. The minimum requirement for a conspiracy theory. Is being a theory. If you can walk down to the hospital. And have your COVID-19 conspiracy disproved. There is no conspiracy. At least in the way you have framed it. Now more than ever. In times like these. Conspiracy theorists need to come together and agree on ONE bizarrely incoherent narrative. Old Testament Sky Wizard playing greatest hits right now. Just play the hits! Our character refused to live up to the standards they set for them selves. And it showed. The heroes are the real heroes here. "Thanks a lot! Yep. Yep. Sure! See you soon! Okay yeah. We'll see!" Sock situation getting weird. A beautiful person's Being is negated. The other must project onto them. A carry over.

A remainder. The residual desire. Left by another. In the past. Beauty is a book. To read. The other's formulation of beauty must be posited into/onto the desired object. This accumulation of beauty. The other's practiced "taste." Their aesthetical *logos*. Their "type." Is learned. It has become a custom. Accustomed. To being performed. Pre-formed. Its origins long forgotten. Simulacra. Beauty is forgetting. The only thing that remains. The repeated form. Empty. Until filled with meaning. Gestures without content. But at least this provides a starting point. New tastes can now be accumulated. But this can only happen. If the individual does not know it is happening. If the person whom the individual attempts to posit their accumulation of beauty into/onto, is not blank enough, then this positing will not occur. Where once there was a man. Alas. Now a beard.

Concern for the poor? What's next? Followers of Wine Maker being decent people? Great time to have Trust Fund. Trust. Fun. Do something bad. To save yourself from the cult of self-righteousness. Existence is forgetting. Forgetting is Existence. Our character looked up at the stars. They couldn't help thinking. They were doing everything wrong. Existence is a distraction from itself. "This is a book. For people who read. To read." – The Author. Philosopher "going pro." Analytic Philosopher taken in the first round. Heideggerian traded to LA Lakers University of Minnesota Amway. Deconstructionist enters transfer portal. Apparently. Our space/timeline. Wasn't the one. Where things could change. Microwaved pizza. Too hot. We don't need studies. To tell us. Who is suffering. We need to stop the suffering. Profound simplicity.

Our character didn't want to write. But nobody else was writing this. And no better options presented themselves. It was a lot like dating. What kind of choice is this non-choice? Look around you. Do you really think "Your Way" of doing things. Is the only way others should be doing things? What do you tell yourself to patch up this *logos*. To stop the flood. What else do you patch up with this justification? What else is in disrepair? The thread that undoes everything. Your justifications. Said out loud. Feel different. Then when it remains. Rattling around. In your head. Always putting it off until another space/time. What you assume space/time will heal. It won't. Or maybe. Don't think it should. And maybe. It will. [It didn't]. Maybe it will fix itself. [It never does. Until it does]. The hope that you are stupid enough. To have overlooked the solution. That will now present itself. *Deus ex machina.* Finding "The One." Etc. Is Christianity working yet? Oh. Maybe tomorrow? Or maybe tomorrow? Etc. *Ad infinitum. Ad absurdum.* What if I buy stuff? Etc. *Ad infinitum. Ad absurdum.* What if I write. More? Etc. *Ad infinitum. Ad absurdum.* We should have kids. Etc. *Ad infinitum. Ad absurdum.* Our character had a working knowledge. Of non-workable solutions.

Our character was watching a movie. Shot from the simultaneous perspectives of two different people (a couple). As they narrate. They break narration. To retell the story that is already occurring (Etc. *Ad infinitum. Ad absurdum*). The conversation driving the story is occurring elsewhere. Off-screen. The audience has to piece together what actually happened based off of the accumulation of simultaneous stories occurring on the screen. In the end. We are stuck with the results of what had happened (the present). The audience only gets different points of emphasis. The average. It keeps folding in on itself. But that is what moves the narration forward. The constant entropy. Welcomes the past. And readily dissolves all meaning. As soon as the meaning has started to be made. Self-similarity. Infinite regress. Etc. Mimetic. Copy of a copy. A *logos*. I'm willing to admit my drugs are a crutch. Why aren't you willing to admit religion is yours? Genius is socially acceptable obsessive-compulsive behavior. I'm new in town. "Where is the good fruit?" "All sounds great." Is it a good idea? No. But it is an idea. And that's always better than nothing? "I'm new in town. Does Ashley live here?" "Anyone else going to CBS Rock and Roll Masturbation Show in Times Square?" "Why would I ask him about this weekend? He knows I've got the sickness between the legs." Our character was still trying to cash in on this mild personality disorder. "I think we need to redefine the term "genius" to include me." I only eat and drink things that have won awards. Stock market falls. Because stock market thought stock market would fall. "I'm Karen, and I'm new in town. Where is the nearest manager?"

Are you saying tapas or topless? Read read read instead of read. To no one in particular. our character mumbles incoherently. We need more lids. Rival Dad hovering too close to grill. Don't flatter yourself. Refugees don't want to live in Freest Nation. They just don't want to be murdered in theirs. Alleged "fruit medley" is 75% melon. Great time for toxic introspection. Overdosed on antioxidants. Both sides agree on "open dialogue." Neither meant it. The episodically overarching narrative. So episodic. It's overarching. Humor is an easier way of achieving the same thing. Plus. It's fun. Avant-garde art. Not always fun. Absurdity and non sequiturs too theorized. I need that pure pure. Her: "My roommate is gone. I can be as loud as you want." Him: "Where did they go?" Romantic love is socially acceptable fetishization. Drink more water. You can't just be clever. But it's a good place to start. Why does it feel like I'm not having sex with you right now? Instead of doing a bad job. Do a good job instead. Yesterday our character was asked to call the branch Branch about some branches. Dedicated to my addictions. Sometimes parents post pics of their kids. To remind others. Their kids are adorable. Sometimes parents post pics of their kids. To remind others. Their kids are adoptable.

Romeo Montague and Juliet Capulet. Not as catchy as Romeo and Juliet. I believe in a post-currency society. So yeah. I can't pay for that. Do you want to see my box collection? Our character HAD to stop being them selves in social situations. Inspired by actual events. Still cautimistic. An odd time to defend the Extremely Normal Money System. One dimensional personalities finally have something to talk about again. Protesters protesting protesters protesting. Back on my bullshit. Crack on my cullshit. I dunno if it's me or it's you? But it's definitely you. Talent no longer rising to the top. Our character didn't know what was funny anymore. Extreme life coach. Another mid-day-wellness seminar. Our character was either striking out. Hard. Or hitting home runs. There was no other explanation. They knew no other way. Our character was genuinely invested in their projects. It was one of their best attributes. And they never knew it. Even if the project ended up being shit. People admired the attempt. Someday. Right now will be millions of years ago. Are Internets getting worse? Art is the process of opening up into another *logos*. Orange Man is proof. Competition doesn't provide the best results. Our character didn't know what they didn't understand. Therefore. It fades into the background. And becomes who they are. Link in bio. Our character had too much to drink. Again.

 When they request nudes. Send pics of others who sent you nudes. They need to learn to be more specific. Communication is key. Never send dick pics. Just chode shots. Band name: Fantastic Everything. DJ name: Acid Pillow. Our character was waiting for Old Navy cargo pants to *swing* back around. Brian Mango Seltzer Orchestra. Be professional. Show her that you get up early. You are goal oriented. And have a spicy seed. Text girls at 6am: "You up?" On the one hand. You got bit. Not everything that slows us down. Is preventing us from what we want. Another speed or direction. Of achieving what we want. One we didn't know existed. If you're afraid of the dark. Become the night. Great art takes you to another dimension. Completely lost. To be found. Again. Later. You don't own your consciousness. Maybe just renting? If you lease today, we can lock-in a great interest rate. Our character's Tuesdays were feeling more like Wednesdays. If you are able to go into other worlds. Then by all means go. As frequently as possible. These days need to be as blurry as possible. A real atheist just agrees. Perpetually recovering. Art should make it possible to live more lives. Our character is now looking back at us. What should we say?

 New continent discovered. Not how you would have thought though. The gaslighters don't know they are gaslighting. Everyone in everyone else's business. Nonsensical string of powerfully woke catchphrases used to sell car. It's almost as if basing a society on perpetual competition wasn't the best way to prepare for natural disasters. Oppressive governments: 0 for 3798343124374182734. MS Word gets font wrong. Again. Our character wanted to assume everyone hated them. So they could be pleasantly surprised. Enemy Nation dedicates large section of history curriculum. On the indigenous peoples of Freest Nation. Every word now the name of a company. TM™. In calling attention to the game. Our character was in danger of never being able to play the game. You've called yourself out. Trust no one. Never let anyone know what you do or don't understand. Admit nothing. Especially in a court of law. Omit everything. Popstar, Orange Man, and CEOs do this all the time. Standard for anyone attempting to hold on to "power." [They couldn't]. Check out this one trick professionals do! Tonight at 8pm! Why shouldn't you? The only thing our character was ever able to find was them selves. Balls as smooth as old Benjamin Button. Insanity merely another way to provide stability. Albeit. Not as appealing. To some. At least. A little daily self-sabotage is okay? [It wasn't]. It takes a village to raise one in every family. You only take the shots you don't hear in the forest. A podcast: "Nobody Asked." This might be nothing, but. . . [It was].

Style is everything. You don't intend. You can never know your style (identity?). Only others can glimpse it. In concert with others. Identity is always contextual. The you. That prevents it. From merely being contextual. I guess identity was a lot of things. Apparently. Shit has always been going to shit. Why did we go to the moon? Lol WTF? We could have cured poverty. Nope. Let's get people to the moon. And then bring them back. Shortly thereafter. "See! We went to place!" Vacation photograph says. Our character still liked it though. Thunderbolts don't exist. Orange Man creating perfect Mexican terrorists. Abstract art in one line: "These random things look cool together." Our character wanted to find out more about them selves. So they traced their way through everything they'd ever heard about them selves. Every conversation. Every result. All so that others could know something about them? When they had to personify them selves. They didn't want to. But you had to give your co-workers something. Without giving them anything. Is there more? Than this infinity loop our character was traveling in. Going to self. Out of self. Into others. And back into/out of self. Etc. This infinity loop was space/time itself. It was also identity. There is no such thing as space/time travel. Only "self-travel." How do you travel through your life? Through yourself? How do you go back to the past or out to the future? The infinity loop provides peace of mind for everything. We know we will not die. But merely bounce back and forth inside the self. This can either be an insanity induced claustrophobic reaction. Or freeing. Or both. [It was ambiguous]. The you that is you is the thing in charge of balancing the two. It must be true (because it rhymed). And in doing so. This is how one dictates space/time. Our character thought: "I do these little things for *next-time-me*." Just in case.

If you want your family to love you. Don't talk about Popstar or Orange Man. In Freest Nation Ever you were free to have your own opinion. Unless you held the opinions our character did. Then you were not allowed to hold your own opinion. I'll get back to you as soon as words matter again. PYT. DTF. We are a riddle for others to figure out. Others including our selves. I'm a riddle *ergo sum*. Here is my handle. Here is my bum. The consensus projection of everyone we have ever met at every moment. Including our selves. Our character's dreams stopped making sense after that. Don't hatch your chickens until you count all the eggs in your bag. Live, laugh, love, divide, and conquer. Hold strong opinions for a short time. Or weak opinions for a long time. Live, laugh, love, and pain is weakness leaving the body. Life is full of hidden solutions. "Has anyone ever had too much syrup? Let me rephrase that. Is anyone here a liar?" Our character was already over this vacation. I am all impulse non-control at this point. Viewer discretion advised. Intelligence is a curse. In a world of idiots. "Do you floss at least three times a day? Let me rephrase that. Is anyone here a psychopath?"

If rich people aren't happy. Sounds like a "them" problem. If our character had money. They would be happy. But because they'd be happy if they had money. They couldn't have any. It takes a different person to get rich. It takes an idiot. If not already an idiot. Being rich will turn you into one. Merhaps. In a "deeper" "philosophical sense" "money" doesn't "buy" "happiness." But healthcare doesn't cost "philosophical" "money." Healthcare costs "money" "money." If people don't have healthcare. They will not be happy. Being unhappy is the opposite of being happy. This sounds simple. But you'd be surprised (you shouldn't be) how many people during our character's space/time couldn't figure this out. If you don't know what to say in conversation. Wait until there is a long pause. Then say loudly: "Survival of the fittest, baby!" As you leave to pretend to go do something else. Channel your creativity through multiplutferms exposurmt. Every victory. I ask. How much will this cost?

Money doesn't "necessarily" help you find your "soulmate." Did anyone ever assume it did? Sounds like a YOU problem. Money DOES allow our character to settle down when they are more prepared to. With a person they aren't forced to be with. Because of money. "Technically." "Money" doesn't "buy" you "happiness." It's only necessary to maintain happiness for any period of space/time. If happiness is the opposite of being miserable. And it's miserable to not have money. Then money is necessary to be happy. *Homo economicus* (once again) turned something into a money-making competition. "Zen for sale inside!" When the imaginary background story becomes all there is. And then the crisis. And now it's real. What does this belief allow you to do? Can we return to our character? Where are they? I'll find them. Let me know if you find them first. Our character finished their novel. It was impossible to tell if the novel made them famous. Was it still being written? On our character's journey.

Space/Time was not linear. It is also possible they were daydreaming about fame. We can question the credibility of our author as well. We can question the credibility of the reader as well. To have read it the right way. Everyone was on trial. So nobody was.

Our character thought their best trait was they were bearable. [They were right]. "I'm not too offensive. Am I?" Thought person who was. Our character hoped they weren't over-selling them selves. [They weren't]. If there is a set sum of money that will make people happy (50k). We don't want people to know it. They can't have a yearly wage. They need to be perpetually trying to add up their hourly rate. This gives them a much narrower perception of numbers/cost/Etc. If you tell someone it will take two years to purchase a car (while still having to pay for everything else in the meantime). That is crushing news. They will stop working. Telling them they will make $8 an hour. Not as bad. $8/hr. sounds much better. When compared to a gallon of milk for $4. But $8/hr. doesn't even make sense. When you put it next to $50,000 a year.

If people knew how much they were going to make each year. They would know how much they will be charged for taxes every year. People would talk. To other people. If everything was standardized. During our character's space/time. All those who profited off the system's inefficiencies (CPA's, lawyers, politicians, realtors, [People who made up the rules.] Etc.). Would be out of a job. And they would be forced to do something useful with their time. Like teach. Or make something. Therefore. Life had to be an anxiety-filled, hour-by-hour game of impossibilities. Our character could win. Or they could lose (like all *the undesirables* around them). Our character started rationing their hours. Since an hour was only worth $8. Which had a direct emotional and spiritual effect. On all their relationships. Which could be measured. If they had the money/time. [They didn't]. If 50k a year is announced. As the baseline. A minimum wage. Everyone will know (without having to add up hour-by-hour wages) how much money/space/time it will take for them to be happy. If everyone knows how much money/space/time it will take for them to be happy. They will demand that amount. Obviously. They will get outraged at housing prices. Obviously. They will not pay their doctor's bill's. Obviously. The insane profits that only benefited trillionaires, would no longer be made. If money didn't buy them happiness. We should take it from them. So they learn to appreciate it. If poors had money/space/time to be educated. This would require trillionaires to actually be educated (not just hold degrees from IvyOxBridge). Which would make them have to work. Just like the poors. Which would defeat the purpose of being rich, having money/space/time, Etc.

College needed to cost an exorbitant amount of money. So they could "give" it to soldiers for "free." So they didn't have to pay college athletes. So they could weed out the individuals who would/could critique the system. Singer unnecessarily differentiates between six and twelve string guitar. Extremely Normal Political Party is doing great things for people. Said nobody. "Nobody is getting out of this goddamn car until Gaga finishes *Bad Romance*!" Our character was no longer constructing witty comebacks. They started writing things down so they could forget them. They could then go back later. To remind them selves. At least. The option was there. Maybe it helped them. To release the burden. Beasts of burden. It was getting heavier by the $8/hr. Should we lighten the burden for our character? Or should we continue to provide more "character-building experiences" during our characters' money/space/time? If only our politicians were as talented as our athletes. Everything has been named. Everything in our character's money/space/time was either terrifying or fascinating. All famous people are troubled. Because everyone is. All great writers have depression. Because everyone does. Famous people. Are just the people we talk about. Of course they are difficult. At/during certain space/times. Of course many people had many different opinions about them. This is merely describing everyone. Who has ever existed. Nothing special about Popstar.

Our character worked in the "service industry" for "character-building-experiences." I suppose we allowed it after all. Let's not make them do this for too long. "Tipping" made them work harder (not softer). It helped make them more obedient. But when it comes to "actual money" they make less. Because of tips. If they worked really hard. It made them think they could "make more." They could make money. While making money. Like the stock market. But not even close. At all. No matter how much they made in tips. Or saved with store discounts (they used to clip coupons out of the "news" paper). It would not be as much as a basic yearly salary. Necessarily. "Perks" are a side show. "Hustle" culture just glorified poverty. Our character could really use a *deus ex machina* right now. Our character's personality is 69% memes at this point. Lol. Nice. Music scene. Dress badly. Sound worse. Almost-useless superpowers. Superhero can tell by looking at people what their dominant hand is. Network does a special on them. Because they are trying to start a campaign against left-handed people. Regulating The Virus? What's next? Regulating assault rifles? "N" onnnnnnnnnnnn keyboard is stuck. This! NNNNNNNance just wanted to make sure Randy had enough sunscreen. No need to get all worked up about it.

You can purchase the book you are reading. Online! Shop Amazon Disney Plus! This Holiday Christmas! Popstar sending a powerful message. About Popstar. Pivotal gay rights anthem unknowingly/unironically sung by thousands of anti-gay redneck Evangelicals at sporting event. "I'm totally punk rock. And I didn't realize it until now!" Everyday we erupt from the void. Every second. Buying in bulk. Was one of those perfectly choreographed capitalistic phenomena. The bad news. The idiots always think they are smarter than you. People: "These are the drugs we need. To make this life livable." Those in power: "We'll sell you some of those drugs as *prescriptions* (lol). So we can make a profit. Other drugs will be illegal because they compete with the drugs we are selling. And other drugs we are going to make sure poor people are on and can't get off. To fund our prison economy. Etc." They aren't even trying to hide it anymore. An artless police state. Redundant redundancies.

  Plant-based equality. Repurpose Nation. Good rough draft though. "Did you say brick and mortar? Or Rick and Morty? I'd rather talk about Rick and Morty in this job interview. If possible?" Our character's own job search wasn't going any better. I don't want to give any clues. If the sentence that follows. Will have any connection to the sentence it proceeds. That the machines started to resemble them was no mistake. They were the ones who made them. If you feel like you've read this before. . . Have you? Our character was only able to accomplish all this. With the generosity of strangers. And the loathing of family and friends. Surrounded or so rounded? The way words are or the waywards "R"? Out of fur pelocity (pure curiosity). If world-class athletes are adhering to pandemic protocols. And breaking world records. I think you can adhere to pandemic protocols at your local Apple Bee's.

7 HOW TO SURVIVE A SHITSTORM

A minimum wage must appear undesirable. It must be a punishment. To those who need it most. An hourly wage insures an hourly obedience. During our character's space/time they would have used a minute-ly wage. If it didn't look too much like the word minutely. Reminding the employees of the "minute" paychecks. If you're late by minutes. You don't get the full hour. "What if the kid at Table 3 doesn't get their tater tots within 5 minutes!" "When I worked at a restaurant, I did everything on time. And in the snow! Both ways!" [They didn't]. We are socially conditioned to be racists and classist. Even when it hurts us most. We don't want to "be" like the people around us. We keep going. We will surpass the people around us. One fine day. If we work hard enough. Etc. If you make the bottom "nearly bottomless" people can see how far others can fall. Overdosing, suicide, shooting up a school, Etc. People need a constant reminder. To keep them motivated. The news helps. If the bottom were merely being momentarily unhappy. Poor people wouldn't constantly put them selves into an anxious, feverish "work" mode. But again. All of this benefits the people at the top. If money doesn't buy happiness. Give me yours.

Fame was fleeting. The fleeting flame of fame. In the hall of lame. Nobody understood what our character's book was doing. Smart people only liked something if smarter people liked it. Stupid people. Were at least. Spared from this. Almost. In the end. Our character didn't like their audience (who could blame them?). And their audience soon forgot about them. For ever. At times our character should have been more insertive. At times they should have been less insertive. Our character was on the brink of grasping the question. Can our character be self-aware enough. To guide them selves through the perfection of a task. But not self-aware enough. To make them selves paralyzed? Lemmon Cellos. New Generation has run out of things to pretend to have invented. iPhone storage bane of our character's existence. The trick to being quick. Is the silence of your movements. Calisthenics are key. Our character planned on eating as much as possible every day. And run sprints as fast as they could. Everyday. All day. And do that forever. They wanted to be an unstoppable wrecking ball of a person. Do at least one smelly thing a day. British version was better.

Our character's visions/versions of grandeur weren't burst (best or worst). They simply hoped there was another level. Another day. In the back of their head. They knew this all along. The people our character was with. Were just as silly. As any group of people. But these people did it. In fancier clothes. And used bigger words. It didn't come as a surprise to our character. They weren't naïve. They wanted a goal to work toward. A reason to be working so hard. At the end. A payoff. They always knew this was a mirage. A curtain hiding the emptiness behind it. Currently (as far as we knew). Our character's personality is based solely on all the drugs ~~I take~~ they take. Opinions overrated. We need a quicker way of getting dirt off our feet. Shoes. Our character was always *trying* to eat right. If you ride around in shiny fast car. With big boom boom guns. You're bound to kill someone. Especially if you get paid. Police should be more like AAA/OnStar/Tow trucks/EMT's. And less like Cobra Commander/Team America. The police should help us. Not kill us. You know, like firefighters and paramedics. Lottery still main healthcare provider in Freest Nation. Our character blamed their sudden lack of motivation. On nothing motivating them.

Our character started forwarding all their bills and debts to the universities supposed to have provided them a career. When everything gets old. There will be something new. The classics gone badly. These standards. Always tragically self-selecting. There is so much more. We have yet to unlearn about ourselves. Our character. Their world. And ours. There will always be a now. Our character would be able to learn from. Merhaps that was comforting? In and of itself. *Per se.* Space/time is learning. Learning is space/time. Faster than the awareness of space/time. The speed of light. Etc. That you are in this body. Pre-remembering. What are the top five things you are? You are not those things. What are you now? Repeat. When we realize we are all living in one person's world. "We are going to invade your country. Because you want to join the UN. To protect you. From us invading your country." Sent back decades. For a moment. We were able to forget about this way of being. We were able to write about it. And talk about it. But once again. Here we are. Now. It was always going to be like this. Our character's friend was a filmmaker. They made a film with an intro montage. Allowing their audience to assume. They were watching an intro montage. But the film remains at this pace. For its entirety. "Note to self." Maybe that will be the title of the film our character's friend was making?

"Do you want to autofill your CV/Résumé by uploading a file to your application?" Yes. "Is this correct?" First and Last Name of Applicant: University College Ave. 3142 Previous employer #3: PhD Skills. In Power Point Ave. 3142 Five years of MA, Georgia. Reference Dr. Microsoft Word. Proficient in Spanish. California. 3 Years. 2015. Published papers. Included other documents. Are you a protected Veteran? Date of last employment. GoFundMe still main healthcare provider in Freest Nation. What is something every guy has pretended to be in order to get laid? And why did you all answer "religious"? Discount Psychiatry. How can we make a world where everyone is happy at/during all space/times? The ultimate hurdle for modernity. What we are all seeking. Even if we deny it. After a while. People can only feel. Through being sad/depressed. A way of happiness. Concealing the end goal. Nobody is happy. But people don't want to tell others. So they tell them selves. They are happy. Etc.

Oh you're an optimist? Name everything going well. Funny how you never hear about the marriage proposals that don't go well. Religion held a special place in Freest Nation. For the worst. The people lacked an "origins story." A clearly defined culture of their own. Traditions connecting them to ancestors. The old ways. People turned to religion. To solve their culture problem. No culture outside capitalistic appropriation. A cultureless culture. The Extremely Normal Money System works perfectly unless something goes wrong. Again. Hiring committee is seahorses. Aim for the moon. To get out of Hillsboro. Extremely Normal Political Party: "Best I can do is neither raising minimum wage nor improving healthcare coverage." Our character was growing weary. The misconception that technology solves problems posed by philosophy. In Extremely Normal Nation they would rather pay millions to make advertisements. About how people shouldn't drink alcohol. Rather than give people money. To solve the problems. That made them drink alcohol. The companies making the anti-drug/alcohol marketing campaigns. Were the same companies. Making the marketing campaigns to sell drugs/alcohol. A never-ending cycle of money making. That would eventually make everyone poor. Even the rich.

Followers of Wine Maker necessarily "backward looking." But only backward looking. In response. To what they have imagined. Is "forward looking." They're imaginations were severely limited. If there is no reality. To either backwards or forwards. Religion makes same mistake twice. If you are going to define yourself by your opposite. Make sure you understand what your opposite stands for. If your opposition doesn't believe history is progressive. You won't have anything to argue against. And therefore, you will have nothing to believe. Fighting windmills. And here we are. Members of the Extremely Normal Political Party believed in the reality of progression. More than progressives did. Politician doing exactly what we'd thought they'd do. Wellp. On to the next life! Fall has fallen. At least our character could spell quarantine now. Extremely Normal Politicians starting to secretly worry about the reputation of their Extremely Normal Political Party. [Too late].

Being a new parent. A hostage negotiator during the day. A secret agent at night. If an unstoppable force doesn't meet another force. It will become a stoppable force. As stoppable as unstoppable. I can't imagine what people see. Who don't understand the rules of football. Must be wild AF. Huge people running as fast as they can at each other. People randomly yelling as loud as they can. Hitting balls as hard as they can. With sticks. A musical act in the middle? Sometimes they take breaks. But for the life of me, I can't understand why. There's another sport where they try to run on ice. This is bananas. It was refreshing when our character realized they weren't the center of the universe. Other people were far more caught up within their own lives. To give our character the negative attention they thought they were getting. So at least that was a good thing? We also forgot our character wasn't the center of this universe. Forgetting (pre-remembering) can be good. They all agreed. Everyone's narrative did not pass through our character. Things are only better or worse. When you contemplate history. As we do. As they did. In the past. We are the experience itself. And maybe that's all we have. Nothing outside that. Our character was getting nothing but blank stares. "No? Just me?" Fucking yikes. Our character's psychiatrist told them they were concerned with their mental health. This disturbed our character. They thanked their psychiatrist for their concern. But they reminded their psychiatrist "I'm not paying you to be concerned. I'm paying you to help me bury this body."

If you give them your best. Tell them it was your worst. If you give them your worst. Tell them it was your best. Always keep them guessing. So long as they can't figure you out. You are ok. If you don't fail often. You are building a false sense of confidence. Religion is the attempt at culture in a police state. Nobody can ever actually "believe" the teachings. The teachings (necessarily) didn't relate to our character's space/time. Detached by space/time. Language. Actual culture. Etc. Their beliefs had to be based on misunderstandings. And bad translations. In order to be beliefs. It was real. In the sense that it was genuinely fake. It wasn't even real when it was being written. All based on what the individual was able to abstain from. A cult of negative identity. Figures. Empty rituals. A memorial. Trying desperately to remain relevant. Going back further. To be relevant. Moving in the opposite direction of anything helpful. Regardless of any other direction available. Sacrificing those it pushes itself off of. To move backward. This cultureless culture. Is a cult of representation *ad nauseam*. Representing what they can't represent. The representation more important. Than Christ himself. If such a character existed. And wasn't merely a Socrates knock-off/reboot. The muted memorial amplified. Personified. Representations of Christ. Have more power. Than he ever did. The sacrifice Christ made. The dramatic death. A rebirth. Christ had to be a young man. Like our soldiers. "New trailer for Socrat-a-verse. Tonight at 8!"

Our character had so much character. They needed to create more characters. And write about them. Extremely Normal Political Party thinks liberal rich bad. Conservative rich good. Because Sky Wizard? We put a man on the moon. But can't feed everyone? We have the means. Yet we don't. A choice we consciously make. Our character assumed it's even worse to complain about people. Who complain about people. So our character didn't include these types of rants in their book. Our character liked to think they weren't one of the robots. But they knew. In a way. They were. A reaction to a force. No different than the force itself. Only mirroring it. Albeit a fun-house mirror. With nothing fun about it. Our character couldn't get anywhere. Opposing the system. Our character had to do something different. Maybe our character was accepting. By seeing. What it was. To get their way. They no longer cared if it was different. They only cared they were alive. The basics. They cared *ergo sum*. Character accepting applications for Character.

Oh good. Another day. Our character can't believe this shit. Here at Amazon Cheeto Pepsi Corp., we are thrilled to announce the publication of *What to Do*. An intriguing romp through the end of days. For the Holidays. Buy it. Follow the link. "Say what you will. It's better than my last book." – The Author (unprompted). You're "uncomfortable" with critical race theory. Imagine how "uncomfortable" it was to be a slave. Highbrow. For idiots. People: "Can we have healthcare?" Nation: "Best we can do is a Marvel Movie." People: "Can we have a non-Marvel Movie?" Nation: "Best we can do is a *Friends* reboot." Never try to do anything. Never try to be anyone. Just be quiet. Go unnoticed. And die quietly. "What's the most pointless thing you've ever done?" When it was our character's turn to talk. They realized they misheard the speaker. Others had been sharing "the most important thing" they've ever done. It took ten people to share. Before our character realized.

Our character was playing doctor on the Internet. Upset stomach, clogged sinuses, existential crisis, depression, lack of sleep, too much sleep, sore muscles, chest palpitations, joint ache, ennui, difficulty breathing, anxiety, loss of appetite, overeating, hurricane of diarrhea, bizarre allergies, weird rash. . . All signs of everyday life during our character's space/time. Everything our character wanted was problematic. Should we have them have no needs? Talk to no one. Trust no one. And never. Ever. Think you deserve anything nice. You don't. Nobody does. Everyone will use everything against you. So be nobody your entire life. There is no such thing as happiness. Only the progenation of the species. Kids' movies are preparing us for when animals will talk. We've always been communicating with them. Talking isn't a big deal. We don't talk to other people all the time. Listen to the unheard sounds of animals that surround us. Everyday. It's the barks you don't hear. Etc.

The collective subconscious. Our character becoming. The people they are. And the people they aren't. If they don't. They will not be able to hear them selves. Let alone. Others. One and other. One an other. No(w)one(an)other. Opposing the word that follows. One nothing. That nothingness. Representations of nothing. The positive aspects of negation. Tonight at 8pm! If you wake up at 5am (EST) every morning, you are waking up at 2am (PST), 9pm in Australia, 10am in London, 6pm in China, 2:30pm Afghanistan, and the equivalent of 5pm (EST) if you work nights. Sorry, what were you bragging about again? Doing *the something different*.

What does it allow? Our character would find out for us. If you find yourself in the same situation. And it didn't work before. Pick the different thing. Sometimes this thing will be nothing. Do nothing. See what happens. If you picked the different thing last time. Pick the same thing this time. It might not seem different at first. But upon closer reflection. Many days after. You'll have forgotten about this incident completely. Our character forgot what they were talking about. Again. We never knew. It was the same thing.

"A fence full of trees." Our character was showering. After working outside all day. They had music on. They got out of the shower. The song they thought was playing. Was another song entirely. The songs sounded nothing alike. And that might be the closest our character would get to understanding everything. Our character couldn't make this connection. It ended up not mattering. All efforts fail. In space/time. The *logos* of the joke itself needs to be a joke. Once you see how language can make fun of itself. You can realize. The target is constantly shifting. Art is another way of practicing mental flexibility. If our character was in an art studio. Doing something to the *tabula rosa*. They were also trying to understand how to undo it as well. If things go awry. [They will]. Our character got better at their process. Continually asking "Should I make or unmake the previous decision?" We'll see if this skill transferred. To flexibility within their personal narrative. Seeing the life of the move. And the death of the move. At once. Our character needed a job. While they applied for a job. Our character needed an apartment. While they looked for an apartment.

"It might be the end of days, but my legs have never looked better." – The Author. If you need Popstar to tell you Orange Man is bad. . . I don't want to live in this country anymore. "This is the best one I've seen!" Our character tolerated Nation. Just as they tolerated existence. If you can't do it in one line. Don't do it at all. Wait. . . Do you remember who you are? Our character reminded us. Youth from disenfranchised minority is glad to see more representations of their culture in movies. Now, if they could only have healthcare. One approach has us spreading out(in)ward searching for everything there is. The other approach has us focus on a center point. That we ourselves put there. The "Truth" bounces from pole to pole. Us and the point. The same answers keep coming back. Inside this echo chamber. But what if the moreness was only more? Of the sameness? "Despite my best efforts, the book is semi-readable." – The Author.

A Greatest Hits of Songs You've Never Heard. And Never Wanted To. If Popstar is only playing the hits. I will too. Last yesterday. The life of the party always pays. Military-grade encryption. Military-grade subscription. Circular. Déjà vus. A pre-remembering. A post-forgetting. Pre-remembering the beginning. Of another cycle. The end of another. Our character saw them selves. As they had already seen them selves. A remembrance of circularity. A re-embrace. By chance. Around the circle with bumps along the way. Living our life loop. Whoever realizes this. Can go in peace. Could our character? Knowing nothing will be lost. No effort wasted in the cycle. To space/time. Difficult to realize. Hardly nobody did. Maybe for good reason. Shop for this book on Amazon Dr. Pepper Bowl Championship and Cleaning Services. You'll be supporting local artists. In a strange way. Hey what's up world? What's your deal? Being able to switch to the ends of the binary construction. An abysmal failure. Or genius perfection. To appreciate both ends of the binary. What the Humanities have sought since their inception. What religion attempts to chase. When directing our character to live via morals. The art our character was working on. Etc. Crossing the binaries. Generating insight and appreciation.

At this point our character wondered if their writing could be turned into an academic book. Maybe Popstar could use it for lyrics? Could post it as a blog? Nobody would read it. Maybe that was a good thing? There must be some dramatic tension. There. Who wants this dramatic tension? Nobody reading thus far (wink). But how do you connect with the reader in a meaningful way? Is comedy your way of avoiding drama? [It was]. When do we start calling it a regime? The bad guys look a lot like bad guys. On the one hand. You got bit. If you build a wall. People will knock it down. If not now. Eventually. The only constant. Walls will fall. Only addressing the symptom. If you don't want refugees. Create a better world. The new normal abnormal. Jenn, say Pa. Great teachers find a way to teach what they don't know. The Humanities should worry less about pedagogy. The Sciences should worry more. Cautious optimist: Cautiomist. Our character was dedicated to their addictions. The loneliest. When nobody believes you. The only thing we ever find. Is ourselves.

"Probably should have never been published. Probably why all publishers rejected it." – The Author. Accepting the journey. An endless spiraling staircase. The insanity of eternal sameness. Something in the sameness. Beneficial? After an individual has passed beyond. The panic as a response to realization. Breaking from Tik Tok time. Sans space. Before returning into the circle. The development of consciousness. Our character. Ready to go beyond them selves. Appreciation of space/time. New narrative expectations. The version(s) one is left to contemplate. Not necessarily the True Self. Or The Truth. Merely a perspective. With which we can move forward. Perhaps the closest our character will get to "knowing." What philosophy/art/literature (*logos*) should provide. But often. Does not. During our character's space/time. Our common motives in *logos*. Unconcealing itself from its concealment. It has always been possible to view yourself in this way. You simply haven't. Yet. Or forgot (pre-remembered). For both "bad" and "good" reasons.

This spring, Ivy League at Oxbridge Saudi Aramco will graduate the four horsemen of the apocalypse, and at least 20 impeachable presidents. "Some words from the book: Are. Is. What. Had. Riveting. And. Etc." – The Author. What does this mean for the future of big business? During our character's space/time they were desperate for qualified workers. But they also weren't hiring qualified workers. Nobody was working. But everyone was also working multiple jobs. There was no oversight. But there was also way too much. Everything was true if it was bad. That's the only thing they could agree on. Inconsistency a hallmark of sanity. Hallmark a hallmark for mediocrity. Another brand of insanity. Existence a distraction from itself. Purgatory is hell. Our character ate the darkness surrounding them. So others didn't have to. Our character wished they were bad at being bad at things. Solipsistic personalities were common during our character's space/time. But not particularly unique. We could try again to know our character through their likes and dislikes. This might yield some information we can be comfortable with.

The fish in the aquarium exists on a level of consciousness that allows them to live in the aquarium. Humans exist on a level of consciousness that allows them to live in the world they create. Living without the equivalent ability to understand it. Is torture. Uninteresting problems deserve uninteresting answers. During our character's space/time, pretty girls took pictures on cliffs. It looked fine. But it made everyone very nervous. Dark matter is the graviton. If we can't find the graviton. And we don't know what dark matter is. Then let's just say dark matter is the graviton. This means gravitons are simply very big. They are black holes. Maybe we are inside a graviton?

Change for the sake of change is regression. Truth is only what you currently believe (duh). The easiest way not to progress. Is to think you already have. Politics oversimplify morals. Morals oversimplify life. Knowledge kept. Is a false sense of possession. There are no necessary evils. Only people who believe evil is necessary. Devil Evil. D'evil. Cruella de Vil. Rationality is the ability to abandon or lessen one's faith in one's own presuppositions when signs of failure appear. Our character looked up at the stars. And couldn't help but think: "We are doing everything wrong." Our character would much rather live in unimportant times. Freest Nation places cameras everywhere. To make everyone "safe." Truth the future. Identity is consciousness. "We love most that which kills us." I know no other way. Our character thought to them selves: "I'm not stupid. I'm just not motivated to think." Remember being scared of the dark? What was that all about? When our categories fail. How do we go on? What thought. Could our character think. That could never harm anyone.

Prison labor just slavery. With extra steps. And so. Life? Goes on? The   that allowed our character to maintain deep friendships. Were the same that enabled the creative process. Both provided effective resistance against neoliberalism. This now. Felt very now. Thought our character. Standardized Poodle. Testing. Testing. 1.2.3. Echo Golf; e.g. Etc. Within the Corporate Academy. You had to BE what you studied. There was a pre-cast mold. Humanities search committee unable to decide on candidate. Jack of all trades. Master of none. Better than a master of one. Our character's advisor told them, "You aren't smart enough to pull that off. You're just perpetually distracted." By convincing them selves they were smart. Our character set unrealistic expectations. They failed. Obviously. Necessarily. But this happened enough times. That eventually they became smart. But they wouldn't have been smart. If they first assumed they were stupid. With space/time. Failure can become success. If given no space/time. Failure is just failure. A good carrot before the cart. But only if there's a horse pulling it.

Kinky kink shaming. Pope gets rid of purgatory. Make purgatory great again! Psychologists get rid of subconscious. Replace it with social media. The people now. Have nowhere to hide. Now, where to hide? Spacetime only makes sense in the past. Having moved through it. Has anyone asked if vampires just have insomnia? Maybe they wouldn't even need blood if they got ONE GODDAMN NIGHT OF SLEEP. Viewer discretion still advised. Viewer discretion being recorded for quality assurance purposes. What we do with the data. We don't even know. During our character's spacetime. People got married to "solve their sex problem." But nobody says: "I had dinner. Hunger problems solved." Marriage. The mirage of stability. Merrily merging with the merely minor mirror mirage of marriage stability. But married people. Are the *most* sexually dangerous. To them selves and others. They believe they've found a solution. And that always creates. The most dangerous kind of person.

Popstar's attempts self-deprecating humor. Uninteresting. Whales are just cows that said, "Fuck land." I bet dogs think cars are wild. Our humans drive them. But they aren't able to stop them that well? Even our own human appears to be afraid of them. When we are walking, they always stay away from them. Our human gets mad and afraid. When we get near the hard ground. Where they drive. They invented this "car." That is the fastest thing I've ever seen. And they didn't wait until they invented a better way to stop them. Before they decided every human needed one? Why doesn't the car start and stop like us, our humans, and other animals? Everything else is good at starting and stopping. But not the cars. Everyone else takes turns. But the cars drive right through. And fast. They are usually only on the hard ground. But sometimes me and my human walk on the hard ground too. I don't know how they know to avoid the cars. Seems like everyone knows where everyone else is going for the most part. But when I don't have my leash, and I'm on the hard ground near the cars, the humans freak out.

Rationing. Obedience. Abstinence. The dark matter that invisibly shapes us. Our thoughts. Daily habits. Etc. It was difficult for our character. To balance. Being open to other's perspectives while also holding on to their own. And pursuing them to their fullest. Unfortunately, during our character's spacetime. To be right about yourself. Others had to be wrong? The balance of seeing others' perspectives. Holding our own. Our character's own. Not a slave to your rhetorical stance. In the non-polarized and ambiguous realm of creative play. To remain open and curious. Address the individual. But not in their singularity. In their ambiguity. Not merely identities restricted to economic terms. The consumer. The entrepreneur. Etc. Our character's life being read while they're living it. Others (us?) constantly reading/writing their story. Reading and re-reading it. Our character was the culmination of all the things others projected on to them. Merely a mirror. Mirrorly. But this is how our character existed. They couldn't complain too much. [They could]. Others will not read this book. Or stop reading it. At least. At some point. Our character will still be here. Long after the reader is gone. If there is a here. Here. Of course lol. Maybe uploaded to the singularity? Why not the multiplicity? Etc.

Commercial provides solution to "pizza emergency." Actual emergencies left to rage freely everywhere. Conservatives tout their freedom. Anyone who spoke English found this odd. Free from what? Self-policing to the extreme. When not asked or required. Especially their neighbors. Is Capitalism working yet? Extremely Normal Political Party takes brave anti-life stance. Never so much money spent on advertising. Never been so useless. Everything was an "experience." "Best underwear experience!" "Best shredded cheese experience!" Rich people bad with money. Don't give them anymore. Newsflash. Extremely Normal Political Party doesn't understand something. Nobody WANTS to get an abortion. Nobody DESIRES to have an abortion. People aren't GETTING OFF on having abortions. People would rather have free healthcare. People wanted the right (luxury?) to choose when and where they had a child. And who they had a child with. Important for the child's upbringing. But Extremely Normal Political Party takes bold stance against free healthcare. That would solve the problem. *Reductio ad absurdum. Ad infinitum.* So we are back at the abortion debate.

Extremely Normal Political Party couches everything under "religious beliefs." To maintain/generate this never-ending "support" for their "cause." Regardless of the mountains of evidence and data against it. Their problem HAS a solution. So rarely does this happen in our universe. But in pretending the solution doesn't exist. And laying the entire burden on individual actions. Extremely Normal Political Party keeps this (now) never-ending "issue" or "controversy" at play. It's not a good plan. But it is a plan. And the Extremely Normal Political Party applies this to all "issues" they take up. They don't stand for anything. All of this would become obvious to more people. If more people received a college education. *Reductio ad absurdum. Ad infinitum.* We HAVE the answers. The problems themselves were not complicated. Or even interesting. This was one of the most maddening things about our character's space/time.

Is sports? How many is hippopotamus? Why sky? And not not sky? Bending spacetime with the creative process. Another method of traveling through spacetime. Our character needed to establish a base-line reality. If not for them selves. For others. To understand. Our character's base-line reality. So others knew how to approach our character. Boundaries must be set. After graduation, PhD in Humanities spent every second proving they earned their PhD in the Humanities. Whether justified/appropriate or not. This was their reality. Like watching a movie our character had seen a long time ago. Only half paying attention the first time. The next time they saw it. They created their own ability to anticipate. Narrative gymnastic training. If enough loud people agree. You could other anyone. Another other. An other. Nother. No other. Older generation promoted narratives of economic mobility. To keep everyone where they were. So their jokes could still make sense. Not very funny. Everyone stayed where they were. For too long. Nomads. No longer. Nomads. Yesmads. Yazz maid. The demarcation between public and private. Only hurts the public. And benefits the private.

They say. You shouldn't eat before you swim. But then again. They say a lot of stupid shit. The lives you don't live. Will live you. Our character was in the middle of every force. Acting upon them. With and against them. If a bear shits in the woods. And nobody picks it up. Do I look like your fucking mother? No one will regret that you stayed in tonight. Freest Nation decides on Democracy and the Freest-market. And stops halfway. Edging. Rich people needed a "special league" to compete in. Aside from the military and police departments (needed to keep the poors in line), the government is only put in charge of things that will be poorly funded and improperly staffed. A government industry doesn't HAVE to be inefficient. But rich people needed the proper context. To be considered wealthy. The poor people had to be protected by the insufficient government agencies that rich people defunded. Except for the military and police departments. Needed to keep the poors in line.

Bouncing ideas off as many different critics as possible. Inside or outside our selves. Sane schizophrenics. Creatives create more "drafts" of the project. To refine the finished work. Before having to present it. Stretching space/time. To make it helpful. Without making it paralyze them. Or their audience. By breaking down the rigid barrier between designer and design. Between author and reader. Etc. The creative process is never over. This can be a relief at space/times. At other space/times it can be a curse. What the creatives learn about their "finished" project. Merely part of a larger creative process. And therefore. Able to let it go. Everyone creates. Few let go. Allowing them and their project to become something other. And more. Beyond the consumer and entrepreneur. Make jorts great again! "As soon as I get this restraining order lifted, I'm going to ask her to marry me."

The people our character spent the most time with. They became them. They become us. Etc. Our character was the undecided one. All their other life trajectories had settled. Our character was the version of space/timeline still searching. Forgetting. What progress had originally promised them. Progress measured. By what it is not. Metaphor is an optical illusion. Narrative is an allusion. Our character didn't know what they didn't understand. Things are only better or worse when you contemplate history. As we do—as we are having them do in the past (now). What's the most pointless thing we could have our character do? And why would we have them do it? Multi-dimensionally space/timed. Going back and reading this. We don't have a strong enough connection to it yet. Perhaps when our character died. They experienced their life at once. No longer in front or behind. Our character was watching regular TV. They just now realized how stupid people had become. How could they warn them? [They couldn't]. Another great "character building" experience for our character.

Writer: "Is there still existence in your space/time, Dear Reader?" Being dragged along. By all our self-interests. How you can get out of a loop of any kind. Keep reading. Sometimes the words are words. And other times the words are words. Etc. There are two kinds of people: those who understand the vicious cycle of poverty and the members of the Extremely Normal Political Party. After every single interaction. With anything. Our character was bombarded by prompts to review the services provided (or not provided). This became more frequent throughout our character's spacetime. But the service was getting worse. Collecting mountains of data. But not knowing why.

Our character wanted the things most people wanted. But that didn't make sense. For us, our character was the only evidenced. Others in their space/time existed (or didn't exist). Our character likes food, playing outside, and sleeping. These were their most distinctive traits. Everyone liked some of these things. Others liked other things. Our writer considered inserting a graph here. But maybe they'll do it later. [They didn't]. Our writer wandered off course. To check on how things are are-ing. Weapons-grade absurdism. If everyone is going to be mad at you all the time. They are setting them selves up for diminishing returns. If you don't hear the complaints of the poor and disenfranchised. They won't hear you scream on the guillotine. They thought writers were the biggest threat to national security in Freest Nation. But really. They were the only thing keeping anything together. Or at least. This book. Etc. Everything happens as it should happen. Become one. To understand how you are not. Words our character tried to Google: "Pretensousness." Our character's spell-check-AI couldn't make the connection. The closest suggestion for their misspelling of "amatures" was: "Armatures, A matures, Matures." Amateurs.

The psychiatrist's receptionist got mad at our character for being overly paranoid, anxious, unable to control their emotions, and poor. "Yes. Isn't that why I'm here?" Our character needed to do their part to help stop the pandemic of self-righteousness plaguing Freest Nation. Our character lost their phone in their house. They thought about calling it. Until they realized [. . .]. Bad guy has Vandyke. Our character went crazy. But so did everyone else. So it was difficult to tell. Wine name: "Earth Son Blood." During our character's spacetime. When you are an adult. Everything fun is illegal. And addictive. Necessarily. In a police state. Everyone needs to be arrestable. At any given moment. If all else fails. They can release you. It's easier to ruin your life. Than miss the opportunity to "hire" essential prison labor. Nobody believes a war will happen. Before it does. Each space/time assumes we are past that point in history. We are not. The false sense of progression. Through space/time. As long as we have a history. We will have violence. At least, it appeared this way to our character.

War. Addressing the past with the past. Blinded by a celebration of modernity. Millions of wars. Are always already waging. You just stopped paying attention to them. We have jobs for that. The news. Reporting nothing new. Compartmentalization allows disassociation. To uncomprehend its inevitability. The cycle needing to complete. Perpetual revenge. You've read this before. Revenge builds every community of people. Revenge brings everyone together. So everyone can be torn apart. All together now! Altogether now. A great personal motivator. If you can forget. Don't forgive? Or. Forget to not forgive. Forget why you started something. Then remember. Then make it not about that. Or nearly like that. But not enough to be it completely. Substantially slippery simulacrum. A corporate slurry. Our character was legally allowed to consume. Illegal Food Science. Tonight at 8!

A kakistocracy and not a meritocracy. Oh well. Another day. *Ergo sum.* Another day inside the graviton. Attempting to please the algorithm. Etc. The center of the universe shifts again. Our character needed to stop trying to be right. And start asking interesting questions. It's the jokes you don't make. That will make you. Etc. It's difficult to be critical without yucking someone's yum. Difficult. But not impossible. Not every judgment you have is worth making. You don't have to hold all the opinions you think. Not everything that offends you. Was made to. Our character tried not to make important life decisions. When things weren't going well. Sometimes, life was just going to suck. Embrace the suck. Survive and move on. Not every task was worth perfecting. But some definitely were. Deciding which is which. Defined our character. Or maybe not. But maybe it made them interesting? How do you not make important life decisions? How do you know which life decisions are important? You didn't. Others did. And the average was the story of your life. Etc. If you've learned from a mistake. You are responsible to share it with others. Our character would do this from time to time. And it was one of their better attributes. Although they never really knew it. No such thing as bad weather. Just wrong clothing. Art is ambiguity. Philosophy without humor is just thinking.

8 PLEASE DIE QUITER
(YOU'RE SCARING THE CUSTOMERS)

If you piss on the floor. You're bound to walk in it. Etc. We measure. We do something. We measure. We do something. We measure. We do something. We measure. We do something. We measure. We do something. We measure. We do something. We release from this self-self. The singular self. Becoming everything around us. When they do this. Our character can experience them selves in different space/times. Looking to the past through a lens in the future. More future than past. At the moment. Now. More past than future. At the moment. The two ends of the binary. Jostle for position. The average self of the selves. Then averaged again. By our perceived perspective of others. Back and forth. Etc. The Book: "Am I one long inside joke?" Author: "Well I hope it's more than that. But I'm open to suggestions." JIF is the peanut butter. So it's pronounced GIF.

Netflix declares war on YouTube. This spring, Ivy League of Oxbridge at Berkshire-Hathaway will graduate at least three future billionaires who will ruin the world. But (down from last year) only two hundred economist who will crash global markets. Fuck Monster. AI spell-check: "This language may be offensive to your reader." Existence is forgetting. Forgetting is Existence. All sounds great. Taxes: working twice for the money you get paid once. Guy who plays classical piano to OutKast songs. This has got to be porn for someone. Can science only prove what we already know? Necessarily. Isn't it impossible to prove what you don't know? Necessarily. If you knew it. You would know it. How can you prove you don't know something? Impossible. There must not be a "before" nor "after" to the experiment. Concealed and unconcealed. Space/time breaks down. *Logos* breaks down. Necessarily. And justified after. Making meaning in any way it can. But that's why we can't always think deductively. Through negation. We need to brainstorm at times. Come up with more possibilities. Not less. Otherwise we might make the mistake. There is one solution. For all space/time. Narrowing to fewer options. Becoming stuck. Fluctuating between the anxiety of limitations and the anxiety of a multiplicity. Humor allows you to slip into the comfort of narrative predictability. Then explodes all possible narrative possibilities into a multiplicity. Causing the laughter. Anything is possible. It always was. But for some reason (what was the reason?). You read into the situation as predictable. What allowed you to do this? The serious comes before the funny. But is only realized. After.

Wine Maker: "I died for this? I died for this shit?" Hot girl must be a bitch. New studies find it's perfectly normal to feel like total dogshit 100% of the time. Ordinary people making an ordinary amount of difference. Nice to be human. Says person on the street. Spinach loves teeth. "Catch and release," but talking about humans. With everything they did. No judgment. Let's provide our character an emotionally free space/time. Where our character does not look down on them selves. Providing the truth that might as well be true. The truth that cannot hurt or harm you. It can't be false. You can only gain from this view. It will not be a waste. Of you. Your spacetime. Comment below. If our character broke all the laws. They wouldn't have time to prosecute them. Deep State cover blown by retirees Frank and Debbie Smith from Homestead, South Dakota. I know just enough. To be really dangerous. Thinks conspiracy theorist. "Original body" left to merely reflexes. Lost focus. Never lost or gained. The days dream of you. The person who remains. Your unconscious. Finally able to peer out. Other thought worlds. Clearer information from the selves. Completely absorbed in the task. Leaning forward out of yourself. Completely silent. Thinking no thoughts. Being. In the same space/time as yourself. Yourself lined up with yourself. For the most part. The perfect alignment. Being death. The final alignment.

Driver relieved environmentally damaging smell coming from car next to them. Pictures show. Thing happened. If our character wanted to be creative. They needed to feel as if they have options to work with. Even if only. To get them started. To give them hope. Through this creative process. They might actually obtain a variety of options. Even semi-original ideas. Perchance. When the overbearing critic isn't present. Refinement. Necessarily. But not yet. Allowing for wide-ranging associations. Cognitive flexibility. But not yet. Creatively and critically. To escape the overly-utilitarian impulse. Of the consumerpreneur. But not yet. White lady scatting at jazz club. Makes everyone uncomfortable. Except for Nance. She thought it was "Actually pretty good." People being really productive in commercial. Should we have the most talented people run Freest Nation? Or no? [No]. Driving car still 108.3% more dangerous than latest local news scare for rich parents. Speaking of speaking in tongues. Our character practiced comedy. To reflect on them selves. Without guilt. Nobody wanted to compete with you. Everyone wanted to be your friend. Everyone you know. Just wanted to love you. Then our character realized. They were simply another person.

The writer went on another break. Does our character recognize these patterns? Or would they be bored if they knew? I'm the character BEING written. Therefore, there is also some of me not being written. Who was the "me" here? Where was the "here" here? What am I beside this narrative? Our character held a new truth: "The reader and I. A step behind our writer (little did they know, they weren't). But what if we were a step ahead instead? Would that make us the writer? What happens when the writer is reading? Or writing. About them selves. As our character? Our writer was trying to write something they would not have been able to write before. Now. Maybe this would make the book something the reader had never read before. Person apologizes unnecessarily for house being "such a mess." Real people not actors. Are really actors. Beautiful person probably really ugly on the inside. A medium amount of awareness of the medium. We have ways of sneaking below. To the moreness. Laughing. Lucid dreaming. Drugs. Etc. But not all the way down. Because that is consciousness. The ability to sink down far enough. To propel us up. On the other side. Teeter-totter. If we were able to reach the extremes. We would find. We are traveling in a circle. The two ends meet. And become the same thing. And then other. Not opposite.

Oh good. Another day. Our character was doomed. To recap all traumatic events that led up to this moment. It didn't help them get out of bed. Though. It did keep them awake. Non-conquering religions made the attempt. To prevent *homo economicus* from invading our every action and thought. Unfortunately, non-conquering religions failed to conquer. There was something inherent to the *logos* of "leading and following" that always upended the project. "Bad trips." The inability of the drug. To overpower our *logocentrism*. But eventually you will. If you give a monkey a typewriter. They'll write something. Or they'll break the typewriter. Something about Shakespeare too. But our character couldn't remember. Just because someone has a stern face doesn't mean they are an asshole. They are an asshole. Because most people are. I'd write in additional characters here. And I'd do it in our character's voice. But I'm overthinking everything. Or not thinking enough. Our character could never tell.

Never before. Had an entire generation. Been infantilized. So thoroughly. They didn't have to change the protest signs. Modern convenience. The problems didn't change. Average citizen responsible for nothing is held to higher standards than the leader of the free world. College Freshman home for the summer identifies as Libertarian. Newly discovered culture pillaged for cookbooks, podcasts, memoirs, sitcoms, protests, inclusive advertisements, cheap National knock-offs, preservation societies, and courses for liberal arts colleges. Mortality rate for humans still 100%. Pandemic-era benefits ending. Restrictive restrictions re-enabled. For poor people. All problems have been solved. And we are all better. The rich people decided. Everyday our character didn't work. They became poorer. Everything adds up. Everyday. If you don't make money. You lose money. Even if you have no money to lose. Somehow you still can lose more. It takes money. To make money. You have to waste money. To make money. Everyone agreed. Nobody could do anything about it. A motivation. Further aligning us with our larger sense of purpose. Forgetting. We are only one half of the equation. And everything we do. Will be undone. Eventual meaninglessness.

Our character woke up one day. Like any other day. In the usual manner. They had always done. And will always do. Then they ate breakfast. They were brushing their teeth now. They thought about their wife, Tamera. And while they were doing this. We were able to escape with them. Out of the pages. And into a fictional scenario of their making. Our character was talking to Tamera. They whispered in her ear, "I love you." They held each other close. For "the last time." Our character woke up one day. Like any other day. In the usual manner. They had always done. And will always do. Then they ate breakfast. They were brushing their teeth now. They thought about their wife, Plamera. And while they were doing this. We were able to escape with them. Out of the pages. And into a fictional scenario of their making. Our character was talking to Plamera. They whispered in her ear, "I love you." They held each other close. For "the last time."

Score one for the dipshits. WWIII sponsored by T-Mobile. Hypochondriac is right. You cannot be good looking and work in academia. In our very modern and Freest Nation. Our character had to move across the country. To get dental care. To keep their teeth. And not be in constant pain. So they could live. We care about your pronouns. But not if you live or die. It's not a dream. Unless you remember it. Everything prohibitive. Prohibition Nation. Is Freest Nation. Feast or famine. Feast and famine. Feast on famine. Race to the bottom. To find the best loser. To reduce the number of jobless claims. They made the claims more difficult to make. All institutions and legal procedures were created to prevent someone like Orange Man from becoming leader of Freest Nation. They failed. And nobody was ready to admit it. Because those institutions and legal procedures wrote the paychecks. Noble Lie. No longer noble. Neoliberal pressures. Limiting us to develop only one side of the dialectic. So far, no healthy and creative ways to work with contradictory extremes. Interviewer thinks that's a fabulous question. Popstar Feminism is sugary panic attack.

Our character was making decisions. In seconds. That had previously taken thousands of years. They were a thousand years ahead or behind. At any moment in their space/time. This hadn't happened before. Had it? Our character felt. They'd been doing emotions wrong. Their entire life. Our character woke up every day. Trying to prove to themselves. They were wrong. That people really were alright. Every day. They were not. Switching the tracks to kill one. Or many. The problem in real life. There is only one track. Everyone is on it. Do you tell them about the train? Pop psychology killing millions. Several things occurred to our character at once. They couldn't tell which happened first. Our character was getting tired of always running back into the past. We were getting tired of sending them. Maybe we should stop? [They didn't. It was too rich a narrative source]. Our character attempted to run forward into the future. But without us.

The task was impossible. Without us. Was it? So little space/time within our selves. Easily distracted. But it's nice to get lost.

Our character (now named "Trish") sat on the edge of her consciousness. And the edge of a beautiful mountain cliff. The summer. Every summer. A summer of summers. The sumerest of summers. A thousand summers to you all! There were things Trish knew. There were things Trish didn't know. This either made her happy or sad. Justified or Unjustified. Here, our attempt to be other people. Was successful. If the reader is still reading. The only thing that counts. "One, two, three, Etc." The only thing of value here. Experiences that make them happy. Maybe they will make the character come alive. In the same sense that we are. Nation's heartland. Is heartless. There's this character I'm working on. They only know actors. From their least known roles. Another pointless superpower. Every writer assumes their space/time is somehow unique. Whether it is. Or is not. Is up to the readers. So either you will write an important book (your space/time *really was* unique). Or nobody will read your book. You can't lose! Tonight at 8!

Economy just pyramid scheme with extra steps. Most people already understand the limitations. They want to hear if something new is possible. But always start small. And never over-play your hand. In these situations. Potential employer. Stalks potential employee's social media. To see if they are "professional" (hot). Movie just really long trailer for sequel. Pouring thing into different container is a fucking disaster. "Here, science starts to look more like science fiction," says documentary. "Living best life," no longer viable excuse. "Whatever it needs to be. I guess." Thought our character. It's amazing. How sometimes. Doing something else. Provides relief. And then also causes more stress, Etc. Although inevitable. As much as you possibly can. Never associate with people. Who do not understand your potentiality. Who are projecting an agenda for your potential that doesn't align with your potential to become happy. They will drag you down. To their perception of your abilities. Or they will drag you up. To a pedestal when you are afraid of heights. And public speaking. Although. Sometimes the challenge can provide growth. Regardless. They do not know your whole story. They have divided you. Cut off a piece. And categorized you. We are doing this to our character all the time. Recognize the type of person others believe you are to them. So you can react accordingly.

Backup player. Not as good at celebrating. As rest of team. Fans love new Popstar. Turns out. Sitting on toilet. Still favorite place. To generate social media content. Sitting on toilet. Still favorite place. To plot death. Of loved ones. In five years. Everyone will live in South Dakota. Kid can tell. When Dad skips pages now. Free Fee. For me? Me? You shouldn't have. No. You SHOULDN'T have. Commercial: "Tree Tea. For Free?

Me?" You don't have to win every game. Just the ones "pretty girls" go to. Go beyond the game. But trust the process? Beyond meat. The part will make sense of the whole. Writing about anything does this. And the whole will make sense of the part. Everything adds up. [Even if it doesn't]. The *logos* of thermodynamics. The thermodynamics of *logos*. We/they/our reader/our character/our writer/Etc. will entrench this smaller sliver of yourself (mining the silver of the self) in a rivalry/competition/partnership /tutelage. You never wanted in the first place. If you're not careful. This situation will consume more of your attention. Than it deserves. You will forget yourself. And thereby. Conceal your potentiality from yourself. Nearly impossible to see any of this. At/in the space/time though. Is butter Alaska or 2x+6y?

Top Questions to Ask at the End of an Academic Job Interview: "How much does this position cost in mental health bills?" Don't waste others' space/time being unnecessarily modest and deferential. With too many caveats. People also want answers. It might appear solipsistic. Self-deprecation might only confuse. Why so self-referential? Becoming the braggart. You are attempting not to be. Not everyone is watching your entire life story unfold. Allow people to become invested in you. You'll need it later. You are never above. A desperate need for patrons. Test drive your thoughts against more critics, more styles, more historically relevant moments, Etc. Provide our selves with feedback. Pop-ups are marketing micro-aggressions. Or just aggressions. Create your own game. Within the game. The large game. Will be lost. Inevitably. Necessarily. To space/time. Gobble. Gobble. Nom. Nom. Defeated through indifference. Defecated through tubes. Hold strong opinions. For a short time. Or weak opinions. For a long time. The only thing. That keeps us. Within the same reality. Is language. The only thing. That keeps us. Outside the same reality. Is language.

Everyone gets their justice. In some form. We all die? Our character felt sorry for all those people. Who would never be able to think like them. "I love the police!" Said. NOBODY. Ever. Take a short, hard look in the mirror. Or a long, weak glance in the mirror. Put all your honey in custard. Put all your money in mustard. This book was really helping our author deal with a lot of things. Not sure what it was doing for the reader. Or our character. 100% joking. Kind of. It might be good to historicize. Especially bad experiences. But not to memorialize. Fine line. Where does it exist? "It's about sending a message!" "What's the message?" "I don't know. We just need to make sure we send it!" Working to include. Our multifaceted selves. Helping us create. An impetus for creativity. For others. By breaking down. The perception that too rigidly defines. Them as creator. Their audience as audience. Vice versa. Versa vice. The audience qua creator: the re-creator bringing it to life. The creator qua audience: their most engaged reader.

Given our (human) ability to measure small things. Far smaller than we are. Far more removed from our consciousness. Our ability to communicate. Etc. Wouldn't it make sense: we are the tiny version. Of someone's much larger universe. Aliens could be dark matter. Black holes could be "higher" Beings. Wormholes could be Sky Wizard. The simulation could be Wine Maker. An evaluative outlook. Laying outside our perception. Generated by the pressure to generate. Role reversal. What works? What doesn't? At some future date (pre-past). You might be the user of your creation. How do we create a good experience for our future-selves? Instead of the cringe? To design something to enable our future-selves. To make something better. It cannot be approached inauthentically. Look around. And notice. The needs of others. Differ from our own. The age of refugees. Is upon us.

Our writer's life. Reduced to writing. Our readers' lives. Apparently. Reduced to reading. Our character? The freest? Top Fifty Questions to Ask in an Interview: "At this company, what drugs are considered poor people drugs? And what are the drugs you all do?" This spring, #IvyLeague @Oxbridge-Microsoft/Tesla will graduate at least twenty railroad tycoons and fifty serial killers. President vows to create best war ever. When our character was younger (earlier in space/time). They remembered dreaming. Let's join them? Somehow, they were running from the "bad guys." In a mall parking lot. 90's-movie-esque. Our character's crew. Obviously the "good guys." Boarded the getaway car/spaceship. But our character (still dreaming) was too young. And didn't know how to drive. They also didn't know how to drive in their dream. A *deus ex machina*. [For all of us]. They knew. They would stand up with the door open. And propel the car forward. As if it were a scooter. One leg pumping the road. Hitting top speeds too. And then we were safe. Dream resolved. Fear subsided. Sleep achieved. The undrivable car. Willing it to move. Reality for adults. Patched together. Strong opinions formed. In the same way. Pushing and pulling the universe together. Every second. For us. To make sense. "Events" in adulthood. Our character lost the thread here.

Universities scrap academic programs to focus more on football. Amazingly tolerant girlfriend pretends to like shitty poetry. Bank attempts to entice new customers. With novelty strategies. Like not killing them. If you don't do drugs. You'll still have the side-effects. Are there going to be snacks? Future will probably look like future. Candy is good for you to eat. Beethoven brought to you by Cocaine Cola and Tim's Truck Ranch. Beethoven bro! Brought to you by [Defunct Phone Company]. Incorporated. Excorporated. Artist attempting to "create dialogue." Existential crisis underwhelming. Rise in crime TV. Reveal desperate attempt at normalization for Freest Nation. Our writer didn't want to write their book. They had no other options. Creativity and inspiration. Promote and require empathy. At the very least. We are pondering the question. And await feedback. Orange Man ensures Freest Nation's lawyers employed in perpetuity. To keep poor people unemployed for perpetuity. Nation outraged at retail theft. Seems fine with Nation theft.

Relationship nightmare fuel. Our character should practice moving outside their rhetorical positions. Their logical anchors. To understand their contingency. Merhaps their agency. Whoa. Let's not get too wild. Enriching the work merhaps. Making the work less narcissistic. And therefore. More helpful. To more people. The inevitable. Restrains our context. The incvitable context of our restraints. Will particularize and prioritize. If you're surrounded by idiots. You're probably one of them. Somedays. Our character thought they weren't ready to have children. Other days. They were drunk. We are the most generous when there is nothing at stake. More like, scin-terrific-theory! Our character recently became a parent. But they told them selves they wouldn't be one of those parents who only talks about their kids. So they won't.

Our character's favorite trick when making art: taking someone's critique (no matter how scathing) and actually using the feedback in a productive way. Regardless of the critics' intentions or motives. Our character got a free "new lens" to view their work. A win win. Our character didn't have to deal with the person. It did not prevent them from gaining a wider view. "Liking" or even "agreeing" with the critic was never an essential part of the process. Our character would not be forced into another exhausting sequence of social interactions/rivalries. They needed more space/time to forget what everyone stands for. This forgetting is one of the best ways for them/us to remember. Our character had been zoning out. And only heard parts of the lecture. It was still interesting. Perhaps even more so. Is it always 1:30pm? Sometimes? Or yes? Is a table always on another table? Tables all the way down. How much more is "A" a table, than "H"?

Why do they make dog food look so tasty? The answer might surprise you. Tonight at 8! Always only do. What people will think you'll do. The least. Tardigrades looking forward to becoming dominant species once again. Our character was smiling too much. Again. They did it to appear non-threatening. They tried to speak in a higher, perky register. To hide the darkness of their soul. How convincing was it? A neoliberal perception of space/time. A pair of blinders on a horse. A stick with a carrot. The carrot was fake. A narrowing of the present and future. With no peripheral or past. An overemphasis. On end-results. A mental shut down. When one is "wrong." Countless. Pointless. Security alerts. Promotional emails. For services. Our character already had. What were they selling? Did the "marketing" "team" know? Self-inflicted/enforced. Misleading at best.

Once identities. Are in the straitjacket of *logos*. Forcing our hand. Responding to a preconceived space/timeline. Created by institutions. Without our best interests in mind. Deciding when relationships are "over." Deciding when space/times are "over." Our character was starting to understand. How much they didn't understand. Maybe that was something. Pressures now appear superfluous. And ill informed.

Lack of sleep and indigestion. Caused by everything. Commendable attempt to carry many things. Fails immediately. Existential crisis that people are misusing the term "existential crisis." The nonlogical processes. Allowing for unintended invention. For mistakes to play a role (roll) in the process of invention. Mistakes make our character's project unique. Keeping the mistake within the work. One way to diverge. From what others have done. From what our selves planned to do. The unintentional. Folded back into the intentional. Get to the point. Where our character is comfortable/playful. Enough to make mistakes. And evaluate them. Before trying to get rid of them. Don't count your chickens. Before you put them in one basket. Give your secrets to the person who will always remember. But forget to tell. The best kind of friend.

Someday. When our character grew up. They wanted to be a regular at a bar. Somewhere. Keep talking MFers. A questioning that asks more. A questioning that asks the most. The biggest questions. Furthest from any answer. The only questions worth philosophizing. To have our character's questioning. Lead to further questioning. Not merely to answers. Not to Sky Wizard. Not to predetermined social constructions. The straitjacket of *logos*. Again. Let's give our character an eternal optimism. In the face of the pointlessness of life. Industrial Strength Existentialism. A cannonball of creativity. A human bowling ball of inspiration. Currently. Our character wasn't in a good mind/space/time. Let's check back in on them later. Or before. Currently. Our character was in a good mind/space/time. Let's check back in on them later. Or before. Etc. The warmth. Our character had not been in the warmth. For so long now. The scents and smells. Home. Where home was. An *ethos*. Filled with *pathos*. Our character was surprised. It could still exist. It still existed. The weight of many years. Had prevented. This softer view. Somehow. Not better or worse. But definitely different. Definitively different.

If our character was an artist. Choosing which things existed. In the universe of their art. Which things did not exist. What voices would our character memorialize? What narratives will they snuff out. Not capturing space/time. But freeing it. The Freest. Not a remembering. But an allowance to forget. Not complete knowledge. But still being a Being. Somehow. Maybe the algorithm got it wrong? What if the doctor read the wrong chart? The computer caught a bug. Maybe these weren't our character's "favorite" things. Maybe they were their "least favorite" things?

How would we know? Without the ability to ask our character directly. Our character: "Why don't you?" Etc. Our character. Was making executive decisions. The best pieces. Fell on the cutting room floor. On deaf ears. Etc. I want to regret them! Come back! If only! Visible ambition. The utmost unattractive. In a neoliberal world. You are required to participate. Our character had no choice. But they weren't supposed to SHOW it. It becomes visible whenever anyone wants to start selling something. So anything anywhere. Everywhere. Everywhen. Selling yourself was one of the most important skills. Maybe this is true of our character too? In the past (of our character's present) they used to call this prostitution. "What's the deal with ambition? It's like, less see. More not see." Audience laughs. "Right? I mean what is THAT?" Audience applauds. There has to be some format our reader appreciates. So our writer wrote in every format. University of California, Chick-fil-A/British Petroleum. Pro-gambling and anti-gambling Ads keeping Ad agencies busy. Business is booming. Busy business is dooming.

We fear death because it might be boring and lonely. Everything is water. It isn't. But imagine if it was. It is. Harvard brought to you in part by McDonald's Viacom Haliburton. If you suspect someone is a con-artist. They aren't. This crack. Is like crack. Princeton Chevy Truck Corporation and Office Leasing District. Stanford Statefarm Doritos University produced by Michael Bay and The United States Air Force. Warning! Human in progress. Makes wide turns. And breaks often. Student human. Behind the wheel. Use extreme caution. Give plenty of space/time. To get out of the way. Accidents will happen. They require a more dynamic perception of mind/space/time. A primordial perception. Moving back to move forward. Being able to listen. To what the moreness. Has to offer. The creative process. The art of *kairos* in *chronos*. Appropriate and sequential space/timing. Exposing our character's investment in logically ordering space/time in a particularly habitual manner. Let's allow our character to rediscover how different they have been. And how different we are going to be. Like reading old love/break-up letters. Simultaneously knowing our selves more. And less. And we become curious of the many different people we have been. And will be.

Walmart lady called our character "sugar" today. And that's the most action they've had in years. Overheard at Big Corp: "Government regulation is killing private business. Alright, HR says I gotta go piss in a cup." Meat Juice. Is soup. Wouldn't living in a computer simulation be ideal? Why this obsession with the myth of authenticity? Are book bans working? Yet? Is everyone perfect? Yet? If we make everyone else stupid. I can buy a third vacation home. Own it for a couple years. Before the world explodes. Because. We made everyone stupid. Nance and Randy thought they packed enough for lunch. Corporation became culture. Their bodies followed. Corruption culture. A brain-thing. Projecting its reality. Outward. What appeared. Appeared to be the physical world. The physical self. Our character was terrified. Of people. Who thought. They were a "better" "person." As if there could be such a thing. People who defined them selves by what they wouldn't do. Or couldn't. And given the circumstance. Really would. Or already have. People who "didn't drink" were terrifying. What were they afraid of? What was going to erupt out of them if they had their guard down? For a couple hours? Has ignoring your issues. Ever helped you resolve them? Although. Our character admitted. Perhaps momentarily. The news doesn't cover the political opinions of children. Why should they cover the political opinions of Republicans?

Our character had been awake for an hour. They were ready to go back to bed. They could already tell. Nothing good was going to happen today. Transform business. Accelerate growth. Data. Models. Policy. Trust. Hadn't our character lived enough already? Enough things had happened. Too many things had happened. Let's give them the option. Not to be. If they don't want to be. From nowish on. Our character is only our character. If they want to keep being our character. Otherwise. Our character was a different character. Nowish. If anything is possible. Why should/shouldn't this be possible? During our character's space/time. Everyone only had enough "free" space/time to fuck everything up. Everyday. If you can put up with someone for long periods of space/time. And they can do the same. That's as close to perfect as it's going to get. Your relatives and close friends will call it true love. Regardless of if it is. It's never been about similar interests. Similar ways of thinking. Only being there. Even when you're not wanted. Especially when you're not wanted. And trying to be everything. The other person wants. While you both recognize. It will never happen. You aren't always going to be. Overthinking can be a terrible thing. Underthinking can be a terrible thing.

Peopling becoming impossible. Guilty until proven. Well. Always guilty apparently. Of something. I mean. Who isn't? Confirmation bias confirms bias of confirmation for confirmation bias. The uneasiness surrounding romance and heartbreak. It's self-constructed-ness. The guilt of an unnecessary primal force. And not even to procreate. For a while. Our character had to say no to the whole thing. Every aspect of it became problematic. There was no sense to be made of it. If you find any success. Everyone will assume you cheated. You did. But everyone does. Otherwise known as an advantage. Or disadvantage. If you are able to be successful despite your disadvantages. They will blame your disadvantages for being unfair advantages. They are. But everyone has them. Verizon Wireless Air Force Charity House Fundraiser. High definition highly defines bad attempt at concealer. Concealer unconcealed. All bachelors are bachelors. Bachelors in the bleachers on beaches are basking with bleach blonde babes.

"Buy this book" – The Author. Halloween candy given more attention than homeless humans. Who don't have food. Our character was going to sell their computer. They purchased a huge typewriter. They typed loudly. As hard as they could. To prove they were getting *serious* work done. "And I'm not enjoying it! So it must be serious! And important!" Disproportions. The foundation of Freest Nation. Private schools and public schools. Financial "success." Everything was being recorded. But quality was never achieved. We've just started to talk about our character. And somehow. We know less about them. Than when we started. They spent so much mind/space/time. Telling the youth to not do drugs. Because they thought. The youth thought drugs were cool. Thereby making it cool. To do drugs. When really. People do drugs. To lessen the anxiety. Caused by everyone who doesn't do drugs. Like the people who think people do drugs to be cool. Thereby making it cool. Etc.

Our character looked out the window. On a train. Moving quickly along the Scottish countryside. Beautiful dark days of rain. Glances of life. Without the laborious details. Dark wood. The smell of pipe tobacco. Live every story you find yourself in. As quickly as possible. So you can get as many lifetimes under your belt as you can. Our character now reflected on their reflecting. This threw them into yet another level of reflection. Etc. Copies without an original. Their own life. What could we say? They enjoyed things most people enjoy. They supposed. But also. At all space/times. They were aware. None of this could be real. Nothing matters. Move onto. The next moment in space/time. Until at least a couple more million generations pass. And humans have been alive as long as dinosaurs. We aren't even close. "Modern" humans weren't even as old as "Early" humans. We aren't even close. Much will be resolved. Or won't be. Etc. We shouldn't worry. We don't know any of the answers now. This implies we will know at some space/time. Can this be comforting? For us to have a conception of not knowing things. There must be an opposite. A space/time where we know things. Hang on. We're almost there! You're in the worst part! It HAS to get better!

Phrases from a five-year old: "Press the backwards fast forward." Comedy is language horror. Willing to settle for bumbling sidekick role at this point. Create a need. Then remove it. Then charge extra to bring it back. To create profit. Create scarcity. People can only want something. If they don't have it. Only be as smart as others are willing to think you are. Never try to be smarter than people don't think you are. Another thing. They never tell you. Essential for survival. Competition Nation can't be helpful. Freest Nation. Slave to competition. It was difficult to determine if our character was likable. Or not likable. Or somewhere in-between. I guess we'll feel these ways about the character at different space/times in the story. Maybe our writer. Could say something to the effect (with no certainty), "Our character was a solipsistic absolutist." They couldn't die. Other people left their plane of existence. But our character stayed there. They always came back into contact with representations of their being in space/time. Simply because. They did. They had been told. At some space/time. The connection will never come back. Until it does. Again. And again. And again. Etc. Some others are never seen again. Maybe these others keep living their own narrative. Permanently separate from our character. Yet to be disproven. And only if life is reduced to what you are currently experiencing. "Nowism."

It only takes misplaced trust in one person. To completely upend our character's entire life. If it could happen. It would happen. And it did happen. [It did]. Our character wasn't mad at the world. Just disappointed. The world did not live up to the standards it set for itself. If our character couldn't do anything right. What was their motivation for trying? Channel your creativity through evolving real world contingency factorization. Trained professionals are standing by to enhance legitimate contact charges through program synergy. Structure free market capital with sound diversification and multiplatform exposurement. Gain new customers with strategic marketplace value feedback. Free-up employee decision-making with circular logic trees. Our character always thought. When they grew up. There would be a lot more reasons to be happy. Our character had been under the microscope for too long. If you look long and hard enough. At anyone's life. You are going to find major problems. Problems our character would admit they had. Nothing new happened for our character. Until they turned the microscope on everyone else. They tried to write a book. The book was a failure by most people's standards. But not our character's?

If everything makes you angry. You won't be long for this world. Anger was the base-line reality of existence. Everything else was extra. You're not really a parent until you've given your son pooping advice. Girls on Tinder: "Ew gross, are you hitting on me?" "Yes?" Historians in 42069: "It looks like they tried to kill the virus with. . . divorce?" Our character could have another version of them selves living in another space/time. And they would never know. There could be another version of our character living in a different country during our character's own space/time. And they would never know. There could be another version of our character living two towns over. And they would never know. They could never know. All odds were against everything. As odds are. Even evens were odd. No proof that anyone exists. Ever. Only through our narrative experience. Our main dimension. That is the structure. Can we do anything outside this structure? Malleable or unmalleable? Others keep living their narrative. Perhaps our character died in theirs? Perhaps our character was never alive in theirs. Making it impossible for them to have died. In the first place.

9 THIS CALL MAY BE MONITORED
FOR NO REASON AT ALL

Feminist loves *The Bachelor*. Currently. Our character's personality was coffee and antidepressants. "Snickers has a pretty cool social media campaign. You guys should check it out," says person to our character. Dependably undependable. Life in a simulation. Brain in a vat. Philosophical problems. Outside the context of "new" "technology." As opposed to how this already happens via *logos*. Etc. Our character had to eat the silence. They had to like it. To live in discomfort. Where/when nobody else could. For people who needed our character to be silent. They sure were prodding them a lot. Countless ways to look for the movie you can't watch. Is three purple? Our character had been reliving the past so much. It was becoming stale. They were starting to experience reality again. In bits and pieces. Reese's Pieces. In fits and starts. It tits and tarts. They could feel it coming back. To pass the time. They wrote an anonymous advice column for the local paper. It got old. They lost steam. Everything comes at a cost. The economics of life. The lie of "part time" jobs. Our character lived in a part of the Freest Nation where there was a disproportionate significance placed on "family" "values." Nobody actually knew what this meant. It functioned similarly to "professionalism." You could never "have it." You could only be blamed for not having it.

Peak brand awareness. Only lasted 30 secs in brand experience. Full release brand experience. Our character was bound to swerve. But as long as they stayed in-between the lines (for the most part). They'd probably be okay? An artist should always know the audience they are serving. As a person. As well. Who you are serving tells you a lot about yourself. It tells you what you currently think is important. If our character was serving something (or someone) they did not hold in high esteem. They should rethink their service. Because they will inevitably disappoint. Do they want to disappoint people who will always be disappointed? Or do they want to disappoint those who might not be disappointed? A need. A narrative that needs an end. Much more convenient then actually dealing with the issue. The bad guys look a lot like bad guys. Our character ran a marathon for a fundraiser. *Doctors Without Borders*. Always read the fine print. Our character was really running all those miles. And raising all that money. For a group of doctors who stand really close to people.

Extremely Normal Political Party has never been right about ANYTHING. Work can put you to sleep. When thought itself inevitably fails. The trauma of not having a shared truth. "I understand I'm angry at gas prices. But alternative energy is for wimps!" "Join us back, now. Ya hear?" Art is the process of accepting the unknown. *Knowing* you will be wrong (or at least, outdated). *Knowing* what you are making. You will disagree with. The cringe. But art is doing it anyway. Is it 75% or 76%? Crunch the data. Perpetual Calculation Nation. Numbers with no context. Are no longer numbers.

Top Ten Questions to Ask at the End of an Academic Job Interview: "What steps did you take to sabotage the previous employee's career? Were they ever able to financially/mentally recover from the trauma you induced?" Two men getting married? What's next? A man marrying his horse? [It wasn't]. Or his dog? Or me marrying my dog? My dog that I love very much? My dog that I want to marry? Look at him walk. Damn. Hot dog. With your art you must find a way for the reader to feel stupid, small, and insignificant. This isn't what you necessarily *want* to do. Especially if you aren't an evil person. But in Competition Nation it is often the only way to get the reader's attention. You must make this sacrifice. Even if you don't *want* to be mean. If you *want* your book to be read. Or taken *seriously*. Just as you might not *want* to write in complete sentences. You might not *want* to insult your reader. But this is the world we live in. You already knew this, potential author. So it would be mean of you. To not be mean to your reader. If you want them to read your book. If the rest of the book has a chance of helping them.

"I voted for Orange Man for religious reasons." What religion? The color orange? Burps are mouth farts. The life of our character. Was like that of many others. They had many opportunities to mess up. But few opportunities to succeed. Or so they thought. Or so it seemed. Or so it was. [It was]. The definition of success and failure was blurry. At best. This struggle was central to their sense of self. Whether it should have been. Or not. At/during other space/times. They forgot about all these things. This kept happening for many years. There are only two emotions. Hopefulness and helplessness. Everything else is fear. But there was a response. In the form of never-ending afternoons. Make Afternoons Great Again. Our character wasn't narcissistic. Were they? Who are we to judge? Our author had to be narcissistic about our character. Our author had to be more narcissistic about our character than our character. So at least our character wasn't as narcissistic about them selves. Maybe that's the right level of narcissism? Orange Man's terrible idea. Still terrible. It never got any better than "Hey Ya!"

If you know this is the way things actually are. You can warn people about aspects of yourself. But they will forget. And then they will blame you. Forgetting you told them. This would probably happen. By warning them. You also plant the idea in their head. They will think they know how to critique you in the future. In Competition Nation this will only end badly. Everything can only end badly. They will blame you. For the thing. You warned them not to blame you for. They will forget.

Everyone forgets. You cannot keep score in Competition Nation. Even though. Everyone else is. If you keep score. You will lose. And not be able to love anyone. Everyone makes mistakes. Even yourself. It's best to be alone. But if you can't do that. Try writing? Something about flannel. Hay and Indian Summers. That's how the story could have started. If it feels like you've read this before. You have. Marriages hold together. When both persons can see them selves dying in the place where they are. Envisioning your future end. The beginning of the end. Like all decisions. Birth. It creates. And adheres. To a field of difference. Not just any. A particular life or Being. That contains a field of difference. Is that all there is? We don't know. But that's all we can see right now. The limits of life. Circumscribing the field of difference.

Freest Nation. Fee-est Nation. Fee Infested Nation. Flea Infested Nationalism. Flat Fee Fleas Flee Nation. André 3000 for President! To get anything accomplished during our character's space/time it took a series of managerial miracles. Red tape. Now red walls. Reinforced blast doors. Weapons-grade barricades. For the most basic services. It took a modern-day Hercules to schedule a doctor's appointment. If you moved ANYWHERE in Freest Nation. It took local healthcare services years to catch up to this inevitable and commonplace occurrence. They could only treat emergencies. Or patients who they had seen for a minimum of ten years. Everyone else was SOL. Everyone else was suspect. Everyone else was a foreigner. Everyone who worked in healthcare had to fight for their healthcare. So what made these outsiders so special? They just receive these services? Without going to war every day? And for free? Not on my watch. They had to go through front-desk-Nancy first. A formidable opponent. There was no ESTABLISHING in our character's space/time. There was simply too much money to be made off of every individual's inevitable inconsistencies. "This was your address last year. And this is your address now?" "Sorry, they are different." "Are you trying to trick us into giving you life-saving medical care?"

Nance and Randy were great at calling out this long con. This scheme of yours to get healthcare. Even if you paid for it. We do not trust you. It is going to take us five million years to process this. And in five million years. We will tell you. You need to reach another department. That'll be five million dollars, please. It's much easier to blame the individual. Plus, people were already good at this. Who are we to stop them? To hire someone with the foresight to plan around these contingencies. Was too expensive. Plus, experts talked funny. And didn't wear the clothes we wear. And didn't like the commercials we liked. Etc. This happened all the space/time. During our character's space/time. There were hardly contingencies anymore. Because they happened every day. Which we would know. If anyone was paying attention. Or was able to work here long enough. . . "Sorry, I've been transferred to another branch. Michelle or Janice will contact you in five million years about establishing a new account with us. They will provide you with no new information. Let us know how we did with a quick customer survey!"

Book bans look very stupid in relation to the burning of the Library of Alexandria. Think of all the millions of works that have already been written. But we need to rewrite. Because we lost the Library of Alexandria. How far could literature go before it became TOO repulsive? Perhaps we haven't even scratched the surface? [They hadn't]. Nuance was impossible during our character's space/time. Our character wanted to post a critical article. About their city's appalling ambulance shortage. But they didn't want to sound like the Extremely Normal Political Party's hysterical/racist/homophobic bemoaning of big cities. Our character couldn't be critical. They wanted to be critical of the current president. But they couldn't. The alternative was Orange Man. Who wanted to destroy Freest Nation. To free it. From being free. The Extremely Normal Political Party: "Defund the people!" If you never hear from me again. I ran out of storage space on my devices. And gave up. PYT DTF. This! British version still better. Maybe this is what they didn't like about our character. Their disregard for the existence of others. Unless they were useful to them. Or posed a threat to their existence. But isn't this how we all treat one another? In neoliberal space/time? Or is this human nature? Limited space/time. How else you expect our characters to act?

At some point all the small stuff becomes the big stuff. And the big stuff becomes the small stuff. The universe makes spheres (atoms and stars). And disks. The disks were merely cross-sections of the spheres. The discs attempt to make a perfect sphere. But are never able to get small enough on the edges. To be anything other than disks attempting to make up the cross section of the sphere. The end points. Preventing the perfect sphere. Perpetuating the process of forming. Things strive to end in a sphere. It becomes closed. Everything is frozen. It has reached the shape it was supposed to become. Space/time has stopped. Why spheres? Sky Wizard likes them? Sky Wizard is them? Pressure is spherical. What's the opposite of a sphere? Dark matter: the non-spherical pressure forming the spheres. Dark matter is the graviton. The God particle. The thing turning everything into spheres. For some reason. Unknown. *Hypotheses non fingo.* Maybe Sky Wizard is bored? That would explain all the wars. Or maybe they just REALLY like spheres. Space. Time. Energy. Mass. Being. All spherical.

Extremely Normal Political Party parents brag. Child back from college. And "Dating a doctor!" Then reject climate change. And evolution. Everything has been named. Rich Older Democrats still trying to find candidate who will change nothing. Which is more difficult? Convincing friends you're an artist? Or not an alcoholic? Our character was anxious about the cost of their anxiety medication. Rich Texans. Still able to get abortions. Out of state. Rich white Southerners. Still able to get abortions. Somehow. Family patriarchs stayed rich and white. Merhaps the opposite of a sphere. Would be this book? [Our writer had tricked them selves into writing again]. The opposite of a sphere would be a Deleuzian rhizome. *Hypotheses non fingo*. But maybe it doesn't matter if I understand it? Maybe it only matters if our reader understands it? Overstands it. Dark matter is rhizomatic. All we know. It likes creating spheres. For some reason. What's the reason? *Hypotheses non fingo*. The missing link. Between the rhizome and the sphere. How to connect them? The assumption. Large scales can work on smaller scales. Scholar sarcastically scales scholastic scoliosis. Maybe we are the medium scale? The medium of scale. The word. And the action. Is the space/time. In-betweenness. Strange space/times call for strange solutions/dissolutions. What if our writer actually did have something to say? Would they have already turned enough people away? Our character could have a noble truth. As much as a noble lie. It could be. As much as it couldn't. And it would take place. . . Etc.

Maybe our writer did have something important to say? Maybe they should write all these things down? Was it morally worse to withhold answers? If they did have them? No one else appeared to have any decent solutions. Our writer would tell others they were almost done writing their book. So that. Maybe they would be. Like promising yourself you'll actually finish this project. It took much longer than everyone (including our writer) thought it would. And it cost much more space/time than anyone could imagine. But that's not too strange: something that is genuinely strange (like this book), would naturally take a strange amount of space/time to make. Forever bound to a strange space/time. The one constant. Just like our character. Idiot who doesn't understand history: "States rights!" Pro states rights. Anti human rights. Pro states rights. Pro regional inefficiency. Pro states rights. Anti future. Pro states rights. Anti American.

The past is a funny thing (so why aren't we all laughing?). The past allows you to "look back." And wonder. How you could have been so blind. But it is only a window. To look but not touch. Torture. A human not able to act. Perhaps not as dramatic as we think. Given another chance. Most of us would probably do the same thing. Over again. Etc. Wincing at lost opportunities. We probably acted. Like we would act today. Given the circumstances. The past. Can only confront. It can't comfort. It can only conform. We know what happened. Or at least. More than the future? More than what will have happened? It doesn't make sense. Unless we are trying to become spherical again. We can look at the whole (hole?). And realize. We survived it. The best way our character found. Was to tell a story. Our character (if they were going to be a writer) knew the story needed to cover the necessary range of information. In a remarkably limited amount of space/time. Without seeming too direct. Or too eager. Or too boring. Etc. Under the cover of narrative economy. Our character was able to do many things at once. This spring, Ivy-Oxbridge sponsored by Arby's Turbo Tax will graduate at least five authoritarian leaders who depend on bad interpretations of history for the genocides they'll carry out. Our character wasn't superstitious. But they were a little stitious. NRA STFU.

During our character's space/time. What was paraded as "freedom" of "choice." Was the inefficiency of the system. Preventing oppressed peoples from organizing or formulating a coherent thought/response/narrative/*logos*. The oppressed stayed oppressed. In the service of "small business." Whose necks they were standing on. Blocking common-sense mergers, consolidations, and ultimately the ability to provide a superior service/product. What difference did it make? If our character watched their favorite show on Netflix or YouTube? What difference did it make which Bank was charging them overdraft fees? Insurance premiums? Etc. Cable and internet. "Choosing" between one or two. Large companies. Making their service worse. To charge for a "premium" "subscription." Products and services were not getting better. But noticeably worse. It wasn't profitable for products to improve. It was only profitable to out-lawyer and out-bank other companies. Lawyers, bankers, and politicians. Realized how worthless they were. [Never happened]. They didn't make a product. They didn't provide a service for people. Which made them double-down on their importance. Little angry napoleons. God's bravest soldiers. Companies were realizing how worthless they were. [They never did]. Etc. Nobody had "brand loyalty." This was a fiction. Their marketing teams had imagined. And then believed. Forgetting they created it. Companies thought they were important. But really. They were boring. As boring as Popstar. Employees didn't have to be proud to work for them. Employees needed a paycheck. And health insurance. And the ability to leave. The "Freest Market" was a shield. A smokescreen. Protecting lawyers, bankers, and politicians. From the oppressed. Which made the fairytale of economic ascension. Even more crucial.

Protesters protesting protesters protesting "wrong." Nance and Randy couldn't wait for their upcoming road trip. Then. They were very happy it was over. It was good to be back home. We could question whether our character was really HERE. Or if they are somewhere/ somewhen/someone else. Virtually plugged into a reality. They forget was there. Enough space/time passes. Enough *logos* passes. Our character forgets it's there. To stay within it. Perhaps they had been using it too much? Pushing to its limit. Never has there been a space/time. That's never been this space/time. Maybe all we can say about our space/time. The most aware humanity has been. Of the inadequacies of humanity. While not being able to do anything about the inadequacies of humanity. Dictators using Gerbils-style propaganda/historical interpretations. In a space/time well beyond it. Come so far. To be so far behind. Our character felt this way. They were no longer young (relative to spans of space/time during their space/time). It's only *as far as we know*. Our character hasn't done this all before. There's nothing that says. Something can't be anything. And so we must be satisfied. By explaining *how* things work. But not *why*. Can you know both? Superimposition? Or regularimposition? In position. Inquisition. The *why*. Long missing. Lost to deep space/time. Maybe we'll find it here. [They didn't]. Grandma. Too fast. Too furious. Internets devolve into thirst traps and pyramid schemes.

Stop dancing. Nance moving things around loudly in the kitchen. While Randy watches the game on the couch. We don't need technological advances. To be lost in spectacle. But currently. Maybe it helps? On our phones. Reading the bible. Etc. All simulacrum. Our character was currently alive. Therefore, not dead. Therefore, cannot have died in the future. Now is all we can know. Eternally in the now. Unless we choose not to be. If space/time doesn't work the way we think it does. Where/when does this leave our character? During our character's space/time. No one could agree on a now. The only thing keeping it going. The only connection within the rhizome. A lack of consensus on space/time. The opposite of a sphere. Space/time is our currency? Hoarding space/time. T-shirt ideas: Beer Thirty (random image of a rhinoceros?). Learn more about our updated Terms of Service. Nance and Randy were surprised how much it rained here. Did it snow in the winter? Still all chickens. Always had been. Hear me out. Who had "trench warfare" for 2022? All emotions. Made sense through deep space/time. Through *logos*.

Discount space/time. Our character could only rent. Anything that didn't make sense in the realm of space/time. Could be too occupied by space. Could be too occupied by time. We need to know how we are time. And it is us. More *kairos*. Less *chronos*. What space/time do you identify as? When we escape into our minds. Virtual reality: a hat on a hat. How many is it? 11? Or 12 and 5? Our character. Furiously attempting to paint another picture of existence. Various rhetorical and literary devices. More to escape to. Out of the thicket. But seriously. We had a good run. Kind of. But surely, we are done. We must be done. We were/are not able to find the next thing. Now everything moves backward and deteriorates. Predicting tragedy has become too easy. We need to keep the populous talented but unprofessional. Or professional but not talented. Do not let them achieve their dreams! It would end the Extremely Normal Money System! There need to be poor. To make the rich. And there I was. Our character had a current love interest. Forever unreachable before them. Disinterested love interest. Previous love interest. Unreachable in the other direction. This tension helped create motivations. Generating distractions. All-the-better. For our character's brainless daily labor.

Click the link below. Comment. Follow. Will you take this survey? Party size. Fun size. Who was the fucking genius. Who decided. Our employers. Should determine. Who gets healthcare? Our character worked really soft. Freest Nation listed as *developing country*. Instead of "rooting" for a team. Our character's son says he is "winning" for a team. And our character liked that better. In our character's biopic montage. They hoped this was the part. Where they were doing some of their best work. This space/time wasn't going to be fun. Our character might as well write (if they were a writer). They weren't going anywhere. During this space/time. But still required them selves to acknowledge these possibilities. That's why it's important. To leave little things. Here and there. That are neutral. Far ahead in the future. Or past. Always gesturing to the unknown. Art is always about art. Art is always about what it is not. The unknown. And yet. There was still something unique and entertaining about relatable characters. With clear themes and motives. It couldn't escape the mind of our writer. Our character. Etc. Our writer didn't even bother. To look back. To see what the name of our character had been. The only good ideas. From the poor and insane. The only ones who HAVE to think them. To exist. Etc. And your knowledge of expansion. Was expanded. Once again. There is the way the box was meant to be opened. And there is the way our character opened it. Nance and Randy were not impressed. It looked better on the brochure.

Submit to the cold quiet comfort of mediocrity. So you won't want to do it for a while. All this wasted space/time. Our character didn't want to do anything. Our character didn't want to go anywhere. Our character didn't want to talk to anyone. Our character found them selves in a town of forgottens. People wanting to be forgotten. But had to keep living. Why? Out of habit. Habitat of habit. Some disease. "Both sides have good points" says "Centrist" (Extremely Normal Political Party). Honesty. Was almost never the best policy. The exigency for a policy. Implied it was not honest. Anyone who lived long enough. Had a history. Our writer could only get lost in work. Our character wanted nothing to do with anyone's plans. Count me out of everything. They did not want to be dependable for anything. If our character could fall asleep. It would be different. They could go to the outer world. Come back refreshed. But they just lay there. Here. Etc. Wake up late. Be unproductive. And crushed. Repeat. Our character had lived this before. If only our character could remember. How they got them selves out of this mess. Last space/time. Throughout our story. There are references. To the accumulation. Of things unrelated. To the main plot. But referencing (simulacrum-like) the main idea of the plot (creating a sphere): small things add up. And create big problems.

Surprising the on-lookers. Who don't notice. Things adding up. But watch. In wonder.

Our character remembered. They knew when their project needed to end. When everyone wanted them to stop. They had worn out their welcome everywhere. It was time again. To be obsessed with their "public image." Every second of the day. Our character did not look forward to this. During our character's spacetime. You had two (panic stricken) weeks (at best) per year to dedicate yourself to something. Semi-important. Everyone could know you by. That could open up possibilities (prior to complete destitution). Leading up to these two weeks, you could work on it multiple days a week. For probably two months before. And two months after. The two weeks of batshit crazy work. The setting must be an Island. Or someplace isolated. We need to get a sense that this is "the world." And nothing exists outside it. Just like. Nothing we know. Exists outside. The actual world. I'm unsure of the place our character "works" (people still "worked" during this space/time). A place they somewhat enjoy? Our character enjoys the people they work with. Enough. Our character says. "This and that." Could be better. But essentially. It's the perfect job. For "right now." "It's fine." "I'm really alright." Etc. Our character has great relationships with their family and friends. Our character felt "known." This first part (which is the intro to the movie) is shot with soft tones. Beautiful scenery. Smooth and precise camera angles and frames. T-shirt ideas: "Quick! Have fun!" Throughout this period. We learn of our character's ambitions. To be some kind of government leader. Our character had high aspirations. And realistic ways of achieving them (believable at least). Our character aspires to study at a prestigious university (there's only one on the island). If you hear a voice. Nobody responds to. They are probably talking to you.

Our character wakes up the next morning. Regardless. Of if it's morning. Our character was one of those who couldn't escape existence. It kept happening to them. At them. With them. Etc. Our character woke up. Already with a story. About how they were still alive. No matter how unlikely. Etc. Vagabonds! Gypsies! These people kept moving west. To get away from their families. In cramped apartments on the East Coast. The poverty and aristocracy of the South. The WASPY North. Etc. Leaving New York, Boston, Florida, Texas, Chicago, South Dakota, Minnesota, Etc. Escaping the Baptists, the Protestants, the Mormons, the Jews, the Old School Catholics, Etc. The puritanical passive-aggressive *ethos*. But not in the wild west. Just people. Trying to be people. The West Coast. Was much more chill. At least, that was the attempt. They were essentially Australians. Our character decided to make things important in their life. That would provide lasting rewards. As long as our character had a purpose. And goal in mind. They told them selves. "They'd be fine." I am fine. I've gotten better at recognizing what has been constructed. By me. By others. Etc. Because of this our character learned how to arrange them selves. To maximize lasting benefits.

The superimposition of meanings. 1s and 0s. It could be both things. In a quantum world. And also neither. The world could be going crazy. And our character could also be going crazy. It didn't have to be one or the other. The two didn't have to be related. Independent of each other. Mutually exclusive/inclusive. The world falling apart. Apparently did not justify our character's actions. *Post hoc.* "Post" already making a problematic assumption of space/time. If only to show our character. They did not have to succumb to the chaos surrounding them. Or could they? States and corporations now have more rights than people. State's surpass women in rights. Oh good. Another day. Public health experts recommend not eating shit. Extremely Normal Political Party responds with poop feast. Extremely Normal Political Party doesn't evacuate wildfire. Because government told them to. All burned. Our character only used what they used. It's not that our character had a bad memory. What? The knowledge our character didn't find useful. They could never remember. Or could they? The problem was. They didn't know. The knowledge was going to be important. At the space/time. Etc.

The games our character played. Might not have a purpose. But they revealed how much space/time our character had on their hands. They made the same mistakes. But recognized them sooner. Covered them up better. As long as their head was above water. More than under. They'd be fine. Our character was thinking of getting into organized crime. Or cage fighting. They would create confrontation. Whenever possible. Probably get more tattoos too. If our character was Sky Wizard. Would a perfect being. Be boring? Everything going their way? Would our character create obstacles? To pass the space/time? Would we? What would satisfy? Their desire to pass along their genes? Babies! Babies! We must have more Babies!!!

Olympic ads. Inspire future brand marketing strategists. Apropos of nothing. Historians in 42069: "Hold onto your asses. Today's lecture is on 2022." In some neighborhoods. Our character was known affectionately. As "that weird white dude." Whenever the background noise got too thick. Whenever our character felt a wall between them selves and specific situations. Whenever they had problems listening to what people were saying. When our character would clumsily drop things. They knew it was time to move on. Impossible to tell. If their novel (Building? Film? Car? Sandwich?) makes them famous. Our character. Daydreaming about fame again. Untrustworthy author. Untrustworthy reader. Our character started writing things down. To forget about them. They could go back later. Remind (preforget) them selves. If they wanted. They wouldn't have to carry it around with them anymore. Our character? Our author? Felt they should write. Because they had a lot to talk about. It seemed they had lived a lot. More or less than others around them? Hard to tell.

This spring, Ivy Oxbridge - Santa Barbra Air Guard will graduate at least ten students who will be found guilty of owning a chain of sex islands. Generations passed. The people forgot. The world went on without them. Communication severed for hundreds of years. Cataclysmic events. Our character assumed one of their biggest flaws was being too sexy. No great inspiring idea. Or higher calling. A greater being. But having nothing. Better to do. Our character always read about these types of trips. The open road. They figured. They'd copy what other people did. Our character wasn't looking for anything. They weren't sure if they should. Our character often wondered. How many times they'd thought of doing this. If they'd already done it before. Was it even their choice? [It wasn't?]. It wasn't an action. Just a reaction. To the world around them. And a situated position. To Be within. Constructing the building. Went well. With our character's constant need for explanation and analysis. A never-ending journey. Tiresome. Full of faults and contradictions. Yet it passed the space/time. A productive and socially acceptable outlet for insanity… Our character could be proud of that. At least?

Studies show that studies show that studies show that. . . Etc. New study. Studied wrong. New study. Studied too hard. Our character sympathized with people that had less than them. Even when it was inconvenient. It was one of their best attributes. And they didn't even know it. It was rumored. In the past. People on the island had left. Nobody knew if this was true. Hard to believe. There was no reason to leave the island. It had everything. Our character encountered a slew of hardships. However. With the help of family and friends. They pulled through. Or pulled through despite their family and friends. Both were popular narratives at/during the space/time. War defeats nuance. Don't write something. For someone who won't read it. They won't read it. And now what have you gained? Ulterior motives can be a good thing. Especially good ones. You've never died before. But think of all the times you practiced when you were alive. All we ever do? A death in life. A life in death. Etc. To prevent your mind. From going there. Things didn't become the way they were. Until they went. Free speech. Costs 10k. Free speech costs too much. Free speech a modern luxury. Etc. Passenger heard that Alaska Airlines might have bought Spirit Airlines. [They hadn't]. "Oh very interesting." [It wasn't]. The passenger continued (to everyone's dismay). [I'll paraphrase.]. It was something about a news report that probably never happened. Reporting about something that probably never happened. But this passenger was definitely one of those people. Who could think it had happened. Etc.

Nobody wanted our author to finish their building. A sign. It HAD to be built. The only one. So rarely could people agree on anything. Maybe this building would bring them all together? Create a common enemy for them? Reverse conspiracy theorist. Unconspiracy realist. So rarely could people agree on anything. And rare things could be expensive. If you knew how to sell them. Etc. So whether the building was good or not. Hardly mattered. It was rare. Or not rare enough. Etc. Our character and the others acted illogically at times. Because their society wasn't logical. Sounds reasonable. You can't reason with the unreasonable. To get what they wanted. During our character's space/time. They had to take it. So they could forget they wanted it. The end goal. A resolution. Dissipating all meaning. So meaning can be made again. The sacrifice. Our character's society. Built monsters. To banished. Ticket sales increased. They always thought. To live correctly. There must be a balance of logic and emotions. Perhaps the Island wasn't accurate with itself. Oh good. Another day. Trying to please the algorithm. Our character took a shower with clothes on. It felt like they were breaking every law. Ever written. Explore our digital environment! New trial period! Don't miss out! Top Ten Questions to Ask in General: "Will this position be cut next year?" How much longer could the Corporate Academy survive? [Not long].

Our character could not shake the fact. The things that happened to them. Had happened to them. And they still had happened to them. When they woke up in the morning. The dreams hadn't. But everything else had. Our character could do nothing about it. For years. So they did something about something else instead. Let's say they opened a bakery. Etc. The things that had happened. Provided great motivation. But not necessarily. Peace of mind. Etc. But it was something? What else was there? For them here? Religion could only tell people what NOT to do. When it came to what To Do. Religion failed epically. If you want to create profit. Create scarcity. There's a lot of weird people. Someone's gotta like you. The sky is an ocean to a bird. Sky fish. All stereotypical names and places. Love story. So has to be in France. Or Italy. Spain? Unspecified Mediterranean? Specific space/time period. Only to show. How universal it is. Classic modern. Our character would fall into a fit of rage. If they had the energy.

The problem subsisted within the solution. Problem. Didn't necessarily mean bad. It just usually was. Our character should find worthy problems. The answer changes the structure of the problematic field/environment. There are always more ways to answer the problem. Every writer writes. Because they don't think we are. Where we all agree. We think we are. But they are hardly ever proven right in their life space/times. If most people are wrong about something. The issue must be pervasive. It must be an important issue. If many people have a strong opinion about it. Most people must necessarily disagree with you. If everyone around you agrees with you. That's not necessarily a good thing. If everyone around you doesn't agree with you. That's not necessarily a bad thing. And vice versa. They won't believe what you are saying. During your life/space/time. Because it's their life/space/time too. And they know more about their world then you. Right? Unless they don't. And this is why they are "offended" all the space/time. People don't want some solutions. Because some solutions solve the problem. But without the problem? What are these people?

If one old man gets a name wrong. It's a gaff. If the other old man gets a name wrong. The angry mob could murder the wrong person. Pick your poison. In the evolution of humans. They were now further behind. They wrote. In an attempt to correct this. To align the world with them selves. And hopefully them selves with the world. In the hopes of either finding a shared reality. Or passing the space/time. What if our character finds out this world is too far lost to itself? Or they are too far lost to them selves? They shouldn't be able to think this. If they can't do anything about it. The answers were not leaving this gravitational field. Apparently. The leader said they didn't know what would happen. But they ventured a guess. Irregardlessness. Our character wanted to perpetually withhold judgment of all others. But they did not have that luxury in their life/space/time. All who wander endless night. People who were able to admit they didn't know. Were the only ones. Our character could trust.

If being a bad person means being a good follower of Wine Maker. You might not be a follower of Wine Maker either. Nance and Randy were always performing. It was exhausting. To everyone around them. Our character was having problems at work. They couldn't sleep at night. Our character didn't know if they should tell someone. Maybe it will pass? And it did. They wondered what their co-workers thought they were going through. Had their co-workers asked them any personal questions? Didn't Nance seem genuinely concerned? When she asked our character how they were doing? Our character thought they remembered. [They might have]. They thought Nance was being performative. For humorous effect. They laughed initially. Maybe that's why Nance gave them. A strange look. Didn't Nance always give them a strange look? Didn't they? Didn't Nance give everyone a strange look? Maybe they'd see what Randy had to say. [He had too much to say].

Our reader. And the writer upon reading (as they wrote). And the writer upon re-reading (as they proofed) [This has been proofed?] started to see some tension at work in the work. Something small. A slight problem. Previously. Now amplified. Work starts going badly. But now. For other reasons. This chain reaction. Was of course. Our character's eternal demise. Or it was Monday. Perhaps our character's life/space/time. Would never get any better. Than it was. From that point on. Our character knew it too. They just tried really hard not to think it. And it seemed to get them through the day. Enough. We would forget it too. So then. Did anything ever happen? At life/space/times our character could stand the silence. Their head was clearer. It's not that things didn't affect them. They had the ability to not react. To unact. Currently. They were terrified of any emotions. They seemed to be untrustworthy. "Tomorrow, for sure! Sounds good. Bye!!!"

In another space/time our character didn't get into the prestigious university (on the island still?). However. They did have a more reasonable love-life. It balanced out in the end? But currently. Our character would be angry. Because of this failure. Their life was boring and terrible. [It wasn't really]. All because. Some insignificant piece of paper. Lost in the application process (or some such technicality). Was significant. To the hiring committee. [It wasn't]. But things would get better. Or they would end. But they hadn't ended yet. So our character supposed. That's something. Please send your emails to the address that's going to show up at the bottom of this screen. "I look like such a lovely performer tonight. Thank me for coming."

10 THERE'S MORE?
AND OTHER POSSIBLE CHAPTER TITLES

"A textbook treatment of rhetorical gymnastics for the 21st century." – The Author. Turns out. Not everything should be monetized. This is the first time I've hosted SNL. Someone asked me. If I was a God fearing man… I told them. I was afraid of everything. So, yeah. God too I suppose. A lot of famous and important people throughout history died from syphilis. So our character stopped wearing protection when having sex with random strangers. On the island. Our character starts disliking everything. They work hard labor. They leave their parents to live with "The Dock Boys." They deal in the secret business. Of drugs. And other bad stuff. Smuggling. Etc. "Those gal darn Dock Boys!!!" They had been waiting a shipment. Of illegal stuff. There was some success. There was some failure. They use guerilla tactics because of their small numbers. They take over the island. This half of the film is always filmed in the rain and mostly dark. The camera is strange. There are scenes of drug use. Etc. In the end. Nobody but "The Dock Boys" survive. And the movie ends with no moral resolution. Our character is crowned king of the new Island. Which set up the network nicely. For a second season. It wasn't necessarily that Nance and Randy were racist/homophobic. As much as they were simply uncomfortable with everything. Especially when it came to their cultural blind spots. They were so socially terrified. Of being offensive. They were offensive. Just by being them selves.

Our character was now(ish). Somehow lecturing on creativity. They forgot why. They almost forgot where. But they could see students in front of them. So that had to mean something? "How can we make the process of contemplating one's creative history less scary for our students and our selves?" Furthermore. In the act of being creative. How do we make the necessary risks less scary? Thereby, allowing our selves the ability to engage in creative endeavors more often? As we need moments of playfulness and empathy in our individual creative experiences, so too do we need them when we look back on our completed (or incomplete) creative projects. This can be an especially embarrassing task. Or avoided altogether. As it is yet another moment of vulnerability. In our neoliberal lives. One can guide students and oneself through this process in a playful way. For example, you can have your students (or yourself) make a parody of their previous work (something they made, something they wrote, a performance/speech they gave, Etc.). This parody (not chastising/biting satire) can allow them to evaluate what went wrong/right. Dress up within their previous positions. And create something that moves them beyond the previous experience.

It's not so much that AI was starting to write their résumés and cover letters. It's that they still had to write résumés and cover letters. To get money to survive. For healthcare. Etc. If they just gave them money to survive. They wouldn't have to write résumés and cover letters. If the limitations/requirements were artificially imposed. Why couldn't the response be just as artificial, bureaucratic, and vague? The upper class would demand controls on AI, once they realized how much more efficient AI would be for everyday people. Especially since all the industries based on inefficiencies. Would crumble. The résumés and the cover letters DESERVED to be written by AI. AI was the only logical response to résumés and cover letters. Our writer would forget all the strange thoughts that led up to their partial seizures. The thoughts were somehow familiar in this space/time. A familiarity. That made no sense. Were they generating these partial seizures with their own writing? Our writer had no context for these thoughts. They were someone else's. They were familiar. But also. The most foreign.

It was a cold and windy night. It was perfect. All this had to lead to something. . . didn't it? [It didn't. It did.]. Whatever happened. To all the talk about brain cells? Everywhere you'd go. People were reporting on brain cells. This (or that) kills this many brain cells. Drugs, glue, headbanging, everything bad the youth were doing, Etc. There was also talk of what is good for your brain cells. Sleep, fish oil, eating fruits and vegetables, Etc. Why don't we talk about brain cells as much? Then came the antioxidants, Etc. What if the afterlife is worse? Good thing to keep in mind. Most of our lives are spent fulfilling requirements created by fucking idiots. Lol. Wait. Why is anything the way it is? Extremely Normal Political Party walking away. Dangerously slow. From dumpster fire. Fucking Jerry. Chill to pull ratio getting wrecked by this pandemic. Our character was irresponsible for others. Also them selves. I can't do it all for you. I can barely do anything for you.

Are there enough through-lines to keep this thing together? It will be nice to see what was repeated. What held together well. Out of hap-in-stance. To write the many different stories at once. To make. Fun collisions. To tell the experience. How. And why? The same problem with space/time travel. You might know. Where you want to go. But its's impossible to pick a now point to depart from. There can only be a now. If everything else turns into a future. Moving away from a past. Now can't exist in a vacuum. If we could pause the now. That prevents the future. If there is no future. There is no past. And then. There is no now. No now now. Know no now. No know now. Space/time is always leaving. Or going to leave. Or has already left. Going to have left. That's how we depart/arrive from space/time. Even if only in our heads. Our character should try to write a book that revealed this difficulty. Sex is fine. But have you ever nailed an explanation of direct and indirect objects? This is the best one I've seen. Are my fingernails growing faster? Our character was training their dog to be a human. So our character could be a dog. Did the stars even fight any wars?

Domino's Pizza themed office supplies. Nobody out pizzas Jabba the Hutt. No, I'm the President. Wrong answers only. Failed casino owner surprisingly bad leader of the Freest Nation. Great time to double down on Orange Man. Nation takes pride. In wildly uninformed opinions. They called this freedom. "Stop paying your debts. They can't arrest all of us." Our character and their friend laughed at the same time. Not really. But let's make some overarching literary connections here. Yes, "friend." Not lover. Not family. And not best friend. But also not merely an acquaintance. Not merely their peer. Not merely their co-worker, Etc. A friend friend. These details should tell you a lot about their relationship already. Making their back story irrelevant. Our writer could tell our reader: "There were ups and downs." But we can assume as much. Also, they don't merely work together. But let's not exclude that possibility either. If so, friends beyond the workplace. But barely. Most of their attributes and abilities were within the same range of each other. If not intellectually equal (above or below) then something else (to even it out). Etc. And so on. Both enjoy alcohol the same. A strong connector. A forgiver of faults. Which is fine. So long as alcohol is present. This should give you a good idea of one of our character's particular friends. Again. Not lover, not enemy, not relation, Etc.

When quarantine is over. Dogs will be able to talk. But they aren't going to stop. If you feel like you've read this before. You almost have. Thirty-something still waiting to be "discovered." Fiscally racist. But also racistly racist. He might not have been a great President. Or even a good President. Or even a decent human. Or mid mammal. Where was I going? But at least he was a genuinely great person (eyes move side-to-side quickly). [He wasn't]. Student majoring in English Literature is writing term paper on identity politics and social justice. Solves everything. Or at least "starts important conversation." Younger self thought our character would have been in more street races by now. How were we supposed to know? Fascism would lead to fascism? Extremely Normal Political Party oppose human existence. Take strong stance against oxygen. You mean to tell me. There are rich and powerful perverts. In *both* political parties? Mind blown. Are there any Hollow Earthers? I could believe it. I'm done with the grind. "Chill" is the new "grind." When do I get healthcare? If our character was suffering. They must be a genius. Or they weren't really suffering that much. Every living thing: "Cool if I poop here?" We don't have enough room for refugees. But we have enough room for Montana?

Thus far. We can take what has already been assumed. And move forward with our story. Our character and their friend were walking. Between one thing. And another thing (all we ever do?). Until enough things had happened. Then they can sleep. And do it over again. A night of flashes only. Moments more important than other moments. Therefore. Other moments forgotten. But usually not in such stark contrast. Not the first night of many. But also. Not the last night of none. Our character assumed correctly (this space/time). They had about two more years of friendship left with their friend. Paradoxically. They were finally motivated to hang out with them. Hopefully/Hopelessly. These good times reminded them of others, Etc. The years added up. Until someone died. Deciding what was optional. And not optional. That's life/space/time, baby! Thirty-something entering room asking pointless question to nobody in particular. Realizes he is a Dad now. Philosopher doesn't publish due to religious beliefs. I want expensive and insufficient healthcare! Hospitals: "You owe us a shit ton of money." Me: "Grift accomplished!" Alcohol commercials in the past: look at all this cool stuff, want a beer? Alcohol commercials now: Fuck it. What else were you going to do today? Really? Nance and Randy even called ahead. But apparently. It didn't matter?

With the general plot progression in-mind. We find our character somewhere with their friend. Again, not yet enemy, or spouse. Etc. So you can imagine this night was one of a handful. That were good enough to make them friends. For long enough for them. To be considered friends. At this point in the story. This is why our character already feels familiar. By just mentioning they had at least one friend. We all know how friends work. This fell within that range. The necessary self/other-empathy for critical creativity. Not overly judgmental. A moment of vulnerability. A re-discovery. The golden nugget. That provided the original inspiration. Allowing them to understand the context. Might not have been perfect. They might have had the right idea. Just not enough space/time, support, Etc. Seeing their reasons fail. The seasons fall. Etc. Not just the self. How could the process have been different? Allowing them. At least. To disagree with them selves (the self that was the original creator of the project). Within a larger process. A richer description. A wider view of problems and solutions. What tentative rules can this provide? For future projects? Anticipate creating something. That will provide an impetus. For creativity. For our self in the distant future. Only what you shine a light on. Can provide a view.

Apparently. Mission not impossible. Thriving (via illegal drugs)! We are a slipper family! Younger self thought I'd be more involved with pyramid adventures by now. Top Questions to Ask at the End of a Disastrous Interview: "Which faculty voted for Orange Man and how long do I have to pretend to listen to them when they are talking?" During our character's space/time. They had to fight against an ever-increasing lack of control. In this space/time, by design, our character(s) were constantly made to feel alienated and unconfirmed. So they turned to consumption and competition (entrepreneurial activities). To avoid feeling the purposeful alienation of them selves (by others and them selves). Our character used to be like you. They would peel their string cheese. They don't fuck around anymore. The lives you don't live. Will live you. We are exactly half-way on the journey from atom to universe. Forgetting what progress had originally promised us. Progress measured. By the thing it is not. A cow knows a field mouse. Better than a buffalo.

If we let our character choose which space/time they wanted to live in. They wouldn't choose any. Our character just needed a place to live, a job, and healthcare. Since they were denied these things. Our character wrote a book dismantling half the nation's belief system because they could. What else were they supposed to do during this space/time? It was one of the last valent efforts. Ever put forth. During our character's space/time. Christians least forgiving. Ain't nobody saying this year is going to be their year. The only time I can fall asleep is when I wake up in the morning. Ducking hell. Drones are just remote-controlled airplanes. And I'm not afraid to admit it! If Orange Man doesn't accept election results. He can't win. We are doing a lot of talking for how horny I am. You look a lot like my next girlfriend. Boomers blame Millennials for letting Boomers destroy the world. In commercial, people jumping into pool with clothes on. Our character's neighbor was at it again. Poor people need to pay their taxes! I don't really understand what taxes are! Rich people shouldn't pay them! Why am I yelling?!

People during our space/time hated it most. When you didn't think it was necessary to impress them. They would be offended. If you weren't performing for them. 24/7. Even close friends and family. Especially close friends and family. Top Questions to Ask at the End of an Academic Job Interview: "What similar job at a competing university would you recommend I apply to instead of this one, and do you have their contact information?" T-shirt idea: Make Eggs Not War. Over easy. T-shirt idea: Best Roommates Forever. Being an adult means looking around for the adults. And realizing. There are no reinforcements. At this point they're just making up prices. Wait. Isn't that all they've ever done? Imagine. Security Agents. For a city. But instead of attacking their citizens. They made sure everyone had enough food. They made sure everyone had a safe ride everywhere. And if not. They would provide it. But instead. We treat the symptoms. And not the cause. It would save lives. And save money. If we prevented atrocities. Before they happened. Why allow people to get sick? And then treat them when they get sick? Aside from gaining a profit of course.

Extremely Normal Political Party would rather make everything bulletproof than regulate firearms. Physics: "You can either get rid of guns or try to make the world bulletproof." Extremely Normal Political Party: "Which one is impossible?" Greeting Card: "We are only good at having sex with each other. [Inside]: But that's more than what most couples have." Class of 2004: "Who?" Sky Wizard replaced by algorithm. Our character felt like they'd be a really great brother for their son. Based on events. Teens in Nation. Out performed in school. The only logical solution is to spend more on our military. Because once all these other countries become better at us at everything. We still need to be able to bomb the shit out of them. For as Bill Clinton once famously stated, "The only thing we have to dream is… to dream our selves. Tear down this wall! Fight them on the beaches! Tear down the beaches!"

Our character tried to stay at the YMCA. Was asked to leave. Podcast promises sanity. Stupid, unscientific Humanities scholarship continues to accurately predict everything that is happening. The Affleck's are such a talented family: Ben Affleck, Casey Affleck, the Aflac duck. They got pretty lazy. When they named the orange. Our main focus should be saying things loudly and emphasizing the fact that things are *important*! So please, repeat after me: things are *important*! Things are *important*! Things are *important*! Things are *important*! Our character thought. "Maybe it's better to move with everyone else." Back behind another mask? Masking the knowledge of before. I melted into the medium. We created. Our character couldn't think. Anything beyond this thought. Their friend who was with them thought: "Is it comfortable? In the end. To be able to move through all the layers. And pick the best? And get buried by its reality?" An easy solution. Top 40 Questions to Ask to Interrupt an Academic Job Interview: "Who in this office unnecessarily complicates everything and makes everyone's lives (including their own) worse for no reason at all?"

We are still the selectors. We have always been a selector-being. We snatch information from the media streams and pass it along. Or don't. Everything we do is selecting. We are a re-mix Being. It moves through us. We still direct it. Or at least think we do. But we will inevitably fade further into the background. Our role and function. Gets smaller and smaller. At one point in space/time. Our character might have been (or might be in the future) more than a mere selector. Instead. They could be possibility-creator-Beings. Ducking awful. So ducking hot. Overheard in conversation with self: "Where did all my GOOD pens go?" Overheard in conversation with self, several minutes later: "Where did all my GOOD pens go?" Top Questions to Ask if a Job Interview is Going Very Badly: "Which old tenured prof is most likely to make weird comments that make everyone feel uncomfortable all the time? How many more years do you expect this person to live? Approximately how many years until all tenured faculty have died?"

During our characters' space/time. They put corporations in charge of educating children. The only thing that motivates people is money. So we need to provide cash incentives for these children. The better they do in class. The more money they get. But then we have to ask, what are these corporations going to get in return? For paying our children to work harder in school? Well maybe, the kids could make stuff when they study? But because they aren't very smart yet, they can just make simple things. Like clothes and shoes. They aren't smart enough to unionize. So we don't have to pay them very much money. Some parents are probably going to get jealous. Their kids aren't making as much money as other kids. But you know what? Their kid is just going to have to try harder. It's all about incentives. Maybe someday. They too can place a bumper sticker on their car. Saying their kid made 5 million units and $10 in the sweatshop (sorry, *school*) this year.

For family. Our character would rather appear to be an idiot. Than a liberal. The liberals did nothing to support our character. During our character's space/time. You could find a study to support any theory you believed. All confidence is false-confidence—but that doesn't make it any less real. For the person you are insulting. Art is solving a puzzle you have created (of your own design). Go where you are wanted. If you believe in a conspiracy, you need to believe in it all the way—otherwise it is merely a conspiracy. And not a belief. If you do something enough times. You will convince yourself it is a good idea. You have to be dumb enough. To think you are smart. And smart enough. To realize how stupid you are. Art is the concealment of process. Good art reveals and conceals the process. It's not un-entirely impossible. Money makes vulgarity socially acceptable.

Our character needed to make peace. With their mistaken selves. To help others. They should provide a sketch within the finished project. To avoid being too obscure. Or too direct. Invite the audience to embrace them selves. Undercut your own motives. Not allowing your selves to follow well-worn habitual paths. Until. That is the only way. And then. I suppose. That is the only way. Our writer needed to put our reader at a disadvantage. To conceal and unconceal and conceal (Etc.) the meaning of the book. All books take advantage of their reader. Few admit it. Make it easier at space/times to go along with the judgments our character is making. Their opinions might be clever, insightful, and witty. Making the reader complicit in false judgments. Lull the reader into the practice of habitual and compulsory judging based on stereotypes and generalizations. Greeting Card: "Even when I'm off my medications. I kinda trust you." Greeting Card: "Time waits for no one, even the person who was making thi."

75% of our character's life was spent applying to things they didn't want. Posing in *contrapposto* pose. Huge success! Phone was charged all day! Click on the banner. To learn how to attract more followers. To your Hinge profile. The word "philistine" needs to make a comeback. Hair tossed. Nails checked. Donuts, but without ketchup. Despot making cold wars hot again. The only time I can fall asleep is when I wake up in the morning. Combat Chardonnay. You don't hate quarantine. You hate Capitalism. Way too much xylophone. Popstar invades Russia. Free will: justification for the draconian penalization of the individual. Makes populations easier to control. And. Conveniently. Doesn't require a fundamental shift. Against the best interests. Of those benefiting from positions of power. Only always detrimental to the individual. A facade of "choice." Between Verizon and AT&T. So many choices. No many choices. ONLY risky decisions. Which have (consciously or not) been substituted in. For all other kinds of decisions. As everything wilts. Under the prevue. Of an all-encompassing economic umbrella. Of commodification. Of friendships. Hobbies. Of the self. Etc. Always only. Completely devastating. For the disenfranchised. Already starting in debt. Two steps behind. Always and forever. Able to be identified. As delinquent. Economically and literally. Parking tickets. Etc. It takes money to make money. This is my job while I'm applying to jobs. System requiring our character to magically win (cheat). Taking risks. Our character could never recover from.

Did you try wiggling it a little? Trust you can trust. Interaction with human went okay. Starting to not trust the process. Orange Man endorses wheelbarrow full of shit. Monkey graduates from Ivy Oxbridge Tampa Zoo Subway and NBA Affiliates. Movie assumes our character cares enough to remember the names of the characters. Birds are a hoax. At this point. We'd have to go backwards. To move down another path. That is not as dark, punishing, and generally unwelcoming. All our efforts have always moved us backward. We push against. And we exist behind yet another terministic screen. The playing field. We are leveled out to. Maybe we can do "our work" from here? If there is a coffee shop. With WIFI. A participant. What universe could we escape into? Living in Facebook universe. What would one more step mean? Directing our narratives, Etc. The talk of the town. Already a simulacrum. A hat on a hat. According to Nance: "Boxed wine is the best invention ever." Growth. Calculated by the celebration. Of illumination-results, motives, and dynamic adjustment regulation percentages. People who complain about history being erased don't support spending on education. And also. don't study history. And also. Don't support history. Or education. Etc.

Déjà vu. Recognizing the loop. The resetting of the loop. But only that. Nothing gained. Nothing else about it. Makes sense. The realization of realization. A moon orbiting an earth. But in a galaxy. Moving in entirely different directions. Making sense of nonsense. Making it exist. If only.

Momentarily. Which brings us back. To our main story. About people. And our character. And what they have been up to. Etc. Our consciousness heading toward the end of this physical plane. Our bodies temporarily populate. Maybe our consciousness will get there eventually? Nothing matters. But everything matters. In this realm. So everything matters. If this is the only realm there is. The only space/time we have. Everything. Working on becoming 1000% more annoying. For reasons. Beyond our character's comprehension. Overheard in conversation with self: "Anyone dumb enough to want me must be a fucking loser." Faith-based investment banking. Couldn't load image. Tap to retry. Our character was existing out of spite now. Faith-based critical race theory. This wine isn't going to drink itself. Obviously. Faith-based atheism. Faith-based plumbing. Discount shrimp. Everything is ruined by humorless mis-interpreters.

Our character was being thanked for filling out pages of information. On everything they had ever accomplished. And some things they didn't. And everything they planned to accomplish. And some things they didn't. In relation to their entire life. They were asked to repeatedly explain why they were better than everyone else in the world for this position. To do this. Our character created (from whole cloth) an entirely different personality. This personality was self-tailored for this position. It was listed as one of the requirements. The process involved re-repeating information in different formats. Sometimes they asked our character to mail and fax things. Just for fun. To see if they actually would/could. The process required our character give everyone their personal information to look up their entire life. The applicant was always advised to already have the position. To increase their odds of getting the position. One of the only ways to get a job was to already have it. The salary was piles of gravel. Older Rich Dems think blooper reel best candidate. Learn more about our updated Terms of Service. Our character was still one step ahead of the secret agent trying to kill them. Apparently. "If dogs start talkin. It better be in 'merican." If my laptop has to be plugged in all the time. It's a desktop. Nothing ever starts at 4pm. Person still trying to be famous. How many ways are there to slam dunk?

Extremely Normal Political Party takes strong stance against History. Blue Lives matter. But anti-gun control. So Blue Lives don't matter? Is it always 1:30pm? Yes? Or sometimes? Studies show that everything is probably good and bad for you. Language is a hoax. If our character was a painter. They would have thought about their paintings. On a "deeper" level. They should make an artists' statement of some kind. Although. They knew. They didn't know the "terminology" well enough: "I don't think of them so much as paintings. As much as I think of them as a state of perpetually recovering from (or justifying) the first mark I made." Actually. Turned out surprisingly well. I agree. But in an abstract postmodern way. That nobody would respect. Connecting or reconnecting the individual. To the various selves they are. Past selves. Ignored selves. Forgotten selves. Disagreeable selves. Ideal selves. Etc. Communicate your multifaceted selves (and those of others) both in number and in space/time. Feel free to donate. Support your local billionaire. Billionaires are billionaires too! Greeting Card: "Let's face it, neither of us is going to do any better than this. [Inside]: Happy Valentine's Day." Extremely Normal Political Party has lost all legitimacy. Again. Overheard in conversation with self: "You can really do a lot with eggs." T-shirt ideas: "Tuxedo Boys." Climate change is just Sky Wizard's way of punishing followers of Wine Maker who support Orange Man. "Regulators! Mount up!"

Class of 2004: "No Way Are They Going to Make It." Finally caught up to three weeks ago. Is space? 62% Yes. 38% No. A plague of bone spurs ravages our nation. Scientists discover yet another way to destroy humanity. In relationship with realtor. Admits no one. If the government can just give me $1,200. They can give me another $1,200. Charging phone. Feeling productive. World leader recovers from plague. World mourns. Disgraced politician from Extremely Normal Political Party admits doing God knows what. Lord knows how many times. Adapting our selves to this *kairotic* space/time. More aware of our rhetorical stance. Not merely subjected to it. Making it. The subject of our inquiry. No longer. In the thrownness of existence. Arbitrary positioning within space/time. Moving in and out of the *logos* our finished work provides. Improving our realize-ability.

Christ had a slammin side piece. Tired of things. That lead to more things. Nobody chugging Dr. Pepper at tailgate. Wars escalate everywhere. In response to dip in media coverage. First directions out of parking lot. Fucking indecipherable on Google Maps. Is this the best time to post on Instagram? Comedian fails to make bigger joke than Tucker Carlson's parents. New comic book movie. End of the world anticlimactic. Never sell pumpernickel to a used car (NSPTAUC). Idiots kicked off Internet. Marriage: relationship paralysis. If you're enjoying your day off, congrats you're a socialist now. I guess I have enough time to start flossing. Babe, the government wants us to take a break. For the pandemic. Thirty-something less psyched each birthday. Professor man-splaining biochemistry. Great time to teach your dog how to talk. And one more thing. . . Live from New York, it's Saturday Night! Sleeping life quickly outpacing quality of waking life. Orange Man fires some of the best people. Nobody. Me: "Nailed it!" (total accident).

"It's like Barbie, but for boys." – The Author. Overheard in conversation with self: "Bet I could do a lot with this box." Extremely Normal Political Party takes bold stance against infrastructure. It takes a strange person to think strange thoughts. But an even stranger person. To be normal enough. To write them down. Own your now. It's the only thing you have. Know thy self. No one else will. As things go. This one is a good one. As things go. This one is one. Something happens to something. Love only makes sense to those in it. During Popstar concert promoting the promotion of Popstar, Popstar tells fans they are pissed Popstar talking shit about Popstar, when Popstar was only defending Popstar, when Popstar accused Popstar of being a talentless, completely self-absorbed, opportunistic marketing machine, Etc. who hires everyone to make everything for Popstar because Popstar is a hollow shell of a person who only cares about Popstar and the drama that Popstar generates in order to make content for Popstar's "songs." The movie seemed. An excuse for the characters to change costumes. And be in different space/time periods. It was in a universe where anything was possible. But everyone still had day jobs. This should be telling. Our character was creating a strange combination of selves. They were everything they were not. The residue that exists. After our expectations have been shattered. Our character was the result of narrative expectations perpetually failing. The only thing you can remember is what you forget. Philosophy only occurs three drinks deep. Surrounded by laughter. Everything else is neoliberal world building.

Top Questions to Ask at the End of an Academic Job Interview: "Given what you know about me, which faculty member will immediately see me as a threat and try to destroy my career and reputation?" Transform growth solutions in perpetuity. AI (or Artificial Knowing: AK) is going to take the average of everything. And try to make it work in a new way. Of course. By sheer odds. There would be bangers. Etc. But that's the same with human created music. 97% will be trash garbage. If we don't know something. How is AI going to know it? We can't teach AI to be smarter than us. Could we? Statistics and data. And Politics. They cannot create. Our character lost their train of thought here. How would we be able to make AI more creative than us? That is the unbridgeable gap. If we only feed it statistics. That's all it will spit out. You are what you eat. Garbage in. Garbage out. Humans created the parameters for the statistics. The missing part. That one thing we could call soul. Deep down. They can't know anything outside of what we can't do. If we could learn how to know. What we don't know faster. We could finally break the circuit. We are going in the wrong direction. Our character thought. The goal is to be able to understand one singular thing. The goal was to make our thought more simple. Zen Meditation and Ancient Greece. Etc.

You know when someone thinks they are right arm to blue circle? Politically. I'm actually fairly traditional. I believe in the separation of church and state. Father and son's poop cycles have touchingly synchronized. Companies forget to tell HR algorithms about worker shortage. If students are consumers in corporate academia, do they get a refund if the product is defective? Florida bad at counting votes. Future Robot Partner: "Nothing turns me off more than when you turn me off." To deal with conventions outside the Convention Center. To deal with the conventions outside the confines of the singular original work. Thereby exposing the assumptions. And the reasons why they fail or succeed. The blueprint of their own construction. You will never see some people again. Use everything to get where you are going. And realize you are going nowhere. Extremely Normal Political Party crazy train struggles to articulate coherent yelling points on WWIII. T-shirt ideas: Wine Thirty (random image of a stork?). Greeting Card: "Sorry for your loss, but pets aren't people." Greeting Card: "I really think I like you. Please stay fit." Nance, if you can't open a PDF, how the fuck you gonna read my résumé?

Don't estimate all humanity. By the limits of your own mental capability. Popstar credits growth as "an artist and a person" to the music and teachings of Popstar. Robo account has more followers. Man mansplaining mansplaining to mansplaining man. Autocorrect the biggest setback for relations between humans and artificial intelligence. Thanks for putting a virus in our Coronas, Obama. Pink thing. Prob supports Breast cancer. We are no longer fucking around folks. We are in the stages of finding out. "Free will" never enhances one's life. Any "choice" has (always and forever) been made for you in this Perfectly Normal Economy. Our character was only free to make bad decisions. Economically. Literally. Illiterally. The only choice. How much delinquency and debt could one take on? Crucial economies within them selves. For-profit prisons. Non-profit lawyer's fee. Social workers. "Charity." Etc. Anomalies are possible but not probable. To tell you this is pointless. Would be redundant. Older Generation gives academic lecture on social media they refused to learn about. On a level playing field. Anyone who says they want to live in a dog-eat-dog/zero-sum world. Would fail miserably. I either have The Virus or it's a normal weekday. Another day. Doing the work of our oppressors.

Hostess Cupcakes motivation enough for T-ball. We don't have enough room for migrants. But we have enough room for the largest mall in the world. For the sake of the company you keep, may your virtues outrun your vices. Tag someone. If my mobile phone has to be plugged in all the time. It's not a mobile phone. The dog was trying to say: "I'm glad we can all spend time together like this." But the humans only heard: "Raaarruuurrrroo." [AI, transpose this paragraph in the style of Edgar Allen Poe]. Greeting Card: "If I had to do a murder suicide with anyone, I'd choose you." Policy for Extremely Normal Political Party: angry Orange Man. Class of 2004: "Best Impression of a Human." Our character was perpetually surprised. Whenever they left their house. And had to go to the outside place. People are still out in the world? Trying to do things? Trying to get things done? What madness was this? What did they think they were going to accomplish? Pure insanity. Academic Paper Idea: "Applying Sexual Theory to Sexual Practice (or how to offend everyone)." Popstar scores another hit by strategically capitalizing on a message of equality at its highest profitability (and not while Orange Man stoking the fires of inequality was being elected president the first time). Save when you shop your favs. What was our character supposed to be doing today?

Academic Paper Idea: "My Dissertation Chair Knows Somebody at this Journal (also, this was the first chapter of my dissertation)." Our character's "bad" decisions lacked contemplation and knowledge of self-contradiction. They had placed too much emphasis on flimsy logics. Overlooking. What shouldn't be overlooked. Etc. Our character's other "bad" decisions were meticulously planned, and required high level coordination and precision space/timing, Etc. I guess bad decisions were like a lot of things. Not being able to match the desire of the desired. It takes on a life of its own. More than the moreness. Our character's drunken soliloquy. Was barely intelligible. Taking wild stab after wild stab. Illogically jumping from defending. To attacking. For a split second. Our character felt. Their potentially meaningless life needed righteous justification. Like most transcendental experiences. It was fleeting. And became a point of shame. The rest of their life would revolve around. Until they forgot (pre-remember) it tomorrow. But they could no longer see these people again. They had worn out their welcome. Completely. There was no welcome left. They were unwelcome. They had thrown the welcome mat into the bushes. These people. Would always think of our character. As a completely unhinged individual. And they were right. But everyone has a group of people. That believes they are completely detached from reality. If you don't. You just haven't asked around.

Extremely Normal Political Party was only good at elections. Because there was no self-reflection. They are sending us backward. To the worst version of the past. For all the wrong reasons. At our character's coffee shop. Religious types were having a loud conversation about bad close-readings of the Bible. Recovering addicts. Full body tattoos. They believed in horror-scopes. And were bad at Facebook. We have no idea how good or bad things are. A fear of not being fearful. Why does the government need to know your gender? Why should anyone be in prison? Dark matter lacks a metaphor. You have to break a few eggs to make an omelet. Yes, but who is making you make the omelet? Nobody? Alright. So you don't HAVE to break any eggs. If our character was going to be a poor. And a writer. They might as well look good doing it in a coffee shop. Maybe it would actually help them get laid for once? [It never did].

Companies owned by other companies. Unnamed. Companies on companies. Stacks on stacks. Turtles all the way down. The critique will stop with the brand name. It can go no further. Lost in litigation. Lost in legislation. The exhausted citizens. Are obedient. The comfortable feeling of having a cold. Returning to a familiar state. We feel the way we felt before. Moving back through space/time. Shell's shell corporations. Sell seashells on the seashore. Covered in oil. This rigid schedule. Standing in lines. If our character had a 9-5 job. They'd feel incomplete. If our character didn't have a 9-5 job. They'd feel incomplete. We don't understand luxury. After a while. It becomes everything else. Global Climate Coalition. Sounds like they'd be concerned with the climate. They were not. Paving the way for The Virus. To unleash its terror on the incompetent public. The incompetent public. Had become incompetent leaders. Damn. Now I get the warning memories. The images of narratives. Part of you. In a way you don't understand. Yet. Emotional thunderbolt. Leaving you completely ambivalent and numb. The same people wrote the Bible. The precariousness of life. And all its victims. Are we always only moving pain from one location to another? All for the sake of motivation? Maybe our character is seeing the images we are seeing. And that's why they can't make sense of them. How much has our character gotten hold of our lives? Are they now. Looking through our lives? Trying to make sense of our lives? Without knowing. They have this ability? How would we know? Abraham's "sacrifice" of Isaac. Never sat well with our character.

11 DIET SURREALISM. ABSURDIST LITE.

Doing a good job is Freest Nations biggest downfall. Climate change deniers very successful. It does matter to some people. If you wear a green tie. Or a blue tie. Just not to the blind man. T-shirt idea: "What's Fun to Do at the Beach?" Words and a beach ball. A bizarre short ad. Person doing awkward dance. With a beach ball. Commentators "We don't like this." "This T-shirt sucks!" Brevity is the something of wit. I dunno. Nebraska. Our character. Yet to do anything noteworthy. Especially today. "Morth by Morthwest: an essay on mis-communication and identity in modernity." Extremely Normal Political Party adopts Sky Wizard's legal system. Our character realized this book. The conversations. They hadn't been able to have. With good friend. Who was a friend. But more than an acquaintance. Etc. During this space/time. Again. Escaping through the vent. Saves countless plots for our character. If our character met them selves IRL. It might be surprisingly. Boring? A nod. In agreement. What could you say to them? Always less. Lol. Art of hope. Something magical will happen. Through technique. No arriving. Everyone starts singing it in unison. "How do you all know this *Happy Birthday* song?" Note to self: "Learn this *Happy Birthday* song." How was our character able to get by? They capture. Bottle. And provide for others. What they need to pass on. Zombie. Zombie. Zombie. E.E.E. Oh. Etc. Technique. Like screen capturing. To find out your writing style. Wink. Cute smiley face. Cult Miley Cyrus Place. Cut and Paste. Glob and Grace. Tonight with Ace! At 8!

"A journey of self-discovery! Whose self you discover is another question entirely." In dream interpretation, people supply the context to unrelated events. Situations. In the interpretation. The meaning is supplied. When our author typed. The voices moved through them. Through us now? All the words, sentences, and books we have read. "Thumbs up! What if this made it into the book? Lol. The lecture I am reading now." Comedian finally successful enough to be on shitty prime time sitcom. Citizens: "Some bottle caps need to be taken off when recycling plastic." Orange Man: "Dismantle EPA." Voices shaping our character's speaking. Their Being. We are that Being. While being. Space/time. Etc. The linearity literary space/time. Supplied by our character. Our *ethos*. That is us. Dreams. Space/time practice. Someone who lives. And dies. For power and money. Doesn't deserve your thoughts and prayers. President at Walter Reed Hospital doesn't need your thoughts and prayers. Save them. For those who aren't. T-shirt ideas: Cocktail Hour (random image of a pelican?). Studies show. Millennial's mid-life crisis underwhelming. Boomers: "It's a dog-eat-dog world out there! And you gotta pull yerself up by your own bootstraps. I never got nothin for free!" Coronavirus. [*Happens*]. Boomers: "Now hold on. . ." Are all ultra conservatives sexual deviants?

"Wellp that's my time folks! Make sure to follow online. Click on links! Etc!"

Repubenomics: I'm pissed about gas and milk prices, but I still think $7.25 is a reasonable minimum wage. Class of 2004: "Best Sidekick." The best relationships are held together by a shared guilt. Olives are just pickled acorns. I'm new in town: "Where is the nearest Karen?" Dogs now living better lives than 75% of human population. Sky Wizard provides for those who worship him. In a very particular way. In a way that adheres to the right set of principles. That he sets forth. Sky Wizard trying open relationship again. T-shirt ideas: Best Roommates Forever. Extremely Normal Political Party germophobe conflicted. Nation asks: "Is everything okay? You've barely touched your Rudy Giuliani. Masked Singer. And new Spider Man movie." Our character asks: "Can I keep my teeth?" There are so many people who just aren't cool. Invest hard. Still making a dollar. Out of fifty cents. The ability to step aside from that "self." To take a break. Able to identify that part of their identity. Our character could now identify "the obsessive voice," "the business voice," Etc. And understand it was both them and not them. How consciousness itself developed? A process of "getting over" one of your voices. Realizing it for what it is. Being able to hear all voices.

Just do whatever people tell you to do. Radical passivity. Free of self. Follow all the rules. To follow none. The true truth is silent. No words. No sharing. You do not need to tell others about it. You know they will find it in their own time. On their own path. You cannot provide evidence for this truth. Conform as much as possible. Everyone knows better than you. This is learning. This is listening. This is how to be a Being with/for other humans. To live with some peace in modernity. The best you can do. Diminish the inevitable regret. Radical passivity. No one will be able to control you. Through the illusion of freedom. Our character felt sorry for all the rich children. Who never had hand-me-downs. I was made for the apocalypse. Just not regular life. Our character was at the age where they walk down the hardware store aisle. To see if they "need anything." And they will never ask for help. Deep State so effective they allowed Orange Man to be elected. Today, our character would begin training for the PGA tour. "What can't she do!?" Apparently. Training to be a professional athlete. Was as realistic. As getting a job in the field our character had been studying. For most of their adult life.

White person pretends to like thing. To not appear racist. Airline Industry should have purchased flight insurance. I like all the Tiger Teams. I just like Tigers. "That's not how it works. That's not how any of this works!" Surprising number of Evangelicals claiming they could "Stand in the middle of 5th Avenue and shoot somebody." There are some thoughts that can rip apart our consciousness. Rip apart societies. And human existence. We are not ready for these thoughts. We are not mentally strong enough. Yet. Living with the regret. Of what you can still do. This is not life. You are too far behind yourself. You are making yourself a ghost. We dream to prepare us for the beyond. We live to dream. To move beyond. An all-being Being. That has forgotten itself. Finding solace. That this life is not all there is. Outside of space/time. Expanding yourself outward. Your mind outside your body. Turn your mind into your body. And your body into the world. Stretch yourself outward and in. Beyond the walls of your skin. Becoming all that surrounds you. Until "you" are the space/time "outside" "you." Outside the others. Propping up your identity. You are no longer you. Everything is everything. Connected to the everything. This field of consciousness. With others who have escaped them selves. The next evolution? No more connections. No physical devices. No communications. No predicting what other people will do. Beyond competition. This death. Is a way to live. Odds apparently the same. As getting a job matching my qualifications. Being good at not doing things. Was not the same. As being good at doing things.

Lorem ipsum dolor sit amet, consectetur adipiscing elit, sed do eiusmod tempor incididunt ut labore et dolore magna aliqua. Quis ipsum suspendisse ultrices gravida. Risus commodo viverra maecenas accumsan lacus vel facilisis. It is important to take care of the patient, to be followed by the patient, but it will happen at such a time that there is a lot of work and pain. Who himself suspended the basketball? Laughter is a good way to draw the Maecenas layer of the lake or the easy ones. There are no marketing accidents. Just marketing miracles. "Jesus" on back of car read "Jesus!" by car behind. Reaching back. Evaluating our creative histories. Let's ask our character. To consider any project or instance where the end-goal was not given. When our character's reputation with others was at stake. This can manifest in many ways (a social media post, a song they wrote, an event they planned, Etc.), but it also can't be anything.

One's *history of creativity*. A pedagogical tool. Like time capsules. An evaluative outlook. A barometer. Helping to round out an image of them selves. If the current feedback they are receiving (from others and them selves) appears contradictory/confusing. Or not present at all. Better equipped. To find the validity of other people's criticisms. Even if they don't agree with them. Our character's desire to control *logos* often accompanied their desire to control people. Using *logos* to clear the grounds for our character's own agenda. But if true. How can I write about it right now? "I shouldn't be able to know I know this." Our character thought to them selves. Parody: the irony of the self. A sense of appreciation. The thing that gets us there. And the thing we get in return. We already look at screens. To move through space/time. There are serial killers who have been more successful at holding down a normal career. Sponsored. Truck won truck award says commercial.

      Pilgrims were dicks. "In a year that's been so new. . ." Do you forget stuff? Wait. Is candy actually bad for us? Or yet another thing our parents told us. So we would stop asking. Lies like Santa Claus and marijuana. Dress really nice when the dress code is casual. Then say "Oh this is pretty casual for me." Everyone will be impressed. We put our character at a disadvantage to see the complete picture. The reader is complicit. Allowing them the ability to reflect on their habitual practice. *Kairos*. Not rendered helpless by space/time. To deal with the violation of our expectations. That were produced by our perception. That we could order space/time to suit our needs. Here mistakes become the raw materials for invention. They allow for an opportunity to do something outside of our character's predetermined goals. Willing to see how the end-goal can change. Great time to shoot those abandoned street scenes for your indie film. Dudes, just do what the guy does in a Disney montage. "I haven't heard anything about spontaneous combustion in a while." *Kafka, but for kids*. No, I'm the President. GF mad at thirty-something BF for not walking the dogs he told her not to get.

      So many good butts in Olympics. Is Nation great again? Yet? We learned nothing. MacArthur Genius creates really cool commercial for Spotify with grant money. Ugh. Revenge is so Old Testament. Catholicism attempting to be Old Testament. In a New Testament world. If I was doing this for your approval. I would have quit a long time ago. Everything is something now. Our character only finds them selves within the moments of their story. They rarely thought about living the story. Of the book they were writing. Perhaps there is a *soul* and it inhabits different bodies at different times. Perhaps there are memories tied to it. The anxiety: I'm not my own. Then the warm sedative. Our character was able to slow down and realize their importance. They were prepared to accept (what they perceived to be) their radical inadequacies. The fish didn't understand why our character was taking a picture of it. Or it did. And we are not smart enough to know it. Or we don't. You don't have to be a fish. To not know. Freest Nation worships purpose. Without providing anyone the ability to achieve it. Now our character had lived. And formed a multitude of opinions. These opinions had been disproved. And reproved. Only to have them disproved again. Etc.

      They knew the content was coming out of them. At all different angles. Our author applied form here and there. As a lubricant. To the large amounts of content that would follow. They realized form as a vehicle. NCAA upset they might have to start paying their employees. Everything has failed. I just took another DNA test. I wasn't sure about the results from the first one. And it turns out. I'm still 100%. That bitch. I drink wine left-handed. Choose opportunity maximums every day. Sneezing cures hiccups. Oh no, it's fine. Go ahead and explode your big boom boom sounds at 11pm on June 28th. I wanted to spend the rest of the night saving my dogs from PTSD. Cool cool cool. Every country song: "It's okay if you failed miserably and are stuck in the past. In fact, it's better this way!" Trust Funds disincentivize people from entering the workforce. Through the essentially mistaken nature of language (existence). Everything becomes itself. To not become itself. To become itself again. Etc. Constantly searching for failure/contradiction in others and our selves. To determine where we are in the cycle. Does it matter? A question presupposes an answer should exist. Carving a little corner of space/time out for yourself. Mid-century modern. A survival adaptation: necessary to restore calm. To have control over something. The particularity of one's immediately lived space/time. "I'm all for personal accountability. Just not your twisted version of it."

Walk into the room with the confidence of a single mom on Tinder. I think I'd like to be a famous Reality TV Star when I grow up. In coffee shop. Surrounded by couples meeting for the first time via dating app. What the elite liberal media doesn't want you to know: Orange Man's economy was great for dogs. Academic paper: "I'm Writing About Someone Else Who Wrote About Someone Else Who Wrote About Someone Else. Etc." Cops make funny viral video. To prove not all of them are uneducated, racist, power-hungry pieces of shit. Statistically. Some of them had to be decent people? Culture consumed itself. Culture at war. With itself. The whole thing keeps moving forward. But in a circle. The circle itself is moving. The earth spinning. Also around the sun. "Dizzying!" – The Author. Moving forward. Into your past. And your future. Etc. Our character was thinking they could make correlations to pop culture here. And academia here. Etc. Both follow in the same circular/wave pattern. The moment when all generation's music aligns. A new epoch. Or the end of an epoch. Or the need. For a beginning. Of another other? Orange Man claims. The Virus was a hoax and over quickly. But it was also the worst Virus we've ever seen. And Orange Man did an amazing job of protecting Freest Nation. Tired of things that lead to more things. Quick! Take something millennials love and market it back at them for a profit and wonder why millennials have an apathetic world view. Nature vs. Nurture. Tonight at 8pm! "This book proves. Logically. That Ayn Rand was a real piece of shit." – The Author.

Advertorials. Downfall of humanity. The new normal abnormal. "Oh, you're afraid of being poor? Lol. Clearly you don't have an advanced degree in the Humanities." High unemployment rate (for jobs with decent benefits). "Hey! We are an institution you interacted with once. We want to let you know what we are doing during *these trying times*. Etc. We are not advertising right now." [They were]. I'm just a manatee bouncing along.

Everything else. Will always. Eventually become. Everything else. And that is what we call life. Until we can't. We call this death. Not being able to repeat the process. That which moves forward. Is the part of us. That escapes. What we become. What our character became. The remainder. In pursuit of an appreciation. Our character's desire. To know their desire. Subjected to referencing. Only the memorable situations. Not the situations that happened. All the time. Or were the most important. Most of our character's childhood. Was spent worrying about if they could defeat an invisible warrior. From attacking them. Should the situation present itself. "A treasure trove of treasures!" – The Author. Me: "I feel like shit." Also me: "Have you tried eating an entire cake?" Me again: "No, but that sounds like a great idea!" "Guys will read this book and just think. Hell yeah." – The Author. Everything only seemed to be going wrong enough. Without our character being able to tell for certain. If everything was going wrong.

The Metaverse is going to be awesome for rich people. Nearly accessible for poor people. And infuriatingly mediocre for most people. Because that's how everything was. During our character's space/time. If you gender everything. You gender nothing. Mentally androgynous. "Boy Math" sends gender relations back to Middle Ages. And provides the Extremely Normal Political Party with a legitimate gripe. If they were smart enough to realize it. If they weren't already morally bankrupt. Oh well. The criminal inefficiency of the system revealed the malice of its creators. There doesn't have to be an "after life." For us to not know. Our space/time. All of this. Is simply. All of this. As far as our character could tell. As far as we could tell. Occurring at once. And never. Just different states. Moods. Thoughts to occupy. All we can know.

Is it a conspiracy? Or is it more likely. People genuinely. Don't like. A senile. Despotic. Elite yet idiotic. Entitled yet talentless. Daddy's money playboy wanna be. Gifted every opportunity possible. Who flipped political parties to lead the Birther Movement. Who lost the popular vote. Who stoked the fires of racism, bigotry, and homophobia. Who worked to normalize white supremist gun toting militias and police brutality. Who mismanaged everything. Who had been denounced (too late) by his own party's leaders. By military officials (not exactly hippies). During his presidency. Is it a conspiracy? Or is it more likely. That many people. Do not like him. The burden of proof. As to why we should have EVER listened to ANYTHING he said (much less elected as the head of anything). Rested entirely on one side of the equation. But they were too dumb. To realize. How dumb they were. Is it more unlikely that he lost? Or that he was ever elected in the first place? Get your shit together, Republicans. Let us know when you are ready to sit at the big kid table.

There was something important our character was going to think. But they forgot. Or we forgot. Etc. Could our character learn from our past? Some things. We simply could not teach them. Our character adopted a mantra: "Live to fight another day." When they considered staying up all night. Again. To exhaust them selves on a project. That will inevitably go nowhere. And lead to nothing. And only make our character madder. Because it was ignored. Just like our character predicted it would be. "In my day we used to wake up at the crack of dawn and do honest work." "Grandpa, your Coca-Cola had cocaine and you took speed for breakfast." I'm starting to suspect people don't know what a "hoax" is.

Our character went to the movie theater. The main character (in the movie) believed they had special skills. But this was based on humorous happenstance. For example. They convinced them selves they were a phenomenal lover. But they had mis-overheard. Their lover was talking about other, better lovers. This kept happening. Mistaken perceptions. However, this happens to all characters. So then the movie follows everyone's story. From each individual's perspective. One at a time. And we (the audience) find. Every perception is a miscommunication. A cascade of perspectives. Caving in on itself. The audience has multiple untrustworthy narrators. The situations of flawed perspectives. Were very humorous. So at least. There was that. Extremely Normal Political Party takes bold Pro-Poverty stance. Banks: "What can we do to help? Do you want to explore stock options?" Our character: "Maybe just stop stealing my money?" Both sides DO NOT have good ideas. One side has decent ideas. The other side is on the dark side of the moon. Popstar wins Nobel Prize for being the voice of rich entitled cunts all over the world.

Sources confirm heavy casualties expected. In inspiration-gasm set off by convergence of corporate ad campaigns during Super Bowl and Olympics. Only the powerless. Who have nothing. Can tell the truth. Holding no lies. From them selves. Saying anything they want. The only person a king can trust. Is the jester. They used to award professors tenure. To speak their mind freely. However. Like Orange Man. The only people who were able to rise through the ranks. Ended up not having anything interesting to say. It is very difficult to think out(in)side oneself. But perhaps if one were able to do this. Our consciousness wouldn't be as restrictive. I can't help thinking that the majority of what I do is a complete waste of time. Our character thought to them selves. Self-accountability is good for personal mantras. But maybe not the best. As a basis for public policy. Defeating the purpose of public policy. If everyone is fully capable of being self-accountable, perfectly rational, moral beings. . . There is no need for public policy. Why is spare tire so small and shitty?

You hate the new Marvel Movie because you are sexist. I hate the new Marvel Movie because the writing, directing, cinematography, and acting was terrible. We are not the same. Elect at all costs. Convert at all costs. "Save, today!" What's the fucking point? What's the goddamn fucking point? Nobody who has ever lived. Has understood how a credit card actually works. You rarely hear about failed wedding proposals. Our character participated in the cult of "self-betterment." Or "self-bitterment." Albeit, with a healthy amount of skepticism. These contradictory positions people embody. To get people places. The cool detachment required to be successful. The baseline happiness our character was striving toward. The fun times footnoted with a hint of incompleteness, shame, guilt, regret. Etc. Why does happiness entail absoluteness? Perfection? Can we redefine happiness? The hero. A person who defies narrative. By forever remaining. Within narrative. Was our character like this? Maybe we'll find out. [They didn't].

Teacher: "Texas, what are you working on?" Texas: ". . . I did an abortion law. . . and voter suppression law. . ." Teacher: "And what are you supposed to be working on?" Texas: ". . . The Virus and the electrical grid?" Teacher: "The Virus and the electrical grid. Good. Now stop being such a shithead." "If this book doesn't get banned in Florida, I've failed as a writer. And a person." – The Author. Concealing the insanity of success. Behind nominally normative norms. A game of appearances. The buy-in: reputations. All bets determined happiness. Space/time revealed the situation couldn't sustain itself. Bad returns. Freest Nation built their economy on buying stuff. But then. Didn't give the people money. To buy stuff. They were not very smart during this space/time. The rich history of rich historians. A very short lecture. Our character was walking their dog. Dog piss. Was their social media. "Oh damn! Did you hear Harold is dehydrated? Wonder if he's doing alright. Smells like he might be going through a rough time. I'll check in on him soon."

The habitual overemphasis on the unnecessary under-emphasis of the essential. A writer could/should conceal/unconceal the subject of the sentence. An impetus. For the reader (pre/post-writer), the writer (pre/post-reader), and the character (pre/post-reader/writer) to create. Take the subject. Move it around. Original purpose forgotten. Merhaps leading to better questions? A synthesis. Realizing the reflexive text. Without detracting from the non-reflexive text (narrative economy of the whole). Could we? Revealing too much emphasis. On recalling the original function. Does the subject retain its intentions? In some small way? The reader (of our character) finding the original subject. Through the canceling contradictions. We can't remember everything exactly. Anything exactly? The exactness was only the potentiality of space/time. Computers should have been able to do this. During this space/time. Instead, they used machines in every other way except this.

Our character had to call into work: "Sorry, I have to take the day off. Storage space on my devices is full. And I can't use anything." Our character contemplated an Entry Level Manager position with Global Life

Liberty National of Columbia United National. Bro. She only likes you for your memes. In writing. Our character constantly confronted them selves. Or their motive for writing, at least. Or they escaped them selves. Etc. How can they write freely? When we determine what they write? Let's have them write something we can't comprehend. *Logos* is conformity. Accepting a tradition of convention. Forfeiting freedom. Fore fitting freedom. Freedom presupposed. Our character would write more later. They went for a walk. Judging other people on their usefulness to them. Has less to do with that person. And more to do with how our character viewed them selves. If they could surround them selves. With those who they found useful. It would help them seem useful. Orange Man teaches us empathy. We now understand what it means to be led by an insane despot in a shithole Nation.

     If you're reading this. I'm not talking about raising your taxes. Our character's glasses got smaller. Or their head got fatter. "Isn't that the guy from that one thing?" [It wasn't]. Thirty-something makes a surprising pop culture reference. Olympians held to impossible standards. Meanwhile. Ocean is on fire. Day turns into impromptu drinking game. The further ahead in space/time, the further you can reach backwards. This is where we go. To think the thoughts. That challenge our existence. The way forward. Is being paved here. Our character could catch a glimpse. But never know. Looks like we've hit dream bedrock. Only dreaming about the dream. No more levels to fall through. Rather than choosing one side of a double-entendre. Don't choose. At all. Instead, know it could be wrong. As in listening to a lecture. Once our character was practiced. They could be understood. What did we not even know we could question?

     Superman was an alien. Figure out what year you live in: year of phone + year of car + year of computer + year you made the most money ÷ 4 = Congratulations! You're stuck in ________ . What keeps us going. The false confidence. That when we wake up. We can actually improve our lives. I know these opinions are controversial. But I am #brave enough to stand by them. I believe we should limit the number of deaths caused by viruses, help poor people, and not be Nazis. We are all on our way to becoming something else. How much you'd benefit from your own advice. A noxious combination of stuff. We can have other ways of being. Art is the negotiation. Your *style* is what you do—despite your best interests. "I like how you negotiated pleasing a particular audience and trying to please no one." The perpetual belief. I am finished with a piece. And the perpetual return. To the piece. To realize I am not. Some space/time it ends. But that happens when it happens. We need not relate our dreams. Back to us. And our world. To see how these narratives operate without us. How unrelated we are. To these stories that occur. Occurring outside our perspective. Or at least. The perspective socially constructed by *logos*. Or the *logos* imposed on our character. The *logos* that creates their life. Etc.

During our character's space/time. The "rich and powerful" didn't have to understand the system. To profit from it. In most instances. They didn't understand. Anything. At all. They assumed superior genetics, their own "work ethic," their culture (or lack thereof), their geographical location, Etc. If they act a certain way. If they took on certain attitudes. If they upheld certain cultural and religious beliefs. Etc. They will remain rich and powerful. When really. The only thing that made them rich and powerful. Was their money. Enter a room with the confidence of a Small Town 7. Call now. Lockdown. I guess we're all going to find out pretty soon. If our neighbors are freaks. Does anyone know where I can get new platinum grillz? Will this be covered by health insurance? [Nothing was]. Workforce replaced by dogs willing to work for treats. But still no health insurance. People who hate people who blame all their problems on others. Support person who blames all their problems on others. I don't have to prove anything. I just have to disprove everything you think. And it's not very difficult. Defense still the best offense.

The radical compartmentalization and overspecialization of society is politically motivated. To disadvantage the Humanities. Created to allow citizens. An understanding of how they were being disadvantaged. Religion's track-record. On guiding philosophy, science, public policy, politics, self-knowledge, Etc. Not great. Not good. In fact. Bad. As if apologizing for their parents, these other fields have had to embarrassingly make excuses for the use of religion within them. For funding purposes. Lip service. Parodies of philosophy and science. Travesties. "Wouldn't it be funny if. . ." (eyes side to side emoji). The need to have two meanings. Two different audiences. People need to start using the word "puritanical" more. McDonalds' ice cream machine down. Rome wasn't built in a day. But the pyramids were built with mustard. When in Ancient Greece . . . do incest? Get your dirty mind in the gutter. I miss the simple days. When we hated Presidents for war crimes. Forgotten password good enough reason to throw device in river. "Jest found out the soap Imma usin is FDA approv'd. Federal goover-ment not gonna tell me wat soap te use! State's rawghts!" The only aspect of being. Was finding being. Our character was no different.

If you find yourself apologizing for being good at stuff. Find new people. IS the thing out there. The thing I have decided. It is going to be? We could communicate these thoughts to our character through various dream scenarios. Almost impossible to receive this message as it is written down here. All we can do. Provide helpful perspectives. In a given space/time. They will be replaced by better answers. And in better questions. But now. We should "do the thing itself." Nationalism making a strong argument as to why IT should end the world. And not the plague. I hope our character was able to fall into something beautiful. When they are lost in thought. The only purpose of waking life? To provide content for dreams. Maybe we work against our own best interests? Because we don't know what our best interests are? And to generate content. Etc. Emergency Announcement from Verizon/AT&T Homeland Security CVS Hospital County Services: "To people in positions of power: It's okay to hire qualified, competent people. You should not feel ashamed about this. If somebody is talented, it's okay to compensate them accordingly. The worst that can happen. They will make everything better for everyone. Including yourself." This message will repeat. "To people in positions of power: It's okay to hire qualified, competent people. You should not feel ashamed about this. If somebody is talented, it's okay to compensate them accordingly. The worst that can happen. They will make everything better for everyone. Including yourself." Dial one to hear more information. Dial two to contact a customer service representative. Dial three to disconnect from the world.

Art is whatever gets you laid. Everyone makes decisions. Everyone is on something. Our character was a complete idiot. Luckily. So was everyone else. Microwave doesn't have 30 sec button. Nobody: "Capitalism is clearly working." HR forgets why they didn't hire you. The Greatest Generation did meth to fight WWII. Marriage: the inability to generate enough reasons to leave someone. The easiest way to create a Latino terrorist problem in the United States: big men with big boom-boom guns break into homes and start randomly tearing apart families and deporting members back to the war-torn countries from which they fled. It's what Sky Wizard and Wine-Maker would have wanted. Something about the Statue of Liberty here. Repubenomics: "I'm pissed about gas and milk prices! But I don't want free healthcare and student loan forgiveness!" Greeting Card: "We should have fucked when we had the chance." Old Democrats back candidate from Extremely Normal Political Party. Extremely Normal Political Party back pure fucking insanity. Great time to invest in stuff. Class of 2004: "The One Who Got Pregnant."

"Some of my best work is hidden in Chapter Eleven." – The Author. Religion has no monopoly on narrative, imagination, and creating a(i)llusions to dramatize our place in the world. To help make sense. Of who we are. Without providing definitive answers. Now. Religion can no longer defend itself from both claims at once. Religion is neither practical enough. Nor imaginative enough. You can teach an ethics course. Without religion. In fact. It might be best to. The faster we get rid of oppression. The faster we can move on from political correctness. No matter what form our character took. They will always. Only be attempting. To pull the world together (for us as well). As they do what we think they want us to do to them. Nebulous particles attempting to become a thing. To remain.

Space/time travel with definitive "now" points hides a realization that everything is constantly happening at once: the past, present, and future flowing through and around us. We inhabit all. For forever. However long. Forever might be for you. The timeless, spaceless, ineffable fabric of soul. The transition from polytheism to monotheism. Back to polytheism. Etc. Oppression sustains itself through perpetually pervasive (and mostly pointless) competition.

In response. The redemption narrative? Proving your worth against all odds. Avenging personal slights. Vanquishing real/imagined rivals, Etc. It works to get our character out of bed in the morning. To work a job they hate. To come home. To an apartment or trailer. Full of people. They had no choice but to see. So they could watch shows that weren't very good. Before falling asleep for not enough hours. Via their drug of choice. That they are always running out of. And wake up. To do it all again. DSM-5-TR: *oppressive depressive anxiety disorder*. Yet another impressive distraction. From generating plausible possibilities. Outside our character's story. It made our job easier. We could keep telling the same story. What happens at the end of Star Wars? Did everyone stop having sex and forget to tell me? If you see something. Say something. If you smell something. See something. Etc. During these trying times. I promise to continue providing pointless content. New York: I can't wait any longer! Pittsburgh: Don't forget to call your mother! San Diego: Wake up early on Thursday! Atlanta: It's for fun! Las Vegas: Your sister lives there! Austin: You're going to be just fine!

Statistically. There are thousands of people who would love whatever weird look you got going on. And your strange personality. That's not rare. What's rare is a mechanism that would allow you to successfully meet these people. But since the economy during our character's space/time was based on generating inconsistencies that kept people nomadic in an agrarian society. They needed relationships to fail. Constantly. Would you rather meet your significant other in a mysterious and dramatic manner? Taking several years. Countless moves. Etc. Or would you rather the mystery taken out. So you can actually meet. And spend time with your soul mate? While you're both still alive? Unfortunately. Too many would prefer the former. And formal. People need to have weddings! Multiple weddings if possible! The more the better. The more houses sold the better. The more condoms sold. The better. The more books on relationships sold, the better. Medications, Etc. It turns out. Our character was only attracted to their (previous) soul-mate's pheromones. The smells you can't smell.

Billionaires running out of things to do with money. Imagine if guns were monitored as closely as my Amazon account. If only banks were regulated as heavily as my glass's prescription. Our character overheard in conversation: ". . . no, it was a Lebanese knock-off mariachi band." Bring back hermitage. Make Hermitage Great Again. Our character said aloud to them selves: "It's a win. I'm considering it a win. Fuck it." This just in: nobody has any idea WTF is going on. Tonight at 8pm! During our character's space/time. Washington DID need a major shakeup. It DID need an outsider to tell everyone to get their shit together. And make our leaders accountable. This unconventional outsider needed a general public willing to look past a lot of their personal shortcomings, the media slams, the missteps blown out of proportion. Etc. However. Simply put. Orange Man was never this character. Narrative illiteracy. Strikes again! Impulsive. With no upside. Reckless. With no benefits. Destruction. Without creative rebirth. Half the Freest Nation "used up" all the forgiveness. Desperately needed for others. None was left. For the people who actually needed it. "Dear Instagram, you don't have to advertise Instagram when I'm on Instagram."

Subscription now subscription based. In our character's future. They wouldn't be able to give data companies ENOUGH access to their information. The opposite of what they thought. Our character also considered raising prices. Due to "inflation." Inflation inflating. Our character had never been to a ball. But they were fine with that. They wouldn't know how to dance anyway. Our radio waves travel out. Our light travels out. Our voices, phone calls, images, Etc. Out into the vastness of the universe. For others. Out there in the vastness. Our civilization will wash over them in waves. Going back in space/time. By traveling out into space/time. If we could out-distance our messages. Faster than the speed of light. And turn around to face the waves. Of all communications. We can relive our past. But it will always be everything. We have always done. At least that's something? Dark matter is what hasn't happened yet. The space/time of silence. That we have not projected on to. Yet. Nothing reflected back to us. Yet. We have not yet projected it. From our past. To see our future. So fast. It's slow. No way to detect it. Dark matter must take more space/time. To become what it is. It is not. During our space/time. Perhaps it will make the universe expand back into itself. Another "first" big bang. What if all statistics were completely misleading? In that. They only told the people of our character's space/time what they already knew. Our character was running. Pushing against the ground. The ground. Pushing back. Everything. A push against. The bit of us that exists in surprised smiles.

Government admits it doesn't want citizens thinking about thinking. Which is more "A": "V" or "H"? The punchline: life needed water to exist. Our character picked up. Where they left off several days ago. Trauma generations. When our character said they didn't like somebody. They often meant "I don't like the person they make me think I am." I wonder what our character thought of us? Writing them. Reading them? To remember you forget. Post remembering. A teacher is responsible for generating and maintaining interest. They need to provide analytical wonderment. Bemusement. Etc. Our character would like to think. They weren't one of the robots. But just in case. They thought they were. At what evolutionary stage was our character's mind? This would only be known by future readers. [It wasn't?]. Everything will come around again. Every day. Really is every day. Sky Wizard might as well exist. Or might as well not. Or both. Our character's car won't start. Their purgatory remains. Once it is fixed. A new purgatory? *Logos* is purgatory. A parody of purgatory. What's the Pope's proclamation? Popstar using platform to talk about issues. *South Park* did it. *Simpsons* did it. Etc.

12 OPINIONS OUT OF NOWHERE
OR EVERYONE SAYS SOMETHING

Our character made a promise to them selves. From this point on. Whenever introduced to the pet of an acquaintance. Our character would assume it was a dragon. And act surprised at how un-dragon-like it was. "Huh. This dragon is a lot smaller than I thought it would be." "Oh weird. This is a small, fluffy dragon?" "This dragon has feathers? Weird!" "I've never seen dragons swim in an aquarium before. Doesn't this prevent them from breathing fire?" Wrong person gets job. Again. I'm too old for this shit. Life hobbyist. Nobody. Capitalism: "Either grandma dies. Or you can buy food. Or you can eat Grandma." Some people don't think it be like it is but it do. Our character was having hot dogs for breakfast. And nobody could stop them. The only thing keeping our character normal. Was the knowledge. A lot of people were crazier than them. It wasn't much to go off of. But it was something?

Our character was outside with their dog. Without words. They shared a fact. "Looks like it's going to rain." They said with a look. Pre-cognitive interaction. A primal understanding. Language unnecessary. The laughing surprise of a joke. Animals get it. How much can a thing be like another thing before it no longer matters? The end of difference. The Ship of Theseus. Noah's Ark. Two ships in the night. Strangers in the night. The end of violence. And perpetually. Too dumb to know what happens next. Including the outside of the work. Within the work. The audience. The unknown. The unintentional. The nonlogical. The other. Etc. Making the impossible. Possible. Others will generate ideas. That go beyond. Leaving the unfinished work within the work. The sketch. An opportunity for others. Including one's future-self. To be. Or not to be. Creative. Writer's strike. Strikes again.

If our character had to meet one more person. They were going to live in the wilderness. For the rest of their lives. Our character's identity. Was being two days behind. On everything. They needed to stop being amazed at the level of wild incompetence. That accompanied supreme confidence. More fucks have been given by lesser fools. Apparently. They were going to try everything. Before they fairly taxed rich people. Emergency room. Is new doctor's office. Poverty-wage employee: scrutinized meticulously. Person running Nation. We'll take anyone. "Never." Was the right time for anything. During our character's space/time. People were always asking our character. If they'd be willing to recommend their business/services. For example. Our character's family and friends. Etc. Multiple times a day. There was a survey after everything. Didn't they have enough information? Was this the moreness? Our character almost made this connection.

Greeting Card: "Wish we could have made it to your party, but we had much better things to do." People love the sound of progress. They spent more time/money on "knowing" the problems. Than fixing them. Elections, research institutes, walk-a-thons, think-tanks, fundraisers, marathons, centers, bumper stickers, slogans, statistics, reports, articles, documentaries, reports, Etc. World hunger still exists. Are you kidding me? So this is what the end of an empire looks like. iCloud storage full. "In my day, nobody got anything for free. And they still don't. Wait. What was I saying? I had to marry my Great-Aunt Linda. In the snow! Wait. What am I mad about again?" Intro to Bank of America Math 101: "You don't have enough money in your account. So we are going to take money from your account. Do you have enough money yet? No? We'll take some more then. Etc." Working several jobs with no healthcare. Capitalism: "Gig Economy." Multiplatform exposerment can channel profits and residuals according to sound investment stratagems and enhanced growth calculations. I don't know who needs to hear this. But.

How much more did the moreness cost? Our character's life was spent honing their ability to detect failure. Sometimes the "winner." Didn't know they won. Who could tell them? The present never present. Never presenting itself. Riding the wake of two opposing forces. To think during the future. To think during the past. To bypass the space/timeline. Remaining in the wake of space/time. Afraid of the expansiveness. Afraid of the claustrophobia. Our character appeared to be a rather durable human. But one never knows. What should our character be working on? It should have been bedtime. Orange Man is "Less racist than Rosa Parks." First Indigenous President never elected President. Our character never understood why people played videogames. Our character played a game: Them vs. the US Economy. Every day. It was tough enough. Broke down and broke down today. Is typing getting worse? A solid 45% of our character's day. Was spent verifying they are who they are. On devices and systems. They used every day. Yet. They didn't feel secure. You can't be anti-woke. There's already a word for that: asleep. Wait. . . are you pro-sleep? Oh, I'm all for that then.

During our character's space/time. Their hand delivered mail was the most or least important thing. The same thing with phone calls. Spam caller. Or once in a lifetime opportunity. Or tragedy. Every institution slowly morphed into a Nigerian Prince. Were they calling about "taxes" or my actual taxes? My "credit card" or my actual credit card? Best. Nation. Ever. Raising the bar for the poor. Lowering the bar for the rich. To be able to reach further back into one's bag. More methods of attack. They could win. Having played the most games. Moving our character a little closer. To a measurement of success. It was that space/time of the year when everyone was surprised it's still baseball season. Goals are dreams with deadlines. Freest Market chooses labor unions. Clip art sales are through the roof. Great time to invest in clip art. There's always money in clip art. How much worse can network TV get? This is going to be wild. An art critic's wet dream. Ineptitude and confidence at all-time high. If you thought it was bad before… Time to sell feet pics. Humanity ain't it fam. Stop trying to impress people. Start trying to impress dolphins.

All these people. Practicing a tough love. They them selves. Could never survive. We study these stories. So when we die the many deaths. We will have a general knowledge of what to do/say. Working far into their future to mend their past. Eventually we will get there. But not in our characters lifetime (a few hundred pages more?). This angst. The cause and definition. Of someone who is *not there yet*. Or perhaps more specifically. A person who already knows. This is not the life cycle that makes it into eternity. What kind of fresh hell will today bring? Unsubscribe. Can't wait to see the latest hot colabs between studio executives and AI. Our character didn't know what they were doing. But they were doing it at full speed. Instagram algorithm under investigation. Healthcare. Try that in a small town. Allow happiness to sneak up on you. I think of social media as a friend. A friend that wants you to remain in the same place you've always ever been. Repubenomics: "I'm pissed about gas and milk prices, but we shouldn't raise taxes on the billionaires I'm paying for gas and milk."

During our characters unprincipled space/time. Our character was surprisingly principled. Nobody would assume this of them. It was one of their best attributes. And they hardly knew it. Emotional boundaries. Conversational boundaries. Our character had surprisingly many. But it turns out. This was a novel our character found on the street. They've simply been reading it out loud. The omniscient narrator misunderstood the story they were telling. Not as omniscient as we thought. Our character had given up reading the novel several months ago. But it was still on their desk. It made them look smart [It didn't]. Aside from the strange book they found, the day was fairly normal. It was one of those summer nights. Where you discover yourself. With enough space/time. You find yourself. Imbibing. On a front porch. Etc. Somewhere. You find yourself in space/time. All of a sudden. There's plenty of it. You could use it. Or not. It's perfect. However. The people who own this front porch. Are giving me a weird look. T-shirt ideas: "East Coast got that meatloaf. Yo."

The most bizarre. Who decided there was a daytime and a nighttime? An appropriate space/time to sleep. An inappropriate space/time to sleep. There is a work week and a weekend. And somehow all of this was normal. During our character's space/time. They marched on. God's Fiercest Little Warriors. Pretending the systems were in place. For a reason. That somehow concerned them. Someone is trying to sign into your Amazon account. We know it's you (it always is lol). But… you know the deal. Lol. Enter this code or something. Note to self: "Practice being good at life." Our character was practicing. A disconnection. From the overarching narrative of a True self. Reflection without guilt. Disconnected from an outrageous sense of mastery. Sighting the many. Releasing from the self-self. Becoming everything that can be. And can't be. Etc. Most dogs had better healthcare than our character. Our character was running for President on a *no homework* platform. They won. Easily.

Businessperson 1: "The Nelson project. Where are we on that?" Businessperson 2: "We need to rethink the whole thing. . ." Everyone is taken aback. Businessperson 3: "Excuse me? What could you possibly mean?" Businessperson 2: "What I mean will be displayed in a presentation my secretary has prepared (nods in direction of 'secretary')." Businessperson 4: "I'm not your secretary. I am the Chairman of the Board." Businessperson 2: "See, this speaks precisely to the problem! What are these titles we carry around with us? We need teamwork people! It's hurting the Neville Project and it's hurting this company!" Businessperson 1: "Did you just call it the Neville Project?" Businessperson 2: "We are so concerned with labels and titles that we forget to inspire and innovate. Synergy! Let's go around the room, and I want you to tell me the first thing that pops into your head when it comes to improving the Neville Project. Let's start with you (points to Businessperson 5)." Businessperson 5: "Bicycles! But with cheese!"

Our character already understood. What they were crafting. Was going to be misunderstood. Did they have a choice? Their Being. An inevitable response. To a problem that had been there for ages. Would the next "them" be better at this than them? Would this other "them" have the kindness they had now? Difficult to say. Was our character's nowness something they should lean into? Or run away from? A reverse superhero story. People who thought they had superpowers. But it turns out they were delusional. And the rest of the story is how they spend their lives dealing with this reality. A book for initiating the uninitiated. And have Fun! To be being without being. Maybe truly terrible. Being without a self and not knowing. Once again, our character suspected a shadowy force working against them. Maybe we should pause the (potentially) pointless introspection? Tinder now mandatory. Greeting Card: "Ceci n'est pas une pipe. [Inside]: It's a Greeting Card!" Extremely Normal Political Party [*Makes government inefficient*]. Also Extremely Normal Political Party: "See, government is inefficient."

An attempt to get rid of mistakes. Instead of listening to them. Listeners of *logos*. The therapeutic qualities of rhetoric. Revealing motives. Hidden by familiarization and clarity. Reinforcing our self-certainty. To sense the unsensed. Incensed incents. I dunno if it's me or it's you, but it's definitely you. Not sure if this book has enough big words. Paraprosdokian. There we go. Idiots will always be in charge because only idiots want to be in charge. T-shirt ideas: Always Glove. FBI Agents are a bunch of liberal snowflakes. Class of 2004 Awards: "He Went Here." Artisanal cocaine. Look for it in an olive oil rosemary soufflé with a ketchup finish. I feel very uncomfortable. Not perpetually worrying. About the President ending the world with a Tweet. Sometimes. Accidentally. There is a little bit of justice in the universe. Our character found it impossible to perform a simple retelling of events in their past. The present kept moving into the future. No fixed point. No grounding in *logos*. Our character could jump from. To jump to. Etc. To get outside of *logos*. Unless. We let them? How would we do this? Even if we could?

Just finished watching that documentary about the guy from Space Jam. At this point. The only trophy I could win. Is for oversharing. When I'm drunk. Overheard Popstar: "I don't like haters. Why can't they all just be rich and happy like me?" Too often. Our character got in their own way. It was their most prominent attribute. Unfortunately. Your brain just wants to get to the next thought. Regardless of what happened previously. Here we are now. All of us. And our character, of course. I wonder what the future me is going to do when they read this. Our character was almost able to think this. Pathways to take. That lead you. Out of yourself. Again. Peering as far out as I could, without losing it all. Slingshotting back into the space/time of possibilities. Through to the other side of grief. Apollo and Dionisius. *Dissoi logoi.* Knowledge becomes wisdom through skill.

Waking up from a reality. Within a reality. Our character on their computerized devices. Living other lifetimes within them. Space/time moved different. In a book, a play, a concert, Etc. WE return. To the most urgent now. There is. Class of 2004: "Best Personality. Or Least Likely to Succeed." For this particular application process. Our character needed to take a grueling standardized test. About stuff they knew. Ten years ago. To see if they could re-remember it? It cost $220. Everything needed a special license. Our character needed a special license. Before they could get a special license. If the overlords liked our character. It meant our character had deceitfully charmed them. So obviously they couldn't trust our character. If they liked our character. And they would get denied. If they couldn't remember anything about our character from the interview. They would try to contact them for additional interviews. But they wouldn't try that hard. Pee in this cup. We own your urine now too. Your chemical history.

Top Questions to Ask at the End of an Academic Job Interview: "Can I have a private side-conversation with the person who has worked here the longest without receiving a promotion?" A cluster fuck of platitudes. A fluster puck of clatitudes. Everyone should have an opinion and vote. Nobody can trust the media. All politicians are corrupt. The four kinds of being: "Cool, Groovy, Hip, and Square." During our character's artistic phase. Overheard in conversation with them selves: "All art is done with one hand. The other hand is needed to fight off society. Preventing your art from being done." Extremely Normal Political Party angry that elite liberal lame stream media is quoting Orange Man verbatim. Punctuality is for poor people. Censorship is for poor people. Apparently. Science is theorem making. The Arts and Humanities are a meditation on a world without theorems. No small task.

In the bathroom. Our character grabbed a container. It moved a vision through them. Of earlier that day. Space/time traveling through the container. The container thought through them. Telling our character about earlier that day. What brings our character back? The present. The place our character is brought back to. The force that forces them back into the space/time they currently are. The present. After the story is over. After this sentence is over. The place we inevitably end up. At the end of the day. Arranged in the same molecular structure. The only one it can be. Given all probabilities in other dimensions. Let us know how we did! Donate! Now! Today! Keep applying! Sure our company/university has a criminal background (anything more than 40 years old probably does in Freest Nation). But you can't do anything about it. And we don't have to legally disclose anything to you. Pee in this cup. I bet Southerners think it's odd. Establishments elsewhere in Freest Nation. Brag about the date they were established.

Hiring committee doesn't understand basic human interactions. Wait, how did WE get OUR jobs? What is a job? How do humans. . . language? "SELF DESTRUCT SEQUENCE INITIATED." "Thank you EARTH for your HUMANS and POTATO-BASED SNACKS." "!Simulation back online!" "!Simulation back online!" "!Simulation back online!" Our character watched the fish in their aquarium. What does the fish know? Does the fish assume this is a regular fish-life? That this is what happens to all fish. More or less? Always walk away from unwinnable situations. Public service announcement. For healthcare. You get band-aides. Good luck! Another day. If that's all this is. Our character might as well engage in the simulation. To get the best results possible. What would ultimate passive-ism look like? #Winning. When asleep. In-accessible to consciousness. But still accessible to being.

Greeting Card: "We are stuck with each other on this planet. Humanity metaphorically. And us literally. [Inside]: It's a good thing I'm dumb enough to love you." Class of 2004: "Most Likely to Live Among Humans." Teach what you don't know. TV is TV again. Police defunding themselves. As entire generation refuses to be racist. If you want to stop crime. Become a History teacher. How many iterations of space/time would have to pass. For our character to live in a space/time. Where they did everything exactly the same? Competition leads to disparity. Not prosperity. Tik. Tok. Clock time bamboozles. Prevents the simultaneous now. During our character's space/time. People could be "early" or "late" for "work" (yes, they still "worked" back then lol). Thinking in straight lines. Roman Generals. When my now. Is the same as your now. Our collective now. Regardless of space/time. Nowness. The only thing we have in common. They had a very themness to them. What is this a commercial for? *Cogito Ergo Sum*. But. *Hypotheses Non Fingo*.

Our character thought today felt like a weekend. Neighborhood giving off "weekend vibes." The center of town felt more like a weekday. Maybe there's a big corporate deadline. Two completely different perceptions of space/time. Only minutes away. Might as well be different worlds. All the people you can't see right now. Might as well be on the moon. It would be the same to you. Except. You probably would have heard about them. If they went to the moon. And you haven't. Have you? Narrative. Fills perceptual gaps. To calm cognitive anxiety. Without a sense of object-permanence. The complete loss of everything. Will your parents return? To care for you? Yelling. Until words come out. Conceptualizing. The experience of space/time itself. Via narrative. Or. This isn't what happens at all. Or it is. Only comedians can deal with hard truths. Soft truths?

Devil. Probably not even that bad. Prob a fine person. Minding their own ggawdmn business. Lol. Devil was just some random dude. Lol. He was so exceptionally average. Everyone hated him. Instantly furious. No fault of his own. A numbers game. "Don't let it get to ya." God needed a scapegoat. Again. Prob why the devil has horns and hooves. I can't finish the book if I keep writing it. Thought our author. But I also can't finish the book if I stop writing it. Etc. And so. This is how our author would get trapped. In their own story. A bargain at the crossroads. Now on sale! Purple Saturday! Our character told them selves: "The odds of success here. Are imminent!" [They weren't]. Legging Generation says skinny jeans are too much. Extremely Normal Political Party when you're holding a beer on social media: "Rabble! Rabble! Rabble!" Extremely Normal Political Party after a mass shooting: "Now hold on. Let's be rational. Let's wait until all the facts are in." Merhaps. One of the reasons we don't know what happens after we die. We haven't a clue what's happening when we are alive.

The secret to life in the Extremely Normal Money System: find addictions that improve your socioeconomic status. Everything based on addiction. Addiction Nation. Addiction Economy. Master your addictions. Never stop. Winners never quit. This is the thing. Our character will be all about. Becomes influencer. Putin attempted to be sarcastic. Putin attempted to tell a joke. He bombed. Falling worse than flat. He already bombed that base-line reality. Putin had no reality left. He could have just as easily believed the thing he said. Than not. Anything was possible for Putin to think. The joke had no grounding. It had nothing to push off of. No context. No juxtaposition. Tyrants and cowards could never be funny. Impossible for them to be Ironic. Only tragic. They would die. We all would. But history would kill them over and over again. Etc.

Our character loved a blank canvas. It was everything after. They'd keep trying to correct. Until they could do no more. Our character wasn't putting things on the canvas. They were trying to take things off. The blank page itself. Another character in our story. Sometimes mocking our author with its silence. Other space/times. Falsely encouraging them to continue. Like a friend entertained by one's misfortunes. *Schadenfreude*. Our character eventually realized this project would never accomplish its objective. Hardly a deterrent. Merely another socially constructed ritual allowing for the practice of projecting oneself outside of finitude into eternity. Or obscurity? The preservation of the soul into an existence separate from the body, Etc. Not mere substitution. But into the nothing of everything. The salvation everyone sought. Albeit taking on many subversive forms. Wait, did we ever decide if all pirates are Irish. Or was that some Hollywood bullshit?

Please review these social media guidelines with your Boomer before they use Internets: 1.) Remind them, if they don't like social media, nobody is forcing them to use it. In fact we would rather they didn't. 2.) If your Boomer doesn't like something you've posted, gently remind them that none of this was created for them. They were never the ideal user and never will be. It might also be a good time to remind them they don't like it. And can quit at any time. 3.) If your Boomer goes on a rant about being "offended," calmly explain to them that sometimes adults need to use "big kid" language to get a point across. Next, get them to agree with you about "freedom of speech." They love that shit. Somehow. It's a great diversion. Use it any time. 4.) If they don't get a joke (or are "offended" by a joke) ask them, "Would you read a book with this humor?" No? Well, think about Instagram as a book and the users as authors. Would you read a book written by someone you deeply despise and whose culture you are hellbent on destroying? 5.) Use the new "Block All Fox News" setting for 60+ to guide your Boomer away from false/dangerous information. Remember they are very impressionable at this age, and they'll repeat anything they hear.

Standing in front of a mirror. Our character finally took the time to check on a pain in their nose. Our character had been vaguely aware of it. A small hole had started on the front of their nose. They moved closer to the mirror. And started to pry around. Our character found the flesh peeled back easily. It was rotten. The pain from their nose came from spiders nesting in it. Thousands started pouring out. Oh maybe our character was dead? Yes, their corpse had been rotting for some time now. They returned back to life. By imagining themself waking up. Which they actually did. And they found them selves back in the space/time that was easiest for them to create/mentally comprehend. They started to write all this down. But they did not get very far. Maybe for the better. Our character held on to the notion that when one created. One was really constructing their eternity. And they did not want their eternity. To be a ceaseless cycle of remembering and forgetting. These spiders in their nose.

Everyone during our character's space/time. Had things they'd admit. Or not admit. On a regular basis. If they had a couple drinks. The scope would change. For better or worse. [Always worse]. Some of the things they could admit. Could make a profit. These were normal things. Other things they couldn't admit. Would not make a profit. The weird things. Philosophy qua ambiguity training. And a necessary step. For our character to imagine a world. Less tied down to the myth of progress. We have to answer. What would motivate them? What would they do during their "down time." One must work to transcend "work." Take it to its absurd conclusion. Our character assumed their narrative defined them. In a very singular, particular way. But it was really their unconscious, their dreams, their mistakes, their multi-personned self, their moreness, Etc. All defying a straight line through space/time. Our memories move us to another period of our lives. Imagine it full. Live in it as long as you want. Fifty Questions to Ask During an Interview for a Job You Don't Really Want: "What happened to the previous person in this position? Where did you bury their body?"

Our character was on a train. They started to think through the thoughts of a woman sitting across from them. A few rows down. "I'm going to think. What I think. She is thinking. About me." It was interesting. But quickly grew inauthentic. Our character suffered a real problem. Running out of illusions. The opposite problem. They originally thought. They would have. In years past. Attempting to rid them selves of all illusions. When the mental condition of perpetual paranoia. And a healthy consideration of multiple possibilities become indistinguishable. And converge to protect your best interests. The mental breakdown. Nobody's life can be summed up. In recounting the details. No matter how many there are. At this point. You might know our character better than your "soul-mate." Could you find the courage to tell them? These decisions, actions, choices, spread out and through the membrane of other realities and parallel universes. But what is our guide? For our character? How do we make these skis? What is pushing us forward? Down this thin plot line. Everything else falls off around us. Why isn't that us? Debris jettisoned by our pilot plot. Polite plot. Plodding. Onward!

During our characters' space/time. The argumentative strategy of the Extremely Normal Political Party: "Problem 1 is not the real problem. The real problem is Problem 2. We will do nothing to solve Problem 2. We hope. By now. You have forgotten what Problem 1 was." Legalese. Not easy. Purposefully hard. Technical technicalities. Worst case scenarios. And the messy statistics. All to justify their xenophobia. Instead of defending their positions. Now their uncorroborated world view is justified by "Freedom." Freest Nation has most people in jail. Our character was watching a documentary. People who lived in a remote, cold corner of the world were showing the film crew their traditional way of making skis. They made a mold to turn the ski into what it was. It wasn't the ski they made first. But the mold. To make a ski. They first had to not make a ski. To make a ski. They made its negative. A creation to enable creation. Our character thought: "Is this what language is?" The thing. That bends everything else. To make the thing what it is? Dark matter? Etc. If a person were to stumble upon the ski mold. It would be nearly impossible to tell its function. It wouldn't be of any use. However. It is essential. The discarded part. That made everything else function. The sacrifice. Our character attempted to think about this. In relation to an art project they'd like to start. There was something there. But it remained vague.

In our character's space/time. People thought. There were good guys and bad guys. The good guys had white cowboy hats. The bad guys had black cowboy hats. The bad guys were bad. Because they sold illegal drugs. To the other poor people. To make their shitty lives momentarily better. At a price they could afford. Conveniently. This made everyone involved a bad guy. Therefore. They could all get arrested. Double the profits! It gave the cops a constant supply of customers. Perpetuating the symptom (crime) by not curing the disease (poverty). Obviously. The bag guys consciously chose to be the bad guys (why else would they wear their black cowboy hats every day?). The bad guys would wake up. And say, "Today. I'm going to be the worst person ever." And then they were. Obviously. They were able to turn their life around. They simply chose not to. They liked the black cowboy hats too much. Conveniently. These were the parameters of the game. The people continued to cycle through the same predictable cycle. The same predictable morality lesson. On personal accountability. The people in charge didn't have to change anything. So nothing changed. It worked well for the guys who wore the white cowboy hats.

Garbage in. Garbage out. What does success look like to you? Institution institutes poorly. The media: "The media is really going crazy about this story." Obviously. The headline. Is the headline. "Heaven is a trip, man." The narrative becomes everywhere. A simulation with no creator. Simulacrum. With each step. A larger calculation. And smaller room for error. Fading back into nothingness. When others weren't around our character. They might as well have been in a different universe. Their technology provided a sense of "knowing" where/when they were in space/time. The *other* imagines the *other*, but only as the *other* imagines them. Our innermost atoms. Unable to touch. At what point do you become the audience of your life? Once. When walking in the backyard at night our character heard a bugler playing Taps. Somewhere in the neighborhood. Our character stood at attention. Looking upward. Paying homage to the stars. The rest of the neighborhood was silent. It was simple. It came and went. With no explanation. No consensus. No committee. The perfect ceremony.

Failure. The perception you will not be able to make another attempt in space/time. An assumption about the future. But we don't have to assign such an emotionally taxing response. What our character deemed their failure. Told us more about our character. Than their actual abilities/inabilities. Our character assumed. They understood everything that happened up to that moment. [They didn't]. But they had a very limited scope of space/time (as did most during this space/time). [As do we]. They were holding onto their failures. It was a knowledge of some kind? Suddenly, our character experienced the fear of the nothing after death. We simply cease. Our character will be left out of eternity. Forever. We will be closed off and final. Everything else goes on. Our character debated writing this down or continuing to nap. An artist's "style" develops from ripping off them selves. A repetition of the self. Same but different.

Neopuritanism. Salvation through busy work. Let's get business cards printed! Older Generation fell in love with busy work. The evidence of work. As opposed to a meaningful finished project. *Homo economicus* had become increasingly difficult to remove from their idea of self. The root of xenophobia. Racism. Scapegoating. Shaming. Etc. The motives that drive us. Instinctually. Different ways to attempt attraction. It needs to keep circulating. For the Extremely Normal Money System to exist. Otherwise, nobody would dream of working so hard. For so little pay. The ending. Makes the story complete. Making the narrative a narrative. Possible epitaph: "Life, three out of five stars." During quarantine, our character would think up these routines. And follow them. More than not? Our character would be surprised. When others didn't know what was going on. Then they'd remember. How strange their routine had become. Our character. Often came close. To realizing. All we ever do. During our existence: attempt to set up routines. And watch them fail. If they don't. Others adjust to our routine. Or we to theirs. Etc.

Every study. Is a study of the past. Of what has already happened. We can pretend to project into the future. But the only way we'd know we projected correctly. Is when it comes back. Everything becomes a mirror of itself. All we know is what's already happened. By knowing it. It moves immediately. Into the past. As soon as our character understood something. The present was gone. It was now something that had occurred. Knowing is the past. Our character had to accept. They might not have this view again. You have learned something so profound. It will stay with you. And then you must leave. The point where the two extremes exist. You must move back into the middle. Of yourself. Closing the logical loop. Revealing it to be circular. To demonstrate how it is done. To explain itself. And therefore. Reveal what the reader learned along the way. Our character's main failure. Was considering their failures. To be failures. It gave them something to be disappointed about. At least it was something? But it kept them in the way of them selves. Our character sought the knowledge that one was subjected to the space/time they were in. They were a different them. At that space/time. And that's fine. There is nothing to be forgiven. By anyone. Nobody was at fault. The thing just was.

Always accept the olive branch. A strict diet of chaos. The contradictions you want to see. Tell us about yourself. Values voting. Could finally be revealed as the sham it was. Placing severe limits on what a human could be. Therefore. It generated nothing "interesting, remarkable, or important." Our character's opinions must be made to reconcile with one another. To converse with the paradoxical opinions within them. But instead. They often kept these opinions siloed off. The more serious they considered the opinion. The taller the silo. What if they spring a leak? The inner voices. That do not mix and mingle. Aren't on speaking terms. Democracy functions. Not by distributing power. But by scattering the perception of power. United by a general disagreement on who we should blame. The illusion of freedom. Present only. When the individual cannot focus the limitations of their well-being onto a singular subject. If our character has no cause to champion. They'd win the championship.

"Do unto others. As you would have others. Do unto you." Would work perfectly. If there weren't any differences between yourself and others. Until then. It prevents us from bridging the gap. Between our selves. In determining everything is predetermined. One forgets. They them selves. Supplied this conclusion. While our ability to communicate has grown. Our capacity to understand has diminished. Taking us further from significant questions. We have too much of everything. And not enough of anything. The purpose of our character's art. Was to make it impossible for anyone to disagree. Or agree with them. Parenting is the slow process of giving in. To everything your child wants. Then self-generating rationalizations. As to why. You "allowed" them to do it. Our character read in an article somewhere that the ability to advertise yourself is more important than what you can actually accomplish. Again. During our character's space/time. They were very stupid. Politicians subjecting them selves. To perpetual campaigning. Instead of actually governing. Our character. If they were slightly more clever. Could imagine a future beyond. A future. Where all we do is advertise ourselves (the beliefs we identify with, Etc.). Nobody would have any actual skills. To accomplish anything. Class of 2004: "Will Never Be This Cool Again."

The athletes on TV were the most *now people* alive right now. They were much more now than our character was. Until now. And now our character is more now than they are. Our character was watching the athletes on the couch. The athletes are now the most now again. The most now in both worlds. And now our character is. Etc. Extremely Normal Political Party astronaut refuses to wear a mask because it is a violation of civil liberties. They wanted the freedom to have their eyeballs sucked out of their skulls. Extremely Normal Political Party now on its casino circuit of shows. That nothing space/time. Of non-decision. Consciousness forces our hand. The narrative. A decision-forcing phenomenon. Every individual has a problem with this. How well we deal with the problem is what people refer to as character. Our character. Our character was done with these difficult thoughts. They went for a walk. They saw people on the street. Who had a great desire to make meaning. Further evidence. Things were meaningless. Hints of failure. However. Maybe only our character's projection. It usually was. With this type of language. Idea for academic paper: "Something Digital + An Ancient Scholar + Opaque Jargon." Academic Mad Libs.

Our author was always a step ahead of our narrator. "Wait, what?" Our reader can know what is going to happen to our character. More than our character. But they can't warn them. Are you guilty for going along with this? For making this reality happen to them? Real or not. Our character could be as unreliable a narrator as the narrator. Or the writer. Or the reader. Etc. But maybe not unreliable on purpose (for profit?)? For-profit nonprofit. We're all dead in the future anyway. It's only the future. When we are dead. What we aren't in space/time when dead. How does that help us make sense of where/when we are now? Our character? Apparently, we haven't died in the future yet. Or maybe we did. In order to make us a now now? Our character would die in the future. But that is not now. Our character: "Wait, what?" But I'm not sure yet how they die. Maybe we will find out if we keep going? [They didn't?] The undeveloped "I" self. Lacks an *ethos*. A home. If monkeys were given a typewriter. In thousands of years. They couldn't produce Shakespeare. Not because of their abilities. But the impossibility of knowing what Shakespeare wrote verbatim; i.e., the mistranslations, lost folios, changes made during performance, contributions from collaborators, the non-canonized editions, Etc.

The wide-open appreciation. Making the cyclical nature of existence tolerable. Our character was on the brink of realizing a new state of mind: "The *other* apart from me is them selves for and to me." Our character's neighbor acts this way. Because they need to be that kind of person for our character. For our character to be our character. This person was good. And this person was bad. This person is this person. For our character to be our character. Our character nearly thought: "Everything and everyone are as they are because they need to be them selves for me to be myself." Our character was exactly who they needed to be. For us. Apparently. "Not necessarily dumb. But definitely annoying." – The Author. Our character had now been alive long enough. To appreciate the difficulty in constructing illusions. As parents for children. And at the same space/time. Our character realized the impossibility of successfully protecting them selves and others with a lasting illusion. In order to further avoid blatant hypocrisy, Extremely Normal Political Party "goes Amish." Nobody complains.

Life sped up drastically during our characters' space/time. Or it slowed down. They couldn't tell. Every year (of space/time) became a new lifetime. Then every month. Every second. Etc. Life is much different than how we learned it. We live for an eternity and never. All versions of eternity are different. All I ask from the Extremely Normal Political Party: to extend to me the same eternal forgiveness they have bestowed on Orange Man. The challenge. To find a way to communicate the profound in a simple way. Without simplification. What good teachers do. What good writers do. Something our character was good at? Let's make this an attribute. Not all complex thoughts are intelligent. And not all simple thoughts are stupid. If we made our character self-aware. They'd only realize their own story was not about them. The cruelest joke? Life's punchline. In the last breath. All we had to do. Appreciate everything. But now you won't be able to. Anymore. At the exact moment. You now know. The most you can about life. But can't do anything. With that information. This is the sense of humor their Sky Wizard had during our character's space/time.

Congress makes headlines by doing their job. The bare minimum. A loving Sky Wizard would not operate within a top-down power structure: I give you nothing, I show you nothing, you give me everything, you show me everything. That's not how a benevolent force operates. A benevolent force is helpful, not mysterious when you need it to be forthright. Not purposefully obfuscating when you need it to be simple. It is understanding. "The Lord works in mysterious ways." But so does the devil. So does everyone. That doesn't appear to be a significant demarcation. If the Extremely Normal Political Party didn't exist, Putin would have invented it. What decisions would our character make, if they had to make the same decisions over and over again? What story would we write if we could only write one? Let's allow our character to live out the rest of their days. Perpetually surprised. At how much they appreciated the space/time. The everything. And the nothing.

Is it all the mumbles? All the things. Our character tried so hard. To not hear. Is that their reality? Or subconscious? Or the book's subtext? Or is that the demarcation. Where the knowledge of our writer, author, narrator, reader, Etc. begins. What is that unknown called? The surface-level unknown. So close to being known. But not. It occupies a space/time. It has gravity. We push against it. And sometimes. The burst. The event. That makes the person. A real person in the world. Our character. Their reality enforced by more people. The more ceremonies you attend. The more real you are. Popstar is real. Everyone knows Popstar. The most real. Of all of us. Overshadowing all our stories. Their story will be remembered. Will ours? Our character did not live in a space/time when everyone was working for the greater good. They had no common enemy to defeat. What if they placed poverty in the crosshairs? [They wouldn't]. That would be their downfall. Or they may have decided humans weren't worth saving. Maybe humans will be worth saving someday. We all have much more "us" to think about than we think we do. The "me" self, the "that" self, the "Fall" self, the "indoors" self, the "angry" self. Etc. Undesirable narcissism turns into anxiety. For the individual to establish their *homo economicus* self. But we have more voices in our life. Demanding we become the more self. Our character needed more practice being them selves. But it's difficult to practice. When playing the game. Our character was in the process of realizing. To love or hate another person (country, Etc.) our character first needed to establish them selves as a unified entity. They had to combine existing stereotypes in society. With the stereotypes they acquired throughout their space/time. With the stereotypes the other person was projecting from them selves. That our character was projecting on them. Etc. To undo this. They should establish them selves as a non-unified entity.

Our character wanted an identity. Their story remembered. But being forgotten completely? Their narrative no longer written. By their life. By the lives of others. Lost fragments. Childhood is old bathtubs. Get your heart broken by as many people as possible. That way you won't obsessively opine for one person during your space/time. You will merely have general regret. Spread over several space/time periods. Eventually too numerous to remember. And at that point, why bother? In the office, our character's co-worker was telling them, "I gave my wife the credit card and told her to get anything she wants at the mall today." We can never know if we are living in a simulation because we can never know if we are living in a simulation. This inability is consciousness. You can only change something if you can change something. Is there one thing? Or two things? Are there an infinity of things? Is there nothing? Is there one thing? Or two things? Are there an infinity of things? Is there nothing? Etc. The importance of doing nothing. Others were admitting our character's truth. Their way. Was becoming a way. Their story was being written again. Not by the past. But in doing. What they've always done. Sometimes it's their turn. Other space/times. They are dormant to the world. Preserving in the nothing. Allows you to remain.

THE END

13 WOULD BE FUNNY IF LEFT BLANK

INDEX

X

Y

Z

ABOUT THE AUTHOR

Michael Richard Lucas is an author of literary fiction and academic scholarship. He teaches courses in professional writing, rhetorical theory, and media production at MichaelTeachesStuff.com. Through playful pondering the author hopes to expand our understanding of ourselves and the world around us. Other published works include: *The Lost Fragments: pointless guidelines for the hopeless* (Sunstone Press 2018), and *Parody and Pedagogy in the Age of Neoliberalism* (Peter Lang 2019). Other works reside at MichaelArtsGood.com.